Developing Cli

Other McGraw-Hill Books of Interest:

Developing Client/Server Applications with Microsoft Access

Ed Jones

McGraw-Hill

New York   San Francisco   Washington, D.C.   Auckland   Bogotá
Caracas   Lisbon   London   Madrid   Mexico City   Milan
Montreal   New Delhi   San Juan   Singapore
Sydney   Tokyo   Toronto

McGraw-Hill

A Division of The McGraw·Hill Companies

1 2 3 4 5 6 7 8 9 0 DOC/DOC 9 0 1 0 9 8 7

ISBN 0-07-912982-X
P/N 032882-X

*The sponsoring editor of this book was John Wyzalek. The editing
supervisor was Scott Amerman, and the production supervisor was
Suzanne Rapcavage. This book was set in New Century Schoolbook. It
was composed in Hightstown, N.J.*

Printed and bound by R. R. Donnelley & Sons Company.

McGraw-Hill books are available at special quantity discounts to use as
premiums and sales promotions, or for use in corporate training
programs. For more information, please write to the Director of Special
Sales, McGraw-Hill, 11 West 19th Street, New York, NY 10011. Or
contact your local bookstore.

To Timothous, who knows very well what he's done to deserve the dedication.

Contents

Acknowledgments

As with any work of this magnitude, this book was the result of the combined efforts of many people. At McGraw-Hill/Professional, I would like to thank Brad Schepp for helping me develop this concept and bring it to light in the publishing world; Stacey Spurlock for her efforts in keeping chapters flowing smoothly during the writing of the book; and John Baker, Scott Amerman, and Suzanne Rapcavage for moving things through the production process. Thanks to soulmate and fellow "family" member Derek Sutton, for being there with a listening ear during a challenging and enlightening year. And thanks to the dedicated members of the Microsoft Access Forum on CompuServe, for answering all those questions that naturally arise during the beta phase of any software product.

Developing Client/Server Applications
with Microsoft Access

1

Microsoft Access and Client/Server: The Sensible Approach to Applications Design

This chapter offers an overview of Access and the object-based nature to which it can be used as a development platform for client/server applications. If you've used Access to some extent and have purchased this book with the view to honing your development skills and applying the use of Access to the client/server environment, you might want to skip this chapter and jump to the chapters that detail the development of applications using Access.

Welcome to Access, a powerful database package and development tool that has established itself as a standard for database management under Microsoft Windows. Virtually any task that lends itself to database management can be handled by applications developed using Access.

Using the capability of Access to attach to files stored on SQL Servers, you can use Access as a development platform to produce applications for enterprise-wide database tasks. The front-end database applications that you can create using Access can be used with any server that is available through the ODBC standard, including Microsoft SQL Server for Windows NT, Sybase SQL Server, and Oracle Server.

Because Access operates as a standalone product with the ability to store data in its own native format as well as to attach to PC-based database files in a variety of formats (including dBASE, FoxPro, and Paradox), you can get productive immediately by developing database applications that store data in a PC-based data format. Later, when your application has been thoroughly tested and debugged, you can move the data to a server and implement that application as a true client/server based one, as described toward the end of this book.

As a package developed from the ground up for Microsoft Windows, Access lets developers create applications that are completely Windows-compliant, with the look and feel of the Windows graphical environment, without the need to become familiar with a complex development language like C++. Because Access uses Visual Basic for Applications, seasoned Visual Basic programmers can develop applications and make use of a familiar language to add robustness and added capabilities to their applications.

Managing Large Application Development Projects

As you utilize Access as a client/server development tool, you'll encounter projects that go well beyond the scope of being small standalone database applications. Access makes it a simple matter to build small applications with a high level of quality; witness the power of the Database Wizards, which can design and implement ready-to-run small applications in a matter of a few minutes. This being the case, the question arises as to why larger projects can become so much more of a challenge. When developing for the client/server environment, one needs to recognize that client/server systems are naturally harder to develop and maintain. Because smaller systems are relatively easy to develop and maintain, the secret to effective management of the development of larger applications is to break them down into smaller parts.

When taking on the software development of a large database project, you need to find some way to divide the project into a series of smaller ones. The overall project will remain the same size, but you can tackle the development of each smaller component as a separate unit. A detailed system used to manage order-entry, for example, initially might be viewed as unmanageably complex for the Access developer. However, if such a system is viewed from the standpoint of its component parts (such as order scheduling, order shipping, credit authorization, and customer file maintenance), the developer is able to get a more realistic grasp of the development tasks necessary for each part. You can take any medium-sized client/server application that you must develop in Access and apply the same methodology to it, taking on each identifiable part of the application as a single unit.

Development Through Visual Programming with Access

Once you choose to use Access as your development tool, you must recognize that the development tasks will be very different than with linear-coding based products of the DOS world that preceded tools like Access. With Access applications, there is no main program consisting of hundreds of lines of code that control the user interface and govern what is and what is not possible. Instead, Visual Basic for Applications code is attached, where necessary, to various events that occur around objects like forms, controls in a form, command buttons, and menu options. A large part of the development task (easily 90 to 95% with most applications) consists entirely of designing objects (such as queries, forms, and reports) visually and tying those objects together by means of macros or Visual Basic for Applications program code.

With Access, you are using an *object-based* development methodology, and this is in line with the object-based nature of Windows itself. The advantage of adjusting to this new way of doing things (and if you come from the xBASE world of database programming, it is definitely a new way) is that you have a tool with which to perform RAD (rapid application development). Using the major design surfaces in Access, you can "paint" the major parts of your application—such as the forms, reports, and queries—then tie the various objects in your application together.

The Process-Oriented Approach

When you start designing client/server systems using a tool for modern times like Access, it makes sense to use a modern approach. An excellent model, commonly used in systems development, is the *process-oriented* approach. The process-oriented approach can be broken down into three stages: *conceptual*, *logical*, and *physical*.

At the *conceptual* stage, you review the requirements of the system and proceed to develop a rough sketch of the project's overall architecture. At this level, processes are viewed from the "big picture" standpoint.

At the *logical* stage, armed with the previous requirements, you consider the business rules that must be applied to the system and begin to plan how the application will satisfy these rules. It is at this stage that mock-ups are created for menus, forms, and reports, detailing what precise sequence of steps will be needed to accomplish a given task.

At the *physical* stage, the design (which to this point exists all or mostly on paper) is transformed into an actual, working system. Forms and reports are designed, code and macros are attached to events, and the database structure is refined. By nature, Access lets you get physical in terms of development very quickly, once you are ready to do so.

How Access Relates to the Windows Environment

Because Access originally was developed for the Windows environment, any applications that you develop using it are going to take on a Windows look-and-feel by nature. As a graphical user environment, Windows follows the CUA (common user access) standards. Command prompts (driven by traditional programming code operating in a linear fashion) has been replaced with menus, dialog boxes, and icons that represent objects within a graphical environment. Windows is event-driven by nature, meaning that the software environment responds to events performed by the user, like clicking an icon or selecting a menu option. Because Windows has become the dominant GUI environment, overall software design has followed its lead. While Windows 95 can't be called object-oriented in the true sense of the term, it has object-based tendencies, and Access follows that overall trend by providing an object-based environment that you can put to use in developing client/server applications.

As a Windows package, Access also supports dynamic data exchange (DDE) and object linking and embedding (OLE), features of Windows that allow the easy exchange of data between different Windows applications. Using OLE and OLE Automation in an Access application, you can pass data from Access to another Windows application, under the control of the Access application. You also can launch and run another Windows application and manipulate the data transferred from the Access application, as will be described in chapter 16.

Installation

It's a good idea to refer to the *Getting Results with Microsoft Access* booklet that accompanies your Access documentation before installing Access; the latest information that you should know before installing the program will be contained in the booklet. Make sure that you have the necessary installation diskettes or the installation CD-ROM on hand. Having done all this, you can install Access by performing these steps:

1. Start Windows in the usual manner, and insert Disk 1 into your diskette drive (if you are installing from diskettes), or load the CD-ROM into your CD-ROM drive (if you are installing from CD-ROM).

2. Open the Start menu, and choose Run Program.

3. In the dialog box that next appears, enter **X**: \SETUP and click OK, where **X** is the letter representing your diskette drive or your CD-ROM drive.

4. Follow the instructions that appear on the screen to complete the installation process.

Summary

In this chapter, you received an introduction to Access as a development environment. In the next chapter, you'll find more of an overview of the actual applications development process used with Access, and you'll find strategies for designing and developing your application.

Microsoft Access as a
Client/Server Development
Platform

This chapter details the overall approach that you will use in developing Access client/server applications, and it provides strategies for efficient application development.

The object-based, event-driven environment that is provided by Microsoft Access means that you must develop things in an entirely different way than with the traditional style of programming. In this chapter, you'll go through the overall steps of complete application development in Access. These steps include data analysis and overall application design, implementing the user interface, controlling the application's processing, testing and debugging, and the delivery of the final product.

Where Do I Start?

When you are in the client/server development environment, it is important to realize that you must consider a number of disparate pieces in the analysis of any overall task that's to be handled by the application that you develop. You must deal with people using multiple workstations on a LAN and with databases that might be located at more than one location on the network.

Contrary to popular belief at some programming shops, the first step in application development is *not* to start writing code. Your first steps in designing and implementing any application is to use analysis to determine exactly how the application should be implemented. First, you'll need to determine the application's purpose (for example, to handle accounts receivable or to manage an inventory.) You also will need to determine the existing status of the application; analysis proceeds differently when you are starting from scratch than it does when you are replacing an existing application running on some sort of hardware with an Access application.

Given the variety of hardware/software combinations that exist in the client/server environment, you also will have to determine what is appropriate for your particular application; choices regarding where the client and server portions of an application are located can greatly impact the overall performance of the application. If you have development tools (such as computer-aided software engineering or version control tools) available, their use must be considered in the analysis equation.

It's important to consider the skill levels of the end users, and their staffing levels, before laying out the design of the application. The most complex and powerful industrial-strength application in the world won't do the users a lot of good if it is so far over their heads that no one can figure out how to use it.

During this "getting started" project phase, you often need to determine who else will be involved in the project's development. Many client/server projects are of such a size and depth that it takes a team of developers to bring the project to fruition. If you are part of a team, your approach will depend on what parts of the project have been directly assigned to you. If you are managing the team, it's up to you to determine which parts of the project go to which programmers. If you are an independent developer, you get to skip this part of the initial analysis, because it all falls on your shoulders by default.

As you work with the application, you can divide the overall development process into three basic phases: *design*, *development*, and *deployment*. You can further break these overall phases into smaller steps, as this chapter discusses in detail.

Determining the Application's Requirements

With any successful application design, you first need to determine the requirements of the application. In simple terms, you must know what the users need before you can meet those needs. In determining the application requirements, you can consider the following important topics.

Data Access

You'll need to determine what tables the application must use for storage and retrieval of data and what operations the application must perform on these tables.

User Interface

You'll need to plan the user interface for the application: what menus and command buttons are needed, what forms they will reside on, and how the users will navigate through the application. If you (or the team member responsible for this analysis task) aren't already familiar with overall Windows user interface techniques, it would be good to do some research in this area as well.

Processing

Analysis in this area means deciding how the application will handle the data that it is allowed to access.

Program Interaction

Here, you must determine whether your application must interact with other programs outside its own environment. For example, part of a design specification might be to use OLE to create Word for Windows documents based on the contents of a field in a particular table.

Output

When performing an analysis of output needs, you must determine exactly what kind of output is needed by the users: what kinds of reports they will need and how those reports should be formatted. If you are replacing an existing application running on older hardware and software, you might be tempted just to model the reporting in the new application on what was provided by the older application. However, be aware that this saves time and effort only when the reporting provided by the older application met the users' needs to begin with (and often, this is not quite the case).

During this phase of the application's design and development, it makes sense to flowchart (lay out visually, on paper) the data access needs, the proposed user interface design, and the program processing and interaction. If you plan to make use of a CASE (computer-aided software engineering) tool to aid in the application's development, now is the time to put it to use.

Mapping the Requirements to Access

With the application requirements established, you next determine how the application will accomplish what it needs to do, using the features that are a part of Access. You'll need to plan the database access, the user interface implementation, the application processing, and the meeting of the output requirements. For each of these needs, you'll have to determine which Access options you'll use to perform the needed tasks.

In accessing the data, you'll need to determine where the data currently is stored, or needs to be stored. With that information in hand, you'll have to plan the ODBC connections to the needed database interfaces.

In mapping the user interface design to Access, you'll need to plan the forms and the dialog boxes that you'll use in Access and how you can use the Menu Builder to design and implement any needed menu options.

In mapping the application's processing to Access, you'll need to determine what events throughout the application you need to track and what Visual Basic for Applications code or Access macros you will need to respond to those events. Most of your work here will involve mapping code or macros to menu options and command buttons placed throughout your application.

In mapping the output requirements to Access, you'll plan the design of reports. You also will need to handle any special-purpose output needs, such as writing output data in the form of a text file or an Excel worksheet. Access offers numerous macro actions and programming code structures that can be used to handle these kinds of tasks.

Designing and Defining the Databases

With the prior steps done, you can move into the actual development phase of the application. A required early step in this phase is to design the required databases (if they don't already exist on a server somewhere).

Assuming your database analysis (back in the design phase) has established the table structures and where they will reside, you can proceed to use the design tools provided with the back-end database of your choice to create the required tables. If you are developing a new system from scratch, the tables can be created locally in Access and later moved to the server. As part of this step of database design, you must make sure that the appropriate ODBC driver for the database interface is installed.

Implementing the User Interface

With the table designs completed, a logical next step is to begin implementation of the user interface. In Access, you'll perform much of your user interface development using the form design tools and the Menu Builder. Following the design that was outlined during the analysis phase, you can create the major forms needed by the application. As you do so, you will use the various tools of the Form Designer and the Menu Builder to add the controls and menu options that will provide a basic functionality to the application.

Controlling the Application's Processing

Here, you take the earlier analysis of your planned events, and you use that analysis to write any needed code and to design the macros that will provide the desired responses to the events. You can attach your code or your macros to command buttons placed within forms, to menu options in menus, and to various events that occur in regard to other Access objects.

Testing and Debugging the Application

During this final step of the development process, you likely will use a number of different approaches to ensure that your application performs its intended tasks. This is one area where there are no hard and fast suggestions as to how you should proceed, because different developers handle debugging and testing differently. To a large degree, specific testing techniques are going to be up to you and your development team. One vital step is to get real users involved, with a subset of real data. Nothing shows up flaws in an application like real-world use by real-world users.

Wrapping Up the Process

After the application has been provided to the end users, you might have a few remaining tasks to handle. Documentation usually is included among these, as is the creation of any backups of the source code and any planning that will support later upgrades of the application.

In considering all of the steps that occur throughout the design, development, and deployment stages of an application, it is important to note that the steps might not always follow each other in a precise sequential order; some tasks might be carried on simultaneously with others, particularly if your application development is a part of a team effort. What's important is that each of these steps do get taken care of at some point in the complete process.

Summary

This chapter has provided an overall examination of the application development process in Access. In the next chapter, you'll see how you can quickly develop an actual Access application.

Introduction to Object-Based Programming

In this chapter, I'll examine the object-based paradigm, how it differs from true object-orientation, and specifically how you'll put the object-based paradigm to use in Access. I'll define the concepts of object-orientation—such as encapsulation, inheritance, and polymorphism—and see to what degree those concepts apply to the Access programming environment. I'll briefly introduce the concept of the event-driven application; Chapter 6 will go into this concept in greater detail. Because learning by doing is one of the best ways to become familiar with any task, I'll present a step-by-step example of a simple application developed using the object-based techniques of Access.

Try It: A Simple Example of an Object-Based Application

Because there's no substitute for real hands-on learning, this section of the chapter offers a step-by-step example of application development under Access. This example application is designed to track customer contacts for sales representatives. The application makes use of two tables. One, named People, contains a record of each customer. The other, named Calls, contains a record of each contact made by the sales rep to that customer. You can create these tables based on the structures shown in Tables 3.1 and 3.2, or you can copy the tables from the sales database in the CD-ROM that accompanies this book.

1. Once both tables exist, get back to the Database window, click the Tables tab, and click People to select it.

2. Click the down arrow beside the New Object button in the toolbar, and choose AutoForm. In a moment, Access will create a default form for the People table.

3. Make the Database window the active window. (You can leave the new form for the People table open for now.)

4. At the Tables tab, click Calls to highlight the Calls table.

5. Click the down arrow beside the New Object button in the toolbar, and choose New Form from the pop-up menu. In the New Form dialog box that appears, choose Form Wizard, then click OK.

6. The next dialog box asks which fields you want included in the form. Click the double right-arrow button in the center of the dialog box to add all the fields to the form, then click Next.

7. In the next dialog box, click Tabular, then click Finish. In a moment, Access will create a form using a tabular design for the Calls table.

8. Click the down arrow beside the Form View button in the toolbar and choose Design view (or choose View/Form Design from the menus).

9. If the Toolbox is not visible, choose View/Toolbox from the menus.

10. In the Toolbox, click on the Control Wizards button if it is not already depressed.

11. In the Toolbox, click the Command Button tool.

12. In the header area of the form, above the Description field, click once to place a command button. In a moment, the first Command Button Wizard dialog box will appear.

13. Under Categories, click Form Operations. Under When Button Is Pressed, click Close Form. Then, click Finish.

14. With the form still active, choose File/Close from the menus. When asked if you want to save changes to the form, click Yes. When prompted for a name for the form, enter Calls.

Table 3.1

Field name	Data type
Contact ID	Text (This field should be a key field.)
Last name	Text
First name	Text
Address	Text
City	Text
State	Text
Zip	Text
Office phone	Text
Home phone	Text
Car phone	Text
Fax phone	Text
Pager	Text
Notes	Memo

Table 3.2

Field name	Data type
Contact ID	Text
Date	Date/time
Time	Date/time
Description	Memo
Open?	Yes/no

In the next set of steps, you'll modify the People form to serve as both a main form for data entry and editing and as a principal means of user interface.

1. Click and drag the right edge of the People form to the right by one inch to widen the form to allow room for a group of command buttons.

2. Choose View Design from the menus, then, in the Toolbox, click the Command Button tool.

3. Near the right side of the form, click about an inch below the start of the Detail band to place a command button there. In a moment, the first dialog box for the Command Button Wizard will appear.

4. Under Categories, click Record Operations. Then, under When Button Is Pressed, click Add New Record. Then click Finish.

5. In the Toolbox, click the Command Button tool. Then click just below the lower-left corner of the button that you just placed to place another button.

6. When the Command Button Wizard dialog box appears, under Categories, click Record Navigation. Under When Button Is Pressed, click Find Record, then click Finish.

7. In the Toolbox, click the Command Button tool. Then click just below the lower-left corner of the button that you just placed to place another button.

8. When the Command Button Wizard dialog box appears, under Categories, click Record Operations. Under When Button Is Pressed, click Print Record, then click Finish.

9. In the Toolbox, click the Command Button tool. Then click just below the lower-left corner of the button that you just placed to place another button.

10. When the Command Button Wizard dialog box appears, under Categories, click Form Operations. Under When Button Is Pressed, click Open Form, then click Next.

11. The next dialog box to appear asks which form should be opened by the command button. Click Calls, then click Next.

12. The next dialog box asks whether the form should open and locate specific data or whether it should show all of the records. Turn on the option titled Open the form and find specific data to display in it, then click Next.

13. The next dialog box asks which field contains the matching data used to look up the information. Under People, click `Contact ID`. Under Calls, click `Contact ID`. Click the double arrow button between both lists of fields, then click `Next`.

14. The next dialog box to appear asks whether you want text or a picture on the button. Click the `Text` option, then click in the text box beside the option and change the text of the button from `Open Form` to `Calls`. Then, click `Finish`.

15. In the Toolbox, click the `Command Button` tool. Then click just below the lower-left corner of the button that you just placed to place another button.

16. When the Command Button Wizard dialog box appears, under Categories, click `Application`. Under When Button Is Pressed, click `Quit Application`, then click `Finish`.

17. Click just above and to the left of the first button, and drag down and to the right of the last button. When you release the mouse, all of the buttons should be selected.

18. From the menus, choose `Format/Size/to Widest` to give all of the buttons the same width.

19. From the menus, choose `File/Close`. When asked if you want to save the form, click `Yes`. When prompted for a name, call the form People.

Finally, you can use the following steps to create an Autoexec macro that will launch the People form as soon as the database is opened:

1. In the Database window, click the `Macros` tab, then click `New` to create a new macro.

2. Move and size the macro window for the new macro so that you can see it and the Database window at the same time.

3. In the Database window, click the `Forms` tab. Then click and drag the People form to the first row of the Macro window, under the Action column. When you do this, OpenForm appears as a macro action, as shown in Figure 3.1.

4. From the menus, choose `File/Close`. When asked if you want to save the changes to the macro, click `Yes`. When asked for a name for the macro, enter `Autoexec`. (In Access, any macro stored using the name "Autoexec" will automatically run when the database is opened.)

At this point, you have the basis of a rudimentary application. Try closing and then opening the database. When the database opens, the form will open automatically, and you can try the various command buttons which serve as the user interface. Figure 3.2 shows the main form for the application.

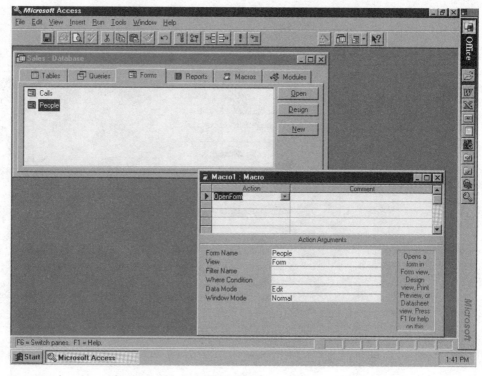

Figure 3.1 A macro with action added to open a form.

Objects, Defined

For a definition of objects, it's helpful to look to the real world. In the world around us, objects are things that you can identify. They have properties (also known as *attributes*), and they have methods (also known as *behaviors*). As an example, consider a car. A car has properties (its color, for example, might be blue), and it has precise methods or behaviors (when you start it, put it in gear, and step on the gas pedal, it moves forward). As the end user, you don't have to know what goes on under the car's hood to use it, because the object (the car) has a certain level of "intelligence," so to speak, built-in. The car is programmed to respond in a certain way to your action of putting it in gear and pressing the gas pedal. In the object-oriented programming world, we take these techniques of objects having properties and methods and use them to develop applications just as we use objects to build things in the real world.

About Object Orientation

While Access is not an object-oriented environment, it does make extensive use of some important object-oriented capabilities. Because object orientation to

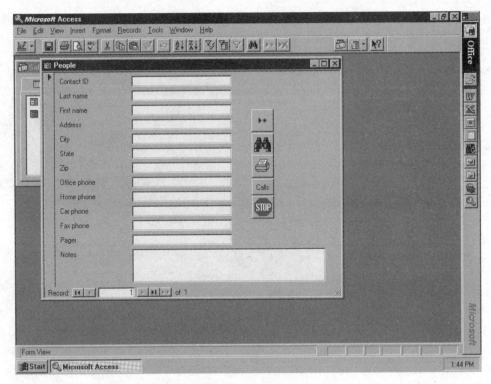

Figure 3.2 The main form for sample application.

the degree that it exists in Access is a vital part of effective application development, an explanation of object orientation might be in order.

Those who come from a traditional (read: linear style of programming) database environment are well aware of the division between data and programming code. With traditional linear-oriented database programming, you write reams and reams of code to manage the application, and this code manipulates the database where necessary, but the code and the data clearly reside on an entirely separate basis.

Object-oriented programming takes a different approach, where the data and the code are combined into reusable units known as *objects*. Objects contain both procedures (or *methods*), which define what the object can accomplish, and data (usually referred to as *attributes* or *properties*). By combining data and code into objects, you create definable units that can be reused throughout an application, and in other applications as well.

Once you enter the object-oriented world, you commonly hear the terms *encapsulation*, *inheritance*, and *polymorphism*; these three concepts are central to the true object-oriented programming environment.

Encapsulation refers to the central concept of object-oriented programming, that data and code can reside together, making up a definable, reusable object. Think of the data and the code as being encapsulated together, within the object. A major advantage of this programming design is that the data and the code don't need to be known to the outside world (the rest of the application); all that needs to be known are the name of the object and its *methods* (the jobs or tasks that it can perform).

Going back to the example of the car used earlier in the chapter, the properties and methods are bound together internally within the car. Hence, you as the user don't need to know the internals of the car to put it to work. This example highlights a major benefit of object-oriented programming; that is, that you need not know (or write code to create) the internals of an object to put it to work in an application. In Access, an excellent example of this is the addition of a command button to a form. Even if you add a button without the use of the Wizards, once you add the button, you can switch from Design view to Form view and click on the button, and it moves up and down with each mouse click and release. The button might not *do* anything, but it does visually move in and out as you click on it. What's important to realize here is that you did not have to write a single line of code to make the button respond to a mouse click. Rather, the intelligence to do so was built into, or *encapsulated*, in the button.

Inheritance refers to the ability of one object to *inherit* the characteristics of another. In environments where true inheritance is supported, you can create classes with descendant objects that *inherit* the methods (or behaviors) of the ancestor objects that they are based upon. This is one of the major traits of true object-orientation that Access lacks. For example, if you create an Access form as an object, then use the Edit/Copy and Edit/Paste commands while at the Database Window to make a copy of that form and then change some aspect of the original form, don't hold your breath waiting for the change to be reflected in the copy. In a more object-oriented environment, you would see changes made to the first form reflected in the copy.

Polymorphism refers to the ability of different objects to behave in their own appropriate manner to a single method. You can think of the method as "morphing" or adapting itself to the different objects. In true object-oriented environments such as C++, a common example is the Print() method, which adapts itself to handle printing of the object in question, without the programmer needing to worry about the details behind printing the object. As with inheritance, polymorphism is not supported by Access. However, because Access does not make use of a large number of methods as do true object-oriented environments, this also is no impediment to the development of robust applications.

Some other terms that aren't so central to the concept of object-oriented programming but are nevertheless heard quite often are classes, class libraries, and instance (or instantiation). A class and an object are much the same thing; you can think of a class as a combination of procedures ("methods" in object-oriented programming lingo) and data ("properties"). You instantiate, or make an instance of a class, just as you might define a variable in a traditional programming language. Once you've instantiated a class, the result is known as an "object."

Class libraries refer to libraries (or collections) of reusable objects that have design characteristics in common with other objects in that same class. In an object-oriented development environment, the ability to make use of multiple libraries of reusable objects often is a major factor in saving time and making rapid application development possible.

If you now are just delving into the worlds of object-oriented or object-based programming, all of this might seem incredibly confusing. (When I made my first foray into object-oriented programming from the xBASE world into Paradox for Windows and then PowerBuilder some years prior to this writing, little of it made any sense, yet it now seems like the only natural way to do things.) Rest assured that you need not understand the intricacies of object-based programming to get productive with Access. After you've worked with Access for a while, building applications by working with objects will make a great deal of sense.

Object-Based Access

Having defined what a true object-oriented environment is (and having established the fact that Access is *not* an object-oriented environment), the question arises as to exactly where Access falls in terms of a development platform. As far as encapsulation goes, Access definitely falls into line in this area, with an abundance of objects that have definite properties and behaviors (methods) built into each object. As mentioned earlier, a command button placed on a form serves as one example, as does the form itself. However, Access doesn't let you create objects with any form of inheritance, and the programming language built into Access (Visual Basic for Applications) does not support inheritance or polymorphism to any degree. Hence, it is most accurate to describe Access as an *object-based* development environment. The extensive use of objects with all the intelligence that you need encapsulated within the object lets you realize the same overall goal as with a true object-oriented development environment: fast development of event-driven GUI applications with no need for writing reams of program code.

The Basic Access Objects

The objects that you commonly use in Access development include your tables, forms, reports, and queries, as well as the macros that you create. (Program code gets stored in modules and is called by the objects that the code is attached to.) Within many Access objects are additional objects. For example, when you manually create a form or a report, you place various objects, called *controls*, at various locations within the form or report. The basic objects of Access are discussed in the following sections.

Databases
These contain your tables, queries, forms, reports, and macros used by your applications. From a development standpoint, it's only important to think

about multiple databases in cases where your application, under the control of Visual Basic, needs to access files from multiple databases.

Tables

Interactive users of Access know that these contain all the data in the form of records divided into fields. From a development standpoint, you can access table data through forms and reports, or you can use Visual Basic code to define Recordset objects to work with table data.

Queries

From a user standpoint, queries are vital for obtaining the specific data needed from one or more tables in a database. From a development standpoint, queries serve as an important data source for forms and reports. A number of different statements in Visual Basic for Applications code can be used to implement and manipulate query data.

Forms

To interactive users, these serve as a window into tables and queries, allowing you to add new data and edit existing data. However, to application developers, forms make up the very basis of Access applications. The overall user interface is centered around the form, with command buttons and/or custom menus attached. That encapsulated ("built-in") intelligence that's in the form relieves you, the developer, of the drudgery of writing program code.

Reports

From a design standpoint, Access reports have much in common with Access forms. You can think of reports as a banded variation of a form, designed to print the data stored in tables and queries. You can Access reports in your applications both through the use of macros and with various statements in Visual Basic for Applications code.

Macros

Macros store groups of instructions that automate tasks in Access. If you're experienced in the interactive use of Access but new to applications development, you'll find macros to be an important part of your design work.

Design Objects

These include smaller objects such as command buttons, graphics, and fields that are placed on forms and reports.

Objects and Properties

In Access, most objects have *properties*. You can change the properties of an object by right-clicking the object and choosing Properties from the shortcut menu that appears. Consider the example shown in Figure 3.3.

The Properties window shown in the figure appears when you click on a field in a form while in Design view and choose Properties from the shortcut menu. In the window, you can click on any of the tabs shown, then click in the desired property to change the property.

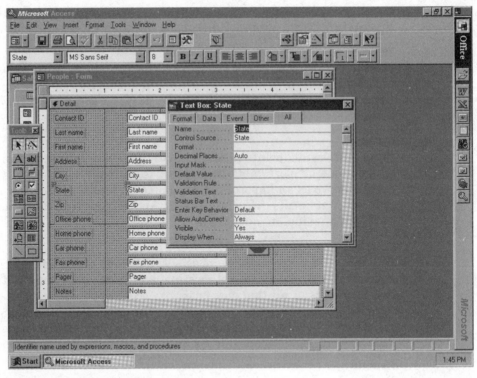

Figure 3.3 Properties for a field of a form.

For developers, it's important to be aware of this property-oriented nature of objects in Access. Most objects literally have dozens of properties that you can modify at will. You often can save time in terms of how much coding you must do by making full use of the properties of Access objects. While Access lacks the methods that some other programmable development environments possess, you still can change the behaviors of Access objects by adding *event procedures* composed of program code to many object properties.

How Access Relates to the Windows Environment

Access originally was developed for the Windows environment to provide database applications with a Windows look-and-feel. As a graphical user environment, Windows follows the CUA (common user access) standards. Command prompts (driven by traditional programming code operating in a linear fashion) has been replaced with menus, dialog boxes, and icons representing objects within a graphical environment. Windows is event-driven by nature, meaning that the software environment responds to events performed by the user, like clicking on an icon or selecting a menu option. Because

Windows has become the dominant GUI environment, overall software design is following its lead. While Windows 3.*x* can't be called object-oriented, its successor (Windows 95) has definite object-oriented tendencies, so the design of Access can be seen as part of an overall trend.

As a Windows product, Access also supports dynamic data exchange (DDE) and object linking and embedding (OLE), features of Windows that permit the easy exchange of data between different Windows applications. Using DDE within an Access application, you can pass data from Access to another Windows application under the control of the Access application. With OLE, you can launch and run another Windows application from an Access application, working with the data transferred from Access inside the other application.

Summary

With Access as your development environment, you're getting a capable object-based environment that you can use to produce robust client-server applications. Any application that you develop in Access will use forms as the basis for your user interface, and you'll design the overall application around a collection of various objects. While much of the design work will be interactive in nature, you also can use Visual Basic for Applications code to work with various Access objects within your application. In the next chapter, I'll look at programming topics central to applications development in Access.

Programming in Microsoft Access

In this chapter, you'll learn about Visual Basic for Applications. (Throughout the rest of the chapter, I'll refer to Visual Basic for Applications as VBA for short.) In many cases, nearly all of the work behind applications development can be accomplished without resorting to Visual Basic for Applications program code; many an Access application has been developed with nothing more than dozens of macros along with the other basic Access objects. Because that's the case, a logical question that arises is, why bother with Visual Basic for Applications? The answer is that the use of Visual Basic for Applications makes it possible to go beyond the capabilities of macros and of the interactive use of Access.

There are a number of good reasons for including Visual Basic for Applications in your bag of development tricks. One point is that the use of Visual Basic for Applications allows tight control over an application. You can perform error handling, which is something that you can't do with Access macros. Another plus is that applications written with extensive use of VBA code are easier to maintain, because the VBA code gets attached to objects like forms and reports, and these forms and reports can be moved around without having to put up with the planning nightmare that arises when you use macros for the same tasks.

For example, if a form that serves as a switchboard has six buttons, all of which are attached to macros, and you decide to use that form as the basis of a switchboard in a different database, you must copy the form and all of the associated macros to the other database. On the other hand, if the switchboard buttons call VBA code stored in a module that's part of the form, you only need to copy the form to the other database.

The purpose of this chapter is to introduce Visual Basic for Applications to readers having some background in programming. That being the case, I assume that you have a knowledge of the basic building blocks of computer programming, including programming structures, calling and returning from procedures, and the use of variables and data typing for those variables. Don't look for this chapter to teach the fundamentals of programming; that topic represents an entire book in itself.

If you've been an interactive user of Access, and programming in general is a totally new topic to you, it might be a good idea to consider a book on general programming principles or on programming either in VBA or its counterpart, Microsoft Visual Basic. You can refer to the *Building Applications* guide packaged with your Access documentation.

What's Familiar and Unfamiliar about VBA

If you are an experienced programmer, you'll find that Visual Basic for Applications bears strong similarities to many high-level structured languages, including C and Pascal. As one might expect, it shares common traits with other dialects of Basic. If you're familiar with other versions of Basic running in Microsoft applications (like Word Basic and Excel Basic in older versions of Excel), you'll find Visual Basic for Applications to be very similar. If you've worked with Microsoft's Visual Basic, you'll find Visual Basic for Applications in Access to be like a familiar glove, because Visual Basic for Applications is modeled on Visual Basic. The statements that you expect to see in any structured language are all there, including the following:

- Select Case structures to test for one condition out of many.

- Do...Loop and For...Next structures to repeat statements a number of times.

- If...Then...Else... structures to test for conditions.

- Exit statements to exit procedures.

- Dimension (Dim) statements to declare variables and arrays.

Users of Microsoft's Visual Basic are likely to be those most familiar with VBA, as the languages are nearly identical. (In fact, you can think of VBA as implemented in Access as a specialized variant of Visual Basic, designed to be used to manipulate Access databases.) Visual Basic and VBA share their leanings toward object orientation, where what the user sees is changed not through the use of a series of procedural statements, but by changing the objects on the Access desktop. The user interface is quite similar between VBA in Access and Visual Basic; both use toolbars and a drawing surface where you can place controls that have procedures attached to them, and the two share many of the same statements and functions.

Where VBA differs from many conventional programming languages is in how it is used; the difference actually has little to do with the language itself and a lot to do with the design of Access. Conventional programming languages traditionally have been used to tightly control everything that happens in a complete system. Often they use coding that results in a procedural or "top down" system design, where a main menu offers certain options, and those options control what can be done by the user within the program. By comparison, VBA is designed to support Access, which is an event-driven database manager with object-based behavior. VBA code can be attached to different objects within Access, and the code runs in response to various events that occur. For example, opening a report or moving the cursor into a certain control on a form can be the event that triggers a block of VBA program code. The code tells VBA to perform a certain operation in response to the event; hence the term, *event-driven programming*.

Understanding Where VBA Fits

One point that's important to understand when becoming familiar with VBA is exactly where the language fits into the grand scheme of application development in Access. Users of dBASE for DOS, FoxPro, early versions of Basic, C, and Pascal might be tempted to learn just the language of VBA and ignore as much of the rest of the Access as possible. This is *not* recommended, because along with the similarities, there are major differences in how Access is used compared to those languages. (Exceptions to this statement include Borland's Paradox for Windows and dBASE for Windows products; the programming languages inherent in those products are tightly integrated with the object-based design of those products, just as VBA is integrated into Access as a whole.)

Many programmers find VBA code to be familiar, because it is a high-level programming language like other versions of Basic, and like Pascal, Paradox PAL and ObjectPAL, and the variants of xBASE. VBA is tightly integrated into the database objects that are present in an Access database. VBA lets you declare database objects (such as tables and query dynasets) as variables, and you then can work with the data in these objects by working with the variables under the control of VBA code. Also, many tasks for which you would need to write code in other database managers can be done in Access with macros or are taken care of by the properties of the objects themselves.

An excellent example is to compare forms used for data entry in Access with their counterparts in older variants of dBASE for DOS. To create a form in such versions of dBASE for DOS, a program file that contains numerous lines of program code is required to place the fields and the labels on the screen in the desired locations. In Access, no code is needed for a data-entry form; all the logic needed to display the fields and the labels and to allow the user to interact with the form is an integral part of the form itself.

If your intent as a programmer is to become only vaguely familiar with the other objects of Access and jump right into writing programs, be warned that this is a poor approach to learning the effective use of VBA as a part of Access application development. The tight integration of VBA with the rest of Access requires the programmer to have a strong familiarity with the other objects in Access, if VBA is to be used effectively.

The unique way that Access is used, and where it fits in, calls for a different way of thinking for many programmers. This is particularly true for those who have written database applications using DOS-based products such as dBASE, versions 1.*x* and 2.*x* of FoxPro, and Paradox for DOS. With these programs, programmers write applications using a top-down or procedural style of coding, where a central menu controls all possible user actions. By comparison, with your Access applications, you should first ask yourself if the code that you are about to write is even necessary. The application's overall design should be implemented in operational form with no code, and code can even be added where needed to provide the advantages VBA can provide.

Macros Versus Visual Basic for Applications

A significant feature of Access when compared to other database managers (even those in the Windows marketplace) is that it offers the user two distinct ways to approach programming: with macros and with VBA code. Macros and VBA code both have distinct advantages in different situations. Interestingly, when Access was first introduced, Microsoft recommended that developers write applications using macros whenever possible, supplementing the application with Access Basic code (Access Basic being the forerunner of VBA) only when absolutely necessary. Currently, Microsoft has moved away from that approach somewhat, recommending more of a mix of macros and VBA code in robust database applications. In fact, if you make use of the Control Wizards to add buttons for performing common database tasks, under investigation you will find that the buttons call VBA code.

Using Macros

It is best to use macros in the following situations:

When you want to quickly prototype an application. You can design and implement an application based on user suggestions or specifications using macros. Switchboards and custom menus can be created, and options tied to forms and reports to provide a complete database application that handles a specific business task. The ability of Access to support rapid application prototyping of database applications has led to its use in demonstrating prototype business applications for local area networks within the corporate setting. After the client or organization agrees that the proposed application is what is desired, the programmer has the option of designing the equivalent application using VBA, or Visual Basic, or an environment optimized for speed, such as C.

When you need to offer custom menus within the Access environment. To have custom pull-down menus replace some or all of the standard Access menus, you have no other choice; you must use macros. The design of VBA doesn't allow custom menus created through VBA code, although you can create switchboards that use VBA code to respond to the switchboard buttons.

When you want to perform simple form- or report-related activities, such as opening or closing forms, or printing reports.

When you want to establish a specific environment upon startup of an application. An autoexec macro is the only way to perform any specific task automatically as soon as a database is opened. The autoexec macro can run a VBA procedure if that's what you want, but the autoexec macro must be used to get the process started.

Using VBA Code

It is best to use VBA code in the following situations:

When you want to tightly control possible errors that might occur within your application. Every professional application must maintain some level of error handling, which governs how the program behaves when something does not occur as it should. Usually, this is because the user does something for which the programmer did not plan—perhaps entering a letter in a dialog box where a number was expected, or pressing the Esc key while a macro is executing. With errors, macros result in the dreaded Macro Failed dialog box, and the user often is left wondering what to do next. Where VBA code is used in the place of macros, you can make an application respond properly to errors, display understandable error messages, and provide users with a clear way out.

When you need to add user-defined functions (UDFs). Many programmers are accustomed to working with user-defined functions, which are customized functions that supplement those made available by the language. Like other programming languages, Access has dozens of built-in functions for providing system values, such as the current date, or for calculating the interest on a simple payment. However, you might need a function that Access does not offer; for example, you might need to calculate the sales tax for an amount, given the names of three different states with different tax rates. If you must perform this same calculation in a half-dozen different forms and reports, it would be best to create a user-defined function to handle the task. That function then could be called from any of the forms or reports as needed to calculate the appropriate sales task.

When you want to perform actions at the system level. With Access Basic code, you can initiate dynamic data exchange conversations to exchange data with other Windows-based applications under the control of a program.

When you want to develop any parts of an application that are simply beyond the capabilities of Access macros. An excellent example of this is the wizards present in Access. All Access wizards actually are programs, written in VBA. The kinds of tasks done by the wizards cannot be handled with macros.

About Procedures and Modules

The programs that you write in VBA are called *procedures*. Each procedure contains one or more *statements*. The statements tell Access what should be done whenever a procedure is called by the object to which it is attached. For example, a command button on a form might have a procedure attached to its OnClick property; when the button is clicked by the user, the procedure runs.

You can have two kinds of procedures in VBA: *function procedures* and *sub procedures*. Function procedures always return a value and can be used as part of expressions. Sub procedures perform operations, but they do not return values. An excellent example of sub procedures are those written by the Control Wizards when you use them to add command buttons to forms. When a user clicks such a button, the button calls VBA code (written by the wizards) to accomplish a specific task. All *event procedures* (which are procedures that are attached to events which occur in forms, reports, or controls) are sub procedures.

One or more procedures can be stored in a *module*. Modules can be database objects; these appear in the Database window when you click the Module button. Access actually lets you have two types of modules: *form and report modules* and *global modules*. Form and report modules are private to the form or report of which they are a part. You do not see these modules in the Database window, and they can be used only by the form or report of which they are a part. Global modules are modules that exist as individual objects in a database. These exist apart from other objects, and they can be called from anywhere within an application. When you click the Module button in the Database window, the modules that you see are global modules.

The Structure of a Module

Each module contains a single *declarations section* and one or more procedures. The declarations section contains any declarations that affect general settings of all procedures in the module. (Usually there is a single Option Compare Database statement in the declarations section.) The declarations section is visible when the module is initially opened. (You can open a global module by selecting it in the Database window and clicking the Design button. Form and report modules can be opened by opening the form or report in design view and clicking the Code button in the toolbar or by choosing View/Code from the menus.) Pressing the PgDn key reveals the procedures that are stored in the module; if there is more than one procedure, pressing PgDn moves to the next successive procedure. When the last procedure is visible, pressing PgDn moves back to the declarations section.

An Exercise: Creating VBA Procedures with the Control Wizards

An introduction to how VBA code can be used to accomplish a task is to use the Control Wizards to add command buttons to a form and study the VBA code that the Control Wizards produce as a result. You can perform the following steps to quickly create and examine VBA code For example:

1. Open the Sales database if it isn't already open, and click the Tables tab.

2. Click the People table to select it, then open the New Object drop-down menu on the toolbar, and choose the AutoForm option to quickly build a default form for the table.

3. When the new form opens, choose View Design to switch to Design view.

4. If the Toolbox is not already visible, choose View/Toolbox to display it.

5. Turn on the Control Wizards if they are not already on (click the Control Wizards button until it is depressed).

6. In the Toolbox, click the Command button, then click in a blank area of the form to place a command button. In a moment, the Command Button Wizard dialog box appears, as shown in Figure 4.1.

7. Under Category, click Record Operations. Then, under When Button Is Pressed, click Print Record. Then, click Finish to add a button that prints the record displayed in the form.

8. In the Toolbox, click the Command button, then click in a blank area of the form beside or below the button that you just placed to add another command button. In a moment, the Command Button Wizard dialog box again appears.

9. Under Category, click Application. Then, under When Button Is Pressed, click Run Notepad. Then, click Finish to add a button that, when clicked, causes the Windows Notepad to appear.

10. Choose File/Save from the menus to save the new form. When prompted for a name, call the form Test Form 1. You can verify that the buttons do what you intended, if you like, by choosing View/Form from the menus to switch to Form view and clicking either button on the form.

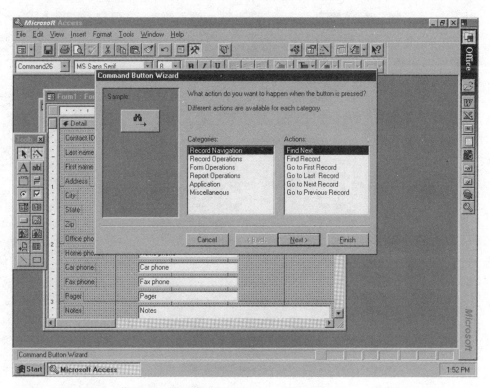

Figure 4.1 The Command Button Wizard dialog box.

Now that the form exists, consider just how the buttons accomplish what they do. Switch to Design mode by choosing `View/Form Design` from the menus. Right-click the `Print` button, and choose `Properties` from the shortcut menu that appears, to open the Properties window for the new button. As shown in Figure 4.2, the button created by the Control Wizards has been assigned a name of its own (this name is a unique name assigned by Access). Similarly, the second button that you added also has a unique name of its own.

Close the Properties window and click the `Code` button on the toolbar (or choose `View/Code` from the menus). A window into the Form Module opens, containing the declarations section of the module, with the following entry:

```
Option Compare Database
Option Explicit
```

In addition to this declarations section, there are two procedures, one for each of the buttons that you added. If you press the PgDn key, you see the first procedure, as shown in Figure 4.3.

This procedure was added by the Control Wizards to respond to the `Print` button that you added. The procedure starts with a line similar to the following (the name of the button in your case might be different):

Figure 4.2 The Properties window for a newly added button.

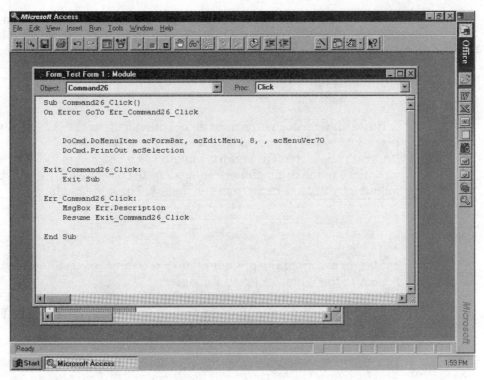

Figure 4.3 The first procedure in a module.

```
Sub Button26_Click ( )
```

and the procedure ends with a line like the following:

```
End Sub
```

Event procedures (such as this one, which responds to a button being clicked) are sub procedures, and all sub procedures begin with Sub and end with End Sub. Everything that falls between these two lines is the code of the procedure. In this example, the second line of the procedure:

```
On Error GoTo Err_Command26_Click
```

provides error trapping for the procedure; it tells Access that, if an error occurs while the procedure is running (for example, the user cancels the print request by clicking the Cancel button in the Print dialog box that appears), program control then should jump to this portion of the procedure:

```
Err_Command26_Click:
    MsgBox Error$
    Resume Exit_Command36_Click
```

This causes a message box that contains the type of error to be displayed for the user. The statements of the procedure that perform the intended task (assuming that no error occurs) are contained in the following lines:

```
DoCmd.DoMenuItem acFormBar, acEditMenu, 8, , acMenuVer70
DoCmd.PrintOut acSelection
```

These statements perform actions equivalent to the Access menu choices needed to select a record and to print the selection. In VBA, the `DoCmd DoMenuItem` statement performs an Access menu command. These particular variations of the command are equivalent to choosing `Edit/Select Record`, followed by `File/Print` from the menus. The statements:

```
Exit_Command26_Click:
    Exit Sub
```

causes an exit from the procedure after the print request has been successfully sent to the Windows Print Manager.

If you press the PgDn key, you see the procedure that has been added by the Control Wizards for the Notepad button you added, as shown in Figure 4.4.

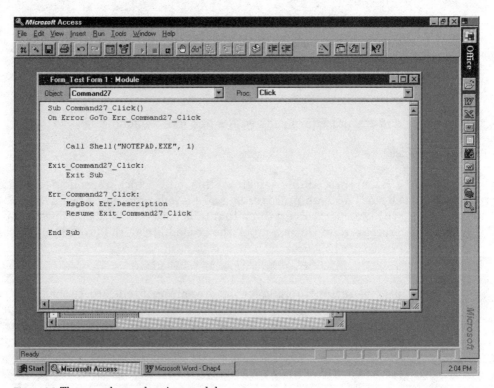

Figure 4.4 The second procedure in a module.

The overall design of the procedure is similar to that of the first procedure shown in Figure 4.3, starting with a Sub statement, ending with an End Sub statement, and containing an On Error statement that references an error routine stored at the end of the procedure. The following statement performs the actual work behind the button:

```
Call Shell("NOTEPAD.EXE", 1)
```

In VBA, the Shell function runs the Windows or DOS program named within the argument of the function; in this case, the Windows Notepad (NOTEPAD.EXE).

The kind of analysis demonstrated by this exercise is an excellent way for those new to VBA to become familiar with the language and how it is used. You can use the Control Wizards to add buttons for different tasks to a form or a report, then open the module window while in Design view to study the code that handles the particular job. If you examine the People form from the Sales database that's stored on the CD-ROM, you can open that form in Design view and examine the modules in it that respond to the buttons in the form.

The paragraphs that follow detail more of the mechanics of programming, including creating modules and procedures, working with the module window, printing modules, loading and saving modules as text, and getting help.

Creating and Opening Modules

You can create new modules or open existing modules by using the following steps. To create a global module, click the Modules tab in the Database window, then click New. When you do so, Access displays a new module in the Module window, as shown in Figure 4.5.

To open an existing global module, perform the following steps:

1. In the Database window, click the Modules tab to see a list of available modules in the database.

2. Click the module that you want to open to select it.

3. Click the Design button. When you do so, Access opens the module in the Module window. (You also can perform Steps 2 and 3 simultaneously by double-clicking the desired module in the Database window.)

To open a form or report module, perform the following steps:

1. In the Database window, click the Form button or the Report button, then click the desired form or report to select it.

2. Click the Code button on the toolbar, or choose View/Code from the menus. When you do so, the form or report opens in Design view, along with its module.

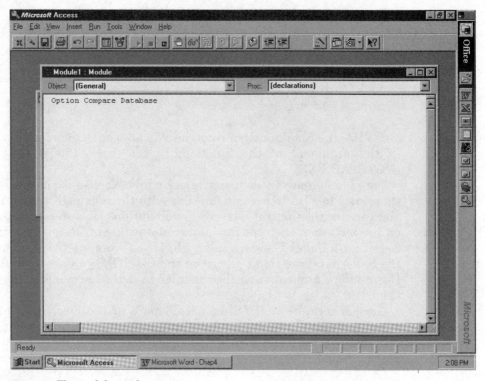

Figure 4.5 The module window.

About the Module Window

Enter all procedures, as well as any entries into the Declarations section, using the *module window*. The module window is a text editor and is very similar in operation to the Windows Notepad. However, it offers features that the Windows Notepad does not. What's most significant is that the module window checks the syntax of your entries as you enter them, and it organizes the code into appropriate procedures. For example, when you type a line that begins with Function or Sub on a blank line anywhere in the declarations section, the module window automatically starts a new function or sub procedure in a window of its own. The module window also contains its own toolbar buttons to work with different procedures and to aid in the debugging process. Figure 4.6 shows the parts of the module window.

You can use the Object and Procedure list boxes to find and jump to a particular procedure or to create a new procedure. In the case of forms and reports, the Object list box displays all of the objects associated with the form or report. The buttons on the right side of the toolbar are used for debugging purposes, and their use is detailed in Chapter 11.

You can enter and edit the text of your procedures as you would enter and edit text in any text editor. Windows cut-and-paste techniques can be used in the module window. Table 4.1 shows the editing keys that can be used in the module window.

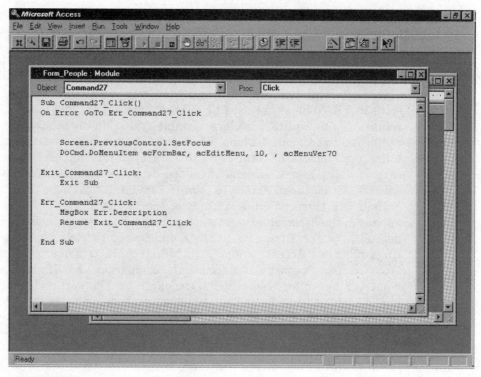

Figure 4.6 The parts of the module window.

Table 4.1

Key	Result
Ctrl–N	Inserts a new line above the current one
Ctrl–Y	Deletes the current line and copies it to the windows Clipboard
PgUp or Ctrl–Up Arrow	Displays the prior procedure
PgDn or Ctrl–Down Arrow	Displays the next procedure
F1	Displays help for the reserved word where the insertion pointer is located; if the insertion pointer is not on a reserved word, displays the Programming Topics help screen
Tab	Indents code

About the Declarations Section

The declarations section of a module is where you make any declarations that affect the overall module. You can declare external procedures (such as those called from the Windows application program interface). Because the declarations section is the first thing seen when a module is opened, many programmers place extensive comments describing the module's contents in the declarations section.

By default, the declarations section of a new module contains an `Option Compare Database` statement and, in Access 97, an `Option Explicit` statement. This tells Access to use the same rules when evaluating expressions in VBA code as are used by the database objects in Access. VBA does not require you to explicitly declare variable types. However, many programmers prefer you to do so; in the long run, being forced to declare data types can minimize the chances of errors due to data type mismatches. You can add an `Option Explicit` statement (added by default in Access 97) in the declarations section to tell Access to require explicit declarations of all variables.

There are three possible settings of the `Option Compare` statement that appear in the declarations section: `Option Compare Database` (which is the default), `Option Compare Binary`, and `Option Compare Text`. These settings affect how Access compares individual characters in a string of VBA code. With `Option Compare Database`, the comparison is performed according to whatever sort order is specified in the database (this setting is made by choosing `View/Options` from the menus and choosing a `New Database Sort Order` under the General category.) You can change this to `Option Compare Binary` or `Option Compare Text`. If `Option Compare Binary` is used, string comparisons are made in a case-sensitive manner, according to the ANSI character set. If `Option Compare Text` is used, strings are compared on a case-insensitive basis according to the Country code that's stored in the International setting of the Windows Control Panel.

Creating and Editing Procedures

In Access, creating new procedures is rather automatic because Access constantly monitors and interprets what you type into the module window. To create a new procedure, open a new or existing module, and on a blank line in the module window type `Function` or `Sub` followed by the name of the function or sub procedure, then press Enter. When you do so, Access automatically adds a new procedure, as illustrated in Figure 4.7.

In the window, you can type the text of the function procedure or the sub procedure. Remember that function procedures accept zero or more arguments, and return a value, whereas sub procedures accept zero or more arguments but do not return a value. Procedure names must be unique (you can't have more than one procedure with the same name in the same database), and procedure names can have up to 40 characters, including underscores, and must begin with a letter.

Tip: You also can quickly begin a new procedure by clicking the `New Procedure` button that's visible on the toolbar when the module is open. When you click this button, a dialog box appears, asking if you want to create a new function procedure or a new sub procedure. Click the desired procedure type, then click `OK`.

As you enter the statements of the procedure, Access checks your entries, so you quickly know if you have made a syntax error or in some other way

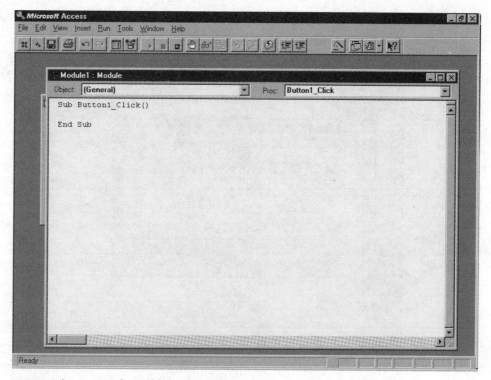

Figure 4.7 A new procedure added to a module.

entered a statement that Access does not understand. If you enter a statement that Access cannot understand, you see a dialog box warning of the problem, and the problem portion of the statement is automatically highlighted. You then can correct the problem.

Changing the Displayed Procedure

By default, Access shows only one procedure at a time in the module window. In a module that contains multiple procedures, you can move between the procedures by pressing the PgUp or PgDn keys. Yet another method (which is helpful if you have a large number of procedures in a module) is to choose View/Object Browser from the menus or to press F2. When you do this, the View Object Browser dialog box opens (see Figure 4.8), showing all available procedures by name.

You can click the desired procedure in the Object Browser list box, then click Show to open that procedure in a window.

Viewing Two Procedures Simultaneously

You can view two procedures in the module window at the same time by dragging the split bar (see Figure 4.9) or by choosing Window/Split Window from the menus. With either method, the module window is split into two parts, as

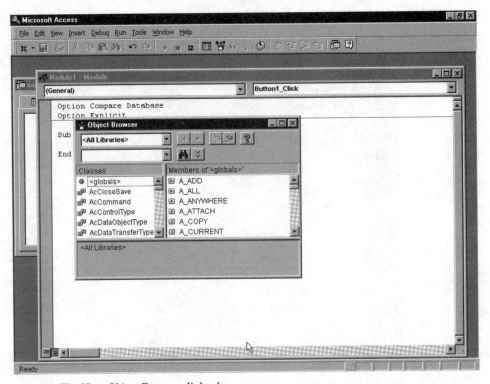

Figure 4.8 The View Object Browser dialog box.

illustrated in Figure 4.9. You can click in either portion of the window and use the techniques noted earlier to change the displayed procedures.

Calling a Procedure

From your other VBA code, you can call a procedure simply by naming it within a VBA statement. For example, a line of code that contains the statement BeepMe(2) would call a procedure named BeepMe and pass a value of 2 to that procedure. You also can use the Call keyword followed by the procedure name, as in Call BeepMe(2), but the Call keyword is optional. VBA does not require its use, but it is allowed as a holdover from earlier versions of Basic.

Private Versus Static Variables

By nature, all variables in a VBA procedure are *private* to the program. A private variable is available only within the procedure that created it; after program control leaves the procedure, the variable is lost from memory. If you want a variable to be available to other procedures, you need to declare it as a *static* variable. Static variables are not released from memory when the procedure that contains them ends. The syntax for the Static statement is

```
Static name as type, name as type..
```

For example, you could declare variable A as a static string variable and variable B as a static integer variable with a statement such as the following:

```
Static A as String, B as Integer
```

Variables that you declare using the Static statement retain their values until you reinitialize them elsewhere or until the program ends.

Passing Parameters to a Procedure

Your procedures can include values passed to the procedure by the calling statement. For example, the following user-defined function, BeepMe, accepts two parameters from the calling statement: the number of beeps to sound and the text that should appear in a message box that the user sees:

```
Function BeepMe(NumBeeps as Integer, SayWhat as String)
    For X = 1 to NumBeeps
        Beep
    Next
    MsgBox SayWhat
End Function
```

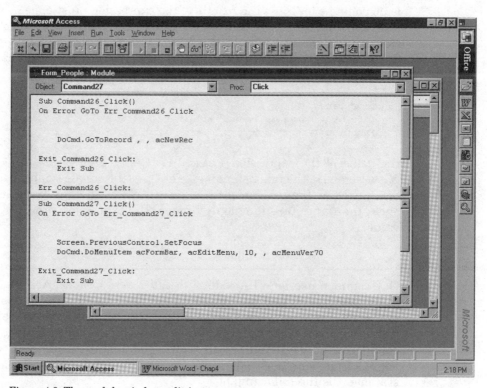

Figure 4.9 The module window split in two.

The parameters are identified inside the parenthesis that follow the name of the procedure. In cases such as this, where there are multiple parameters, separate each parameter with a comma. If this function were stored in a global module, VBA code elsewhere in the application could call the function with a statement such as the following:

```
BeepMe(10, "No such filename")
```

The result would be 10 beeps, followed by a message box that contained the text string "No such filename."

Using Expressions in VBA Statements

Expressions, which are commonly used in calculated controls that appear in forms and reports, also serve as the basis for the functions you create in VBA. A difference is that with VBA, you include an equals sign and the name of the function to create an *assignment statement* that assigns the desired results to the function. In an example of a `DateDue` calculation for a video store's rentals tracking database, placing an expression in a specific control such as `=[Date Rented] + 2` is all that's needed. Because the expression is assigned to the control when you type it into the control or into the Properties window, there is no doubt as to where the results of the expression must appear. With a VBA function, it is not so obvious what should be done with the results of an expression. An assignment statement is used, with the function name, followed by the equals sign, followed by the expression; therefore, the result of the expression is assigned to the function name. In the following text:

```
Function DateDue( )
    DateDue = Forms ! [Rentals] ! [Date Rented] + 2
End Function
```

the value of the expression `Forms ! [Rentals] ! [Date Rented] + 2` is assigned to the function name `DateDue` (the equals symbol between them being used as the *assignment statement*). When another Access object references the `Date Due` function by name, the expression provides the needed value.

Calling Macros

One common use for VBA code is to call macro actions. At first, this might seem unnecessary because you could call the same macro actions from within a macro. However, the advantage of using VBA is that you can maintain tighter control over the application, including error trapping, while still relying on macro actions with which you might be familiar. Call macro actions from your VBA code using the `DoCmd` statement. The syntax for this statement is the following:

```
DoCmd actionname [argumentlist]
```

where *actionname* is the name of the macro action and *argumentlist* is the list of arguments, if any are needed. Whenever the argument list takes multiple arguments, separate them with commas. For example, if you followed the exercise earlier in this chapter that created a form with command buttons, you saw code created by the Control Wizards with statements, such as the following:

```
DoCmd Print 1    `Print SelectionB
```

In the case of this macro action (the Print action), the arguments specify the type of object to be printed and the name of the object. Keep in mind that you can get help for the names of all possible macro actions and arguments by searching the Help system for the name of the desired macro action.

Exiting a Procedure

By default, procedures end when program control reaches an End Function or an End Sub statement. You can force an early end to a procedure by including an Exit Function or Exit Sub statement elsewhere in the code. When a procedure terminates, all variables that were private to the procedure (that is, any variables that were created within the procedure) are lost. Therefore, if you want to use values generated by a procedure elsewhere within your application, you should assign them before exiting the procedure and declare them on a global level.

Saving a Module

To save a completed module (and all its procedures), choose File/Save from the menus. A dialog box appears, asking for a name for the module (if you are saving it for the first time). Enter the desired name, then click OK; after saving the module, you can press Ctrl–F4 to close the module window. Remember that the need to save modules under a given name applies only to global modules. Form and report modules are a part of the forms and reports to which they are attached, and they are saved when you save the form or the report.

Printing a Procedure

To print a procedure that is part of a global module, click the desired module in the Database window, and choose File/Print from the menus. To print a procedure that is part of a form or report, open the form or report in Design view, choose View/Code to open the module window, then choose File/Print. In either case, printing the module prints both the declarations section and all the procedures contained in the module. If you just want to print a single procedure, find that procedure, and select the entire procedure (click and drag from the beginning of the procedure's code to the end). Then choose File/Print, and in the Print dialog box that appears, click Selection, then click OK to begin printing.

Saving Modules as Text

You can save procedures as text, with the `File/Save As Text` command. This command (available from the File menu whenever a module is open) can be used to save the contents of a module window as a text file. To save the contents of a module as a text file, open the desired module, and choose `File/Save As Text`. When you do so, the Save As Text dialog box appears (see Figure 4.10).

Under File Name, type the name of the file that contains the code that you want to save, or choose a filename from the list box. (Use the Directories and Drives list boxes to navigate your drives and directories.) After entering or choosing a name, click OK to save the module's contents as a text file.

Adding Comments to Procedures

Comments are a recommended aspect of most programming. In VBA, you can create comments by prefacing them with a single quote (`). VBA ignores any text that follows the single quote character until it reaches the end of the line. For example, you might have a statement in a module such as the following:

```
x = Shell("NOTEPAD.EXE", 1) ` This line loads the Notepad.
```

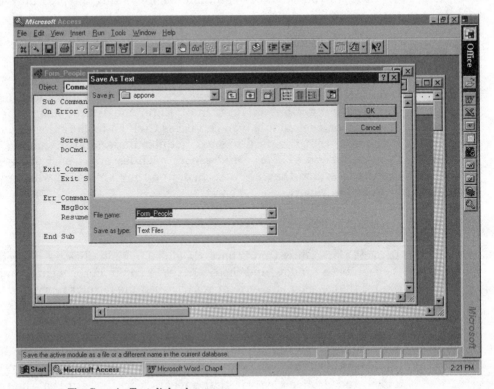

Figure 4.10 The Save As Text dialog box.

The portion of the statement following the single quote would be ignored by Access; it serves only to identify to the programmer what the line of code is used for. You can begin a line with a single quote, in which case the entire line is a comment. Note, too, that VBA lets you use the Rem keyword to begin a comment; Rem is the equivalent of the single quote and is familiar to those who have programmed in dialects of Basic in the past.

Getting Help

Like any structured language, VBA requires you to follow a specific syntax. Adhering to that syntax can be challenging, but the online help available in Access can be a big aid in this area. You can get specific help for any reserved word in VBA by clicking anywhere within that word in a module and pressing F1. The Help system displays a window that contains the appropriate topic for that word. You also can open any help window, click Search, enter Visual Basic for Applications as a search topic, and click the Show Topics button. The available topics that you see include a Functions Reference, a Methods Reference, a Reference and VBA Topics List, and Programming Topics. Click any of these as desired, then click the GoTo button to see more on the specific topic.

Examples of Procedures

Because VBA is used differently from database programming languages outside the Windows environment, it is impossible to demonstrate the use of VBA around any sort of procedural approach, as can be found in books that demonstrate programming in dBASE for DOS or Paradox for DOS. One of the best ways to become familiar with when and where VBA code should be used is to study existing examples of VBA procedures. The remainder of this chapter highlights some examples of VBA procedures used in different applications; you undoubtedly can find others by opening the module window in applications made by others (such as the Northwind Traders application shipped with Access) and examining the code contained within.

The Utility Functions module in the Northwind Traders database contains a number of different user-defined functions; one of these is highlighted here, and you might want to spend time examining the others. This function is designed to tell a VBA routine whether a particular form is loaded. Its code is as follows:

```
Function IsLoaded(ByVal strFormName As String) As Integer
 ' Returns True if the specified form is open in Form view or Datasheet
view.

    Const conObjStateClosed = 0
    Const conDesignView = 0

    If SysCmd(acSysCmdGetObjectState, acForm, strFormName) <>
conObjStateClosed Then
        If Forms(strFormName).CurrentView <> conDesignView Then
            IsLoaded = True
```

```
        End If
    End If

End Function
```

The calling VBA routine passes the name of a form to the function as a string variable. The function returns true if the form is loaded and false if the form is not loaded.

As yet another example of using VBA to solve a real-world problem, consider the need to calculate the number of working days between two dates. There is no built-in function in VBA that determines the number of working days between two given dates, but you can get this kind of information with a user-defined function written in VBA. The function shown here includes the start date and the end date, so the number of days between 01/03/96 and 01/12/96 equals 7 (because the sixth and seventh of that month for that year fall on a weekend).

```
Option Explicit
Function WorkDays (StartDate as Variant, EndDate as Variant) As Integer
    Dim TheWeek as Variant
    Dim CountDates as Variant
    Dim EndDays as Integer
    StartDate = DateValue(StartDate)
    EndDate = DateValue(EndDate)
    TheWeek = DateDiff("w", StartDate, EndDate)
    CountDates = DateAdd("ww", TheWeek, StartDate)
    EndDays = 0
    Do While CountDates <= EndDate
        If Format(CountDates, "ddd") <> "Sun" and
            Format(CountDates, "ddd") <> "Sat" then
            EndDays = EndDays + 1
        End If
        CountDates = DateAdd("d", 1, CountDates)
    Loop
    WorkDays = TheWeek * 5 + EndDays
End Function
```

To call the function, you would pass it either a valid string or an actual date value (in Access, date values are enclosed in # signs). The following shows two ways to call this function from the Immediate window (for more on the Immediate window, see Chapter 11):

```
? WorkDays(#06/02/94#, #06/07/94#)
4
```

This chapter's last example of a potential use of VBA is shown in the code for the following function, which accepts a date value, and returns the last day of the month for the month in which that date falls:

```
Function FindEOM(TheDate)
    Dim NextMonth, EndOfMonth
    NextMonth = DateAdd("m", 1, TheDate)
    EndOfMonth = NextMonth - DatePart("d",NextMonth)
    FindEOM = EndOfMonth
End Function
```

The following expression could be used in a form or report:

```
=FindEOM(MyDate)
```

assuming that MyDate is an existing variable containing a given date value.

Summary

This chapter has detailed VBA programming in Access on an introductory level, with coverage of creating and saving modules, using procedures, passing parameters, using statements, and calling macros. As the chapter has outlined, a significant part of development in Access involves understanding where VBA fits into the picture. With both macros and VBA as development tools, you have the flexibility needed to meet your development needs.

Designing Access Forms for the Object-Based Development Environment

In Access, forms provide both a means for adding and editing data and a foundation for the user interface for any application. Forms in Access can be created quickly with the New Object button on the Toolbar or by means of the Form Wizards. You also can design forms manually by means of a Form Design window, which lets you drag objects (such as fields and text) to any desired location. Figure 5.1 shows a table's datasheet and a form for editing that table's data. In this case, the form was created in a single step, using the Toolbar's New Object button.

Developers accustomed to database products from the pre-Windows days are accustomed to forms that provide data and text labels but, with Access, you can do much more. You can use forms to display graphics, such as drawings, photos, or corporate logos. Calculated fields can be included to offer totals or other summations of numeric information. You also can display data from related tables; for example, a form for customer orders could show one record for a specific customer from a customers table and all associated sales calls placed to that customer. Figure 5.2 shows a form of this type.

Forms also offer the flexibility to display a specific subset of data that's appropriate for the occasion. You might have a number of different forms using the same table, offering different views of the needed data. For example, consider the two forms shown in Figure 5.3.

In this case, a table of sales contacts supports two different forms, both designed to serve the different needs of a single application. One form shows primary data for the contacts, and another shows contact phone numbers. To place all this information in a single form could make the form awkward to work with; having separate forms enables users to quickly get at the information that's relevant in a particular setting.

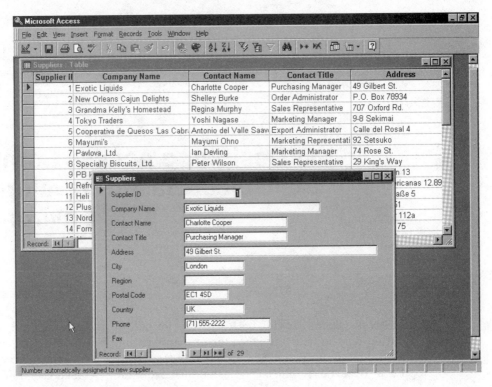

Figure 5.1 An example of a form.

To most interactive Access users, forms are the easy way for adding and editing data to a table. However, this use of forms represents just one of the many capabilities of forms within Access. A very common use for forms in applications is as *switchboards*, or main menus that provide the users with ways to reach different parts of the application. If you open the Northwind Traders database (it's included with your installation of Access), click the Forms button in the Database window, and open the form titled Main Switchboard, you will see an example of a form used as a switchboard (Figure 5.4).

Clicking on any of the buttons shown in the form causes a corresponding macro to run. The macro then performs other necessary actions (such as the opening of additional switchboards, the running of queries to retrieve data, or the printing of reports).

Forms Should Be Based On...?

One point that you'll need to decide early on in the forms designs process is whether the forms should be based on tables or on queries.

Because Access lets you base forms on tables or on queries, some advance planning might be a wise idea to help make the most effective use of forms. When creating forms with any method but the toolbar's AutoForm button, Access displays a New Form dialog box at the start of the process (Figure 5.5).

You use this dialog box to indicate which table or query the form should be based upon. If you intend to use the form to examine any or all of the records in a single table, base the form on the table. If you need to examine data from multiple tables or if you need to examine a selected subset of data, base the form on a query. You can later change the underlying table or query that a form is based on by changing the form's RecordSource property. You'll find details on how to do this later in the chapter.

Tip: When you base a form on a query, Access runs the query as the form opens. Hence, forms based on very large tables and/or complex queries can be slow to open.

About the Form Views in Access

Access offers three different views as you work with forms: *design view*, *datasheet view*, and *form view*. You can easily move between the different views by clicking the down arrow beside the Form View button in the toolbar and choosing the desired view.

Design view is used to make changes to the design of the form or to change the properties of the controls and other objects that are in the form.

Form view is the view that you use as you work with the data in the form; you can view, enter, and edit data, typically in a record-at-a-time format.

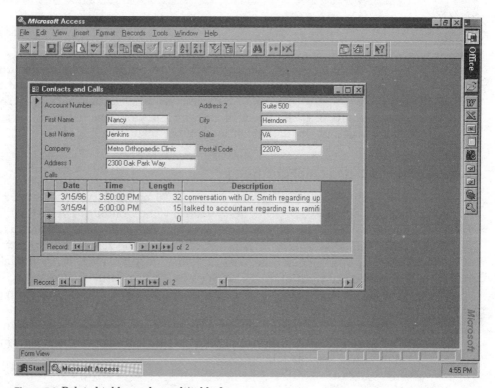

Figure 5.2 Related tables and a multitable form.

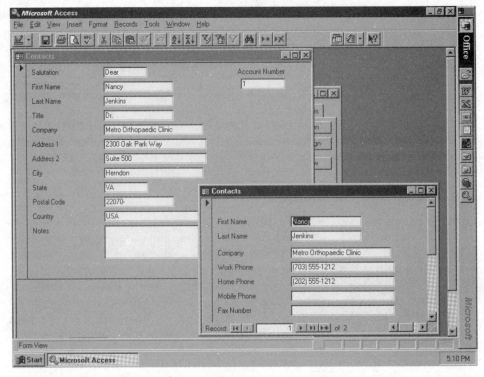

Figure 5.3 Multiple forms using the same table.

Datasheet view displays the data in the familiar row-and-column format, identical to that of a table's datasheet or a query's dynaset. The datasheet view of a form carries the same limitations as other datasheet views: You can't see the contents of OLE Object fields, and you can't use list boxes or combination boxes when in the datasheet view of the form.

Creating a Form with the AutoForm Button

The simplest way to create a form is to make use of the AutoForm menu option of the New Object button on the Toolbar. The AutoForm option builds a default single-column form for whatever table or query is selected at the time that you click the button. Open the Database window (if it isn't already open), click a desired table or query to select it, then click the down arrow to the right of the New Object button, and choose AutoForm. When you do so, Access builds a default form for the table or query; an example of such a form was shown earlier, in Figure 5.1.

The type of form that you get with this approach is a single-column form. All fields appear in a column aligned at the left side of the form, and the field names are used as labels.

Creating a Form with the Form Wizards

Access provides an automated way to create a wide variety of common forms with the aid of the Form Wizards. Like other Access wizards, the Form Wizards step you through the process of form creation by asking a series of questions about the desired form. The overall steps, which are described in more detail in the paragraphs that follow, are these:

1. In the Database window, click the Forms tab.

2. Click New (or choose File/New from the menus) to display the New Form dialog box.

3. In the Select A Table/Query box, choose the desired table or query that you want to base the form upon.

4. Click Form Wizard in the list box.

5. Follow the directions in the Wizard dialog boxes. In the last dialog box that appears, click the Open the form with data in it option, then click Finish to begin entering or viewing data in Form view, or click the Modify the form's design option, then click Finish to see the structure of the form.

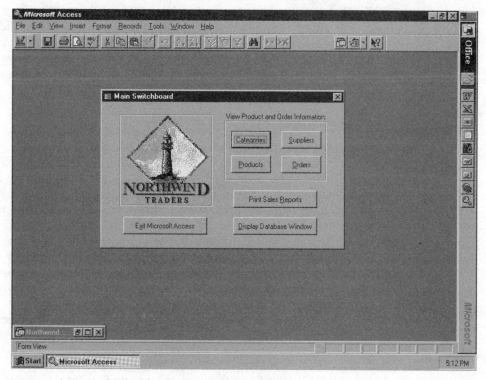

Figure 5.4 An example of a form used as a switchboard.

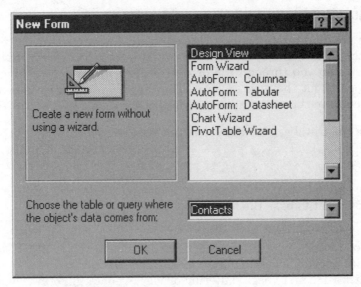

Figure 5.5 The New Form dialog box.

When you click the Forms tab in the Database window and then click New (or click the New Form option of the New Object button in the Toolbar), the New Form dialog box appears, as shown above in Figure 5.5. Click the down arrow in the Select a Table/Query list box to display all the available tables and queries in the current database (you also can type in the name of the table or query). In the list box, click Form Wizard, then click OK. Once this is done, you see the first dialog box for the Form Wizards (Figure 5.6).

Choosing the Tables and the Desired Fields

When working with this dialog box, you can use the Tables/Queries list box to select which table or query is needed as the data source for the form. As you choose a desired table or query in the Tables/Queries list box, all the fields in that table or query appear in the Available Fields list box. Click on any field to select it, then click the right-arrow button to add the field to the Selected Fields list box. Also, you can double-click any field in the Available Fields list box to add it to the Selected Fields list box. You can add all of the fields in the Available Fields list box to the Selected Fields list box at once by clicking the double right-arrow button. If you make a mistake and add a field that you don't want, you can click it to select it in the Selected Fields list box, then click the left-arrow button to remove it from the list.

If you need to base your form on more than one table, first add all of the needed fields from the first table. Then choose another table (or query) in the Tables/Queries list box, and add the desired fields for that table or query. When you've finished adding the needed fields, click Next.

If your selected fields are all from a single table, you'll now see the dialog box shown in Figure 5.7. This dialog box asks you to choose a layout for the form,

with choices of Columnar, Tabular, or Datasheet. With Columnar, all of
the fields are arranged in a single column at the left side of the form. The
Tabular option gives you a form with a table-like appearance but with space
surrounding each field. The Datasheet option results in a form with an
appearance like that of a datasheet. Choose the desired option in the dialog
box, and click Next.

If you chose fields from more than one table or query in the first Form Wizard
dialog box, you'll see the dialog box shown in Figure 5.8. With the options provided here, you choose which table should be the parent table or the main table
used to view your data. (You make this choice by clicking the desired table or
query in the upper-left portion of the dialog box.) You then choose Form with
Subforms if you want the data shown on a single form, or you choose Linked
Forms if you want the data shown on multiple forms. When done with the
options, click Next. (If you chose Form with Subform, you'll also be asked
whether you want a Tabular or Datasheet layout for the subform.)

The next Form Wizard dialog box, shown in Figure 5.9, asks which style you
want for the form. Access provides 10 different styles. (You can think of these
as background designs.) Choose a desired style, then click Next. Be warned
that some of the more colorful styles can be very slow to open on machines
with limited memory.

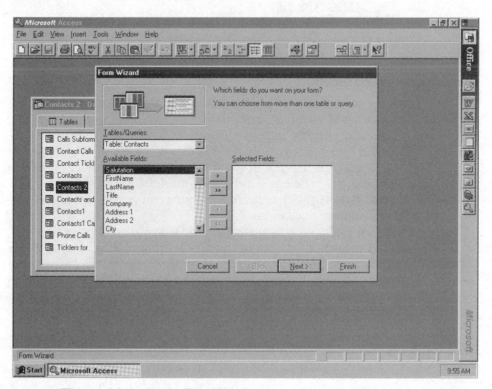

Figure 5.6 The initial dialog box for Form Wizards.

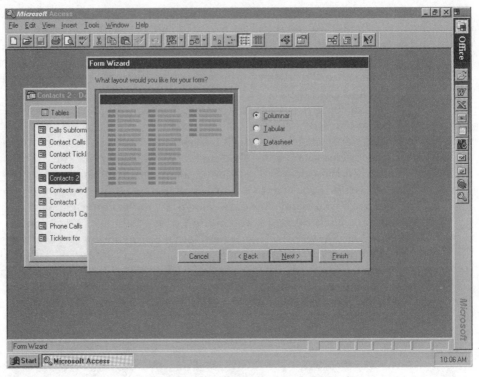

Figure 5.7 The second Form Wizard dialog box (used for single tables).

Completing the Design Process

In the final dialog box presented by the Form Wizard (Figure 5.10), you see a box for entering the title for the form (and subform if one is used), along with Open and Modify buttons. The default title is the same as the underlying table or query, but you can change this if you want. After entering a title, click the Open the form to view or enter information option, then click Finish to use the new form with your data. You also could click Modify the form's design, then click Finish to open the form in Design view and make additional changes.

When you close a new form for the first time, Access will ask if you want to save the form. Click Yes in the dialog box, and Access will ask you for a name for the form (you can use any name of 64 characters or less, with or without spaces). Enter a name for the form and click OK. The form then will be added to the list of forms that appears when you click the Forms tab in the Database window.

Designing Forms on Your Own? Use the Wizards Anyway...

Sometime you will prefer to design your own forms, but this doesn't necessarily mean that you should ignore the use of the Form Wizards. If you use the Form Wizards, you often can save time and effort by quickly creating a form that is close to what you would design manually. Use the wizards to create a form, then switch to Design view and make the desired changes to the form.

Designing Forms Manually

As detailed earlier in the chapter, any form can be opened in Design view by selecting the form in the Database window and clicking the `Design` button or by double right-clicking the form by name in the Database window. When you open any form in Design view, the sections of that form are visible, as shown in the example in Figure 5.11. Each form has a detail section, that contains the information that is displayed in the main section of the form. All objects placed within the form are *controls*, and they can be used to display information from fields, offer feedback to the viewer, or provide methods of interacting with Access.

In addition to the detail section, forms can optionally have form headers and form footers. In the case of multipage forms, you can include page headers and page footers. In the form, you might or might not see grid dots, horizontal and vertical rulers, a Toolbox, and a Field List. (The Toolbox and Field List appear if they were visible when the last form was put away after its design. The Toolbox, Field List, grid dots and rulers all can be turned on or off by choosing their respective options from the View menu.)

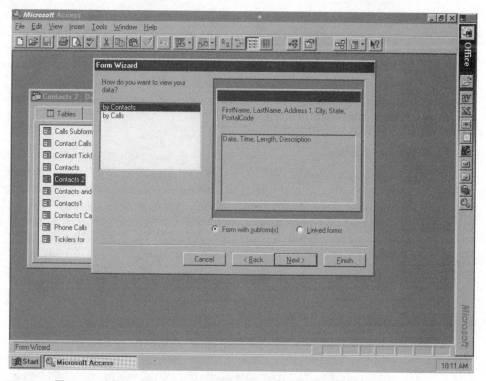

Figure 5.8 The second Form Wizard dialog box (used for multiple tables)

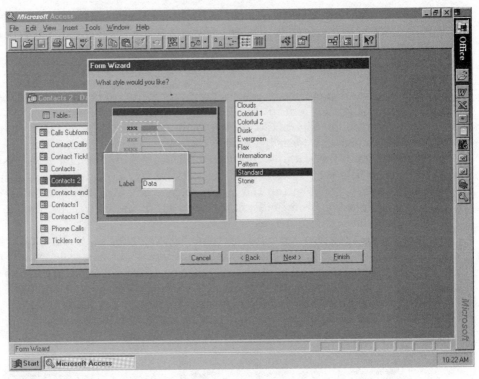

Figure 5.9 The third Form Wizard dialog box.

If you are familiar with Microsoft's Visual Basic, you will find much of the environment used for designing forms to be familiar. The visual design surface, the Toolbox, the Toolbar, and the Properties window are all borrowed from the Visual Basic environment.

Form Headers and Footers

The headers and footers of a form, when present, contain any information that appears at the beginning or end of the entire form. (With large multipage forms, the header information appears once at the start of the form, but not on each page of the form. The footer information also appears once, just at the end of the form. Typically, form headers are used for titles, and form footers are used for any summary information that is desired. You can add form headers or footers to an existing form's design by opening the form in Design view and choosing `Format/Form Header/Footer` from the menus.

Page Headers and Footers

Access also offers the capability of adding page headers and footers to a form, but these are rarely used in form design. (Page headers and footers are far more common to reports, where they often are needed to provide page-specific information.) When added to a form, any information inserted into the page header appears once at the top of each page of the form, and any information in the page footer appears once at the bottom of each page of the form. In a multipage form, you might include a title in a page header so that the title of the form would be visible on every page of the form. Page headers and footers can be useful when designing very complex types of forms; an example is the Suppliers form provided with the Northwind Traders database, shown in Figure 5.12. In this form, the form footer includes command buttons that are used to open other forms.

You can add page headers or footers to an existing form's design by opening the form in Design view, and choosing `View/Page Header/Footer` from the menus.

The Design Surface

When you open a blank form, it opens to a default size, as illustrated in Figure 5.13. A grid composed of dots fills the drawing area, and rulers also appear at the top and left edges of the form, unless these options have been turned off. You can turn the rulers and the grid on or off, by choosing `View/Ruler` or `View/Grid` from the menus.

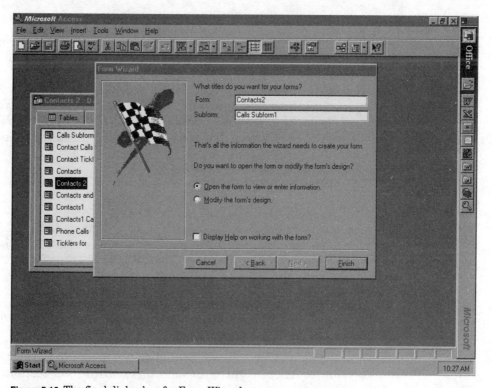

Figure 5.10 The final dialog box for Form Wizard.

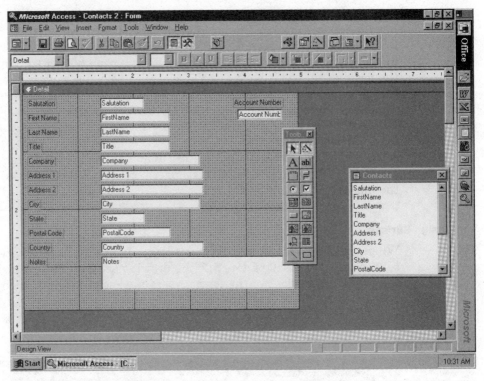

Figure 5.11 The sections of a form.

Tip: You can change the grid spacing (the fineness of the grid or the number of dots per square inch or square centimeter). To do so, open the form in Design view, and from the menus, choose Edit/Select Form, then choose View/Properties. Change the Grid X and Grid Y settings (you can find them under All Properties or under Format Properties in the list box). The higher the numbers, the finer the grid.

Sizing Sections in a Form

You can increase or decrease the height of form sections individually, but the entire form has just one width. If you change the width of one section, you change the width of the entire form. You can change the size of the sections with these steps:

1. In the form's Design view, change either the height or the width by placing the pointer on the bottom edge or right edge of the section. The pointer changes to a double-headed arrow.

2. Drag the pointer up or down to change the height of the section, or drag the pointer left or right to change the width of the section. To change both the height and width of a section simultaneously, place the pointer

in the lower-right corner of the section until the pointer changes shape to an arrow with four heads. Drag the pointer in any direction to adjust the section's size.

Adding Controls to Forms

All objects placed on forms are *controls*. If you are accustomed to using older database managers, you might be used to building forms by placing fields in a drawing surface of some sort. You can liken controls to fields in those programs, but controls offer much more than fields. Controls can display the contents of a field, but controls also can display calculations, text, list boxes, combination boxes, and command buttons. Controls can run Access macros or call programs written in Access Basic, and they can contain embedded OLE objects, such as an Excel spreadsheet or a video clip.

In Access, you can add three types of controls to forms:

- Bound
- Unbound
- Calculated

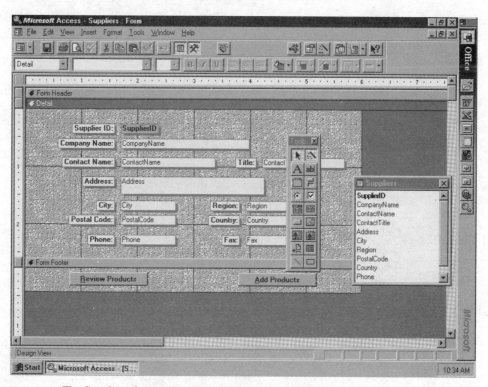

Figure 5.12 The Suppliers form in Northwind Traders' database.

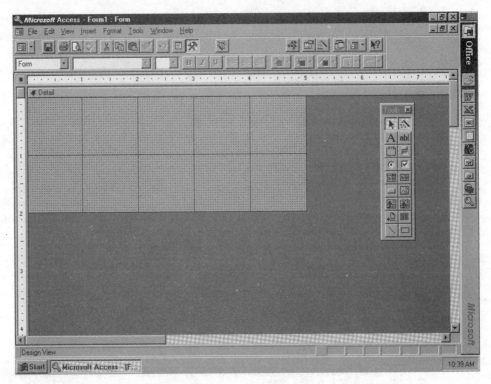

Figure 5.13 The default size for a new form.

Bound controls are controls that are tied to a field of a table or query. When the form is in use, data entered into the bound control is stored in the corresponding field in the table or query. In forms built by the Form Wizards, the text boxes that contain the contents of fields are bound controls. Text boxes are the most common type of bound controls, but you also can have toggle buttons, check boxes, and option boxes bound to Yes/No fields, and you can have bound OLE objects that can display graphics or contain sound or other Windows data stored in an OLE Object field.

Unbound controls are controls that are not tied to any data source. Such controls can be used to receive data, but the data is not stored in any particular field. (You might choose to act upon data that's stored in an unbound field by means of a macro or by Access Basic code.) Unbound controls also can be used to display ordinary text. In forms built by the Form Wizards, the titles that appear in the form header sections are unbound controls. Labels that contain descriptive text that you might add to a form would be unbound controls, as would any lines or rectangles that you might add as design elements.

Calculated controls are a special type of unbound control whose contents are based on calculations. The expression used to perform the calculation generally is based on one or more fields of the underlying table or query. For example, a table of video sales might contain a field for Sale Price, and a field for

Quantity. A calculated field called Total Cost would multiply the contents of the two fields, with an expression like [Sale Price] * [Quantity].

Access provides two tools that make the addition of controls to a form easy: the *Toolbox* and the *Field List*. If these tools are not visible when you are designing a form, you can show them by choosing View/Toolbox or View/Field List from the menus. (You also can click the Toolbox or the Field List buttons on the Toolbar to bring either of these tools to the foreground.) Figure 5.14 shows the Toolbox and the Field List. In a nutshell, the Field List is used to add bound text boxes that display the contents of the field to a form, while the Toolbox is used to add any type of control to the form. The Toolbox controls are detailed further in Table 5.1.

The precise method behind adding controls using the Toolbox will vary depending on the type of control, but the overall process consists of these steps:

1. In Design view of the form, display the Toolbox.

2. If you do not want to use the Control Wizards to help create the control, turn them off by clicking the Control Wizards button in the toolbox so that the button is up (not active).

3. In the Toolbox, click the type of control you want to create.

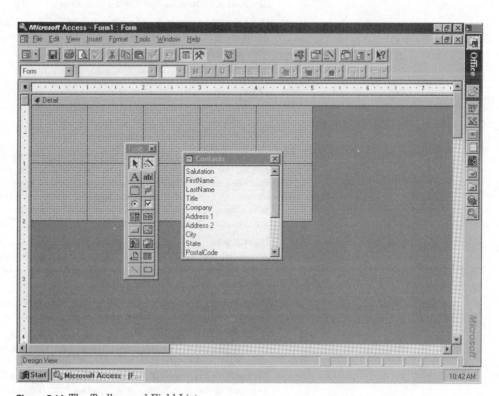

Figure 5.14 The Toolbox and Field List.

Table 5.1

Control	Description
Select Objects Pointer	Used to select, move, or size objects within the form. If another Toolbox tool was previously selected, clicking the Select Objects Pointer deselects that tool.
Control Wizards	This button turns on (or off) the Control Wizards. (Control wizards provide help in adding some types of controls, such as list boxes, combination boxes, and command buttons.)
Label	Used to add a label, such as descriptive text, titles, captions, or instructions. Labels can be attached to text box controls to serve as descriptions, or they can be completely unattached, used only for informational purposes.
Text Box	Used to create a text box that displays the contents of a field or the results of an expression. Text boxes are usually *bound* (or attached) to a field in a table or a dynaset.
Option Group	Used to add option groups. Option groups are used to store two or more option buttons, toggle buttons, or check boxes; only one of the options in an option group can be selected at a time.
Toggle Button	Used to add a toggle button. Toggle buttons are buttons that look like they have been pushed down when selected. They are used within option groups to select one choice from many, or they can be used individually to specify a yes/no choice.
Option Button	Used to add an option button. Option buttons are circles that are darkened in the center when selected. You can use option buttons (also called *radio buttons*) within an option group to chose one choice from many, or you can used them individually to specify a yes/no choice.
Check Box	Used to add a check box. Check boxes are small squares that contain an X when selected. You can use check boxes within an option group to chose one choice from many, or you can used them individually to specify a yes/no choice.
Combo Box	Used to create a combination box. Combination boxes serve as a combination of a list box, and a text box. With a combination box, you can choose values from a pull-down list that appears in the box, or you can type in a value. The choices in the list are generally taken from rows of a query, but they can also be based on SQL statements or from a list of predetermined values.
List Box	Used to create a list box. You use list boxes to choose values from a predetermined list. The choices in the list are generally taken from rows of a query, but they can also be based on SQL statements or from a list of predetermined values.
Graph	Used to add a graph to a form. Using this tool starts the GraphWizard, which you then use to design a graph based on values in the underlying table or query.
Command Button	Used to add a command button. (Command buttons carry out one or more commands, and these are normally attached to macros or to Access Basic routines. If the ControlWizards are turned on, adding a command button causes a wizard to appear that helps in the creation of the desired type of command button.)

Table 5.1 *continued*

Control	Description
Image	Used to add a frame that you can use to display a static (graphic) image.
Unbound Object Frame	Used to add an OLE object created by another Windows application to the form. Unbound object frames are routinely used to display graphic elements (such as a corporate logo) in forms.
Bound Object Frame	Used to display the contents of an OLE field from the underlying table or query in the form.
Page Break	Used to insert a page break into the form. Page breaks force the beginning of a new page when a form is printed, but they do not appear in Form view.
Subform	Used to add a subform to a form. For example, if a form displayed the names of video club members, you could use a subform to display a detail table of all video rentals in a given month for that member.
Line	Used to draw lines in a form. (Note that you can use the Palette, which is available by choosing View/Palette, to change the width and colors used by the lines.)
Rectangle	Used to add rectangles or squares to a form. (Note that you can use the Palette, which is available by choosing View/Palette, to change the width and colors used by the rectangles.)

4. Click in the form where you want the upper-left corner of the control (not its label). The control appears in the default size for the selected type of control. Drag the pointer to size the control as desired. If the Control Wizards are on and apply to the type of control that you selected, you will see the first of the Control Wizard dialog boxes, which will assist in the creation of the control.

Changing Properties

Every control has its own properties that you can modify at will to affect the behavior of that control. To change a control's properties, select the control, and open the Properties window by choosing View/Properties or by clicking on the Properties button. Figure 5.15 shows the Properties window for a selected text box—the most common type of control.

You can get an idea of what properties can be manipulated throughout a form if you open the Properties window, move it off to the side so that you can see it and the form simultaneously, and click on various objects within the form, such as the controls, the labels, and the sections of the form. As you click each object, the properties for that object appear within the Properties window.

Besides the control properties, the sections of a form also have properties that can be modified for specific needs, and you can set properties for the

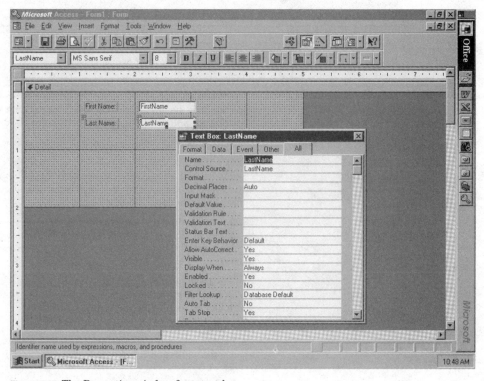

Figure 5.15 The Properties window for a text box.

entire form. The paragraphs that follow describe the important properties in forms that you will want to work with. In a nutshell, to modify any of the properties used by the form, you perform these steps:

1. In Design view for the form, choose the control or section whose properties you want to set. Click the desired control to select it, or click in the section to select a section. To select an entire form, choose Edit/Select Form from the menus.

2. Open the Properties window by choosing View/Properties or clicking on the Properties button in the Toolbar.

3. Click the property whose value you want to set. If an arrow appears in the property box, click it and choose the desired value from the list box. You also can type the appropriate setting or expression directly into the property box. Note that, if you need to enter an expression, you can create the desired expression, using the Expression Builder.

The common types of control properties that you might want to change in your forms are detailed in the following paragraphs.

Control Source. This property binds the control to a field in a table or query or names an expression that creates data displayed in the control. If you create the control by dragging a field from the Field List, the name is set automatically. Optionally, you can right-click in the property and choose `Build` from the menu that appears to display the Expression Builder, which can be used to build an expression.

Format. This property specifies the desired format for displaying or printing the data. Depending on the type of data displayed by the control, different formats will be available. Click in the property, then click the down arrow to open the list box, and choose the desired format.

Decimal Places. This property, used in conjunction with number or currency fields, determines how many decimal places to use when displaying numbers. Your choices in this property are `Auto` or 0 to 15. If you choose `Auto`, the numbers appear as specified by the Format property setting. If you specify 0 to 15, the digits to the right of the decimal point appear with the specified number of decimal places. Digits to the left of the decimal point appear as specified by the Format property setting.

Input Mask. This property controls how data displayed in the field appears. For example, if you set this property to `(000) 000-0000`, a phone number stored as `7185551234` would appear in the form as `(718) 555-1234`.

Default Value. This property lets you specify a default value for the control. With forms used for routine data entry, a default value can be a time-saving feature. For example, if you are using a form to add names and addresses to a sales table and most of your customers live in a particular city, you could enter the name of that city as a default value for the City text box of the form. That value automatically would appear in the field for every new record added using the form. As users would add records using the form, they could either accept the default value or change it to something else.

Validation Rule and Validation Text. Use these properties to validate data entered into a form. The Validation Rule property contains an expression of your choosing that validates the data, and the Validation Text property contains the text that appears as an error message if the data entered is not valid according to the validation rule.

For example, a number field that contains salaries might use a validation rule like `between 12.00 and 18.50`, and a date field that contains hire dates of employees might use a validation rule like `between #4/30/94# and date()`, which would translate to between April 30, 1994 and the current date according to the computer's clock. Note that, if you set validation rules for the control in a form and for the underlying field in the table or query, both validation rules are applied by Access when data is entered or changed in the form.

Status Bar Text. This property specifies the text that appears in the status bar when a control is selected; it can be useful for adding explanatory messages that help your users understand the purpose of the different fields on the form. You can enter a maximum of 255 characters for the Status Bar text.

Auto Tab and Enter Key Behavior. Use these properties to determine the behavior of Access when you fill a field with allowable characters and the behavior of the Enter key. If the Auto Tab property is set to Yes, a tab is generated (the focus moves to the next field) when data fills the field. If Auto Tab is set to No, the focus does not move when the field fills with data, and the user must press Tab to move to the next field. With the Enter Key Behavior property, you can choose Default or New Line in Field. If the Enter Key Behavior property is set to Default, Access uses whatever setting exists in the Move After Enter option in the Options dialog box. If the Enter Key Behavior property is set to New Line in Field, then pressing the Enter key in the text box creates a new line in the text box, where you can enter additional text.

Visible. This property determines whether the control will be visible or not. (Typically, you might change the Visible property of a control from within a macro or within an Access Basic procedure.)

Display When. This property can apply to individual controls or to sections of the form. It determines whether the object or section is displayed or printed. In this property, you are given three choices: Always, Print Only, and Screen Only. If you choose Always, the object or section appears both in Form view and when the form is printed. If Print Only is chosen, the object or section is hidden when in Form view and appears only when the form is printed. If Screen Only is chosen, the object or section is hidden when the form is printed and appears only when in Form view.

The Display When property can be useful with forms that you want to print that contain command buttons. To prevent the buttons from printing with the rest of the form, you can set their Display When properties to Screen Only.

Enabled and Locked. Use these properties to determine whether a control can have the focus and whether edits will be permitted to data through the control. If the Enabled property is set to Yes, a control can have the focus. When you set the Enabled property to No, the user will not be able to move the focus into or out of the control while in Form view. The Locked property, when set to Yes, prevents any changes to the data in the control. If the Locked property is set to No, data displayed within the control can be changed.

Tab Stop. This property determines whether you can use the Tab key to move the focus to a control in Form view. When set to Yes (which is the default), you can tab into the control. When set to No, you can't tab into the control.

Tab Index. This property determines the tab order for the controls within the form or which control successively gets the focus each time you press the Tab key. In the property, you enter a numeric value ranging from zero to one less than the total number of controls in the form. For example, if a form contained five controls, valid Tab Index values would be 0, 1, 2, 3, and 4. The control with a tab index of 0 would be the first control to get the focus, followed by the control with a tab index of 1, then the control with a tab index of 2, and so on. When you are designing complex forms with multiple controls on the same horizontal line, you can modify the tab index of the controls to force the focus to "flow" through the form in a way that you prefer. (Note that you also can change the tab order of controls on a form by opening the form in Design view, choosing Edit/Tab Order, and selecting the desired tab order in the dialog box that appears.)

Scroll Bars. Use this property to add a vertical scroll bar to a control. The property provides two options: Vertical and None. Scroll bars can be useful if you have a control for a field with large amounts of text (such as a memo field), yet you do not want to size the control so large that it takes up a prohibitive amount of room on the form. If you set the Scroll Bars property to Vertical, a vertical scroll bar appears at the right edge of the control, and the user can use the scroll bar to scroll the text displayed within the control.

Can Grow and Can Shrink. These properties can apply to controls or to the sections of a form. Use them to determine whether a control or a section will be allowed to grow or shrink vertically to accommodate data of varying size. (For both properties, your choices are Yes and No, and the default is No.) If Can Grow is set to Yes, the control or section will grow vertically as needed to accommodate the data. If Can Grow is set to No, the control or section will not grow beyond the size allotted as part of its design. If Can Shrink is set to Yes, the control or section will shrink vertically as needed to accommodate the data. If Can Shrink is set to No, the control or section will not shrink beyond the size allotted as part of its design.

For most objects, you can specify background and border colors and styles in the Properties window, although this is more easily done by means of the Palette. You can define events that should take place when certain things occur, such as when an object is double-clicked or when the insertion pointer moves into a text box. In the case of text box controls, you can specify the control source (where the data in the text box comes from), and you can establish validation rules for data entered into the text box. To find out what any property can be used for, open the Properties window and click inside the property in question, then press F1. A help screen will appear explaining the purpose of that particular property.

Setting the Default View and Views Allowed Properties. Two useful properties that affect how your users see the forms are the DefaultView and Views Allowed properties. If you choose Edit/Select Form, and then you choose View/Properties to open the Properties window, you see both the Default View and the Views Allowed properties in the Properties window. Use the Default View property to determine whether the form opens using a single form view, a continuous form view, or a datasheet view. You can use the Views Allowed property to determine which views the user will be allowed to switch to while using the form; your choices here are Form view, Datasheet view, or both.

Changing the Form's Title Bar
By default, a form's title bar contains the same name that you saved the form under. You can change this name to anything that you want by changing the Caption property for the form. With the form open in Design view, choose Edit/Select Form, then choose View/Properties. Click the Caption

property in the Properties window, and enter the desired caption. The new caption will appear in the Title Bar when you switch to Form view.

Making a Form Modal

At times, you might want to design a form so that the user can only work with that form until the editing is done; you want to prevent the user from switching to other Access objects until he or she puts away the form. You can do so by making a form *modal*. When a form is modal, you cannot click on any other forms until you close the current form. To make a form modal, open the form in Design view, choose Edit/Select Form, then choose View/Properties, and change the Modal property to Yes. Note that changes to the Modal property setting take effect only after you close the form, save the changes, and reopen the form in Form view.

Tip: Making a form modal also can prevent accidental changes to the form, as the Design button is dimmed in the Toolbar when a form is modal, and a user cannot easily switch from Form view to Design view. (Design changes to a modal form must be made by closing the form, then selecting it in the Database window and clicking Design.)

Removing the Scroll Bars and/or the Record Selector

For small forms, or for forms that are to be used specifically for adding data, you might want to hide the scroll bars, the record selector buttons at the bottom of the form's window, or both. You can easily do so by opening the Properties window for the form (choose Edit/Select Form, then choose View/Properties), and setting either the Scroll Bars property or the Record Selector property. With the Scroll Bars property, you can choose Both, Neither, Horizontal Only, or Vertical Only. With the Record Selector property, your choices are Yes to display the record selectors or No to hide them.

Selecting, Moving, and Sizing Controls

Once a control has been placed in the drawing area, you can select it to work with the control. To select a control, click anywhere in the control. When you do so, the control becomes surrounded by handles, indicating that it's selected. With most controls, the handles include move handles and sizing handles. Most controls, including text boxes, have two parts: a label and the text box itself.

To select a group of adjacent controls, place the pointer at any location outside the top or bottom control in the group, then click and drag the pointer around or through the desired controls. To select nonadjacent controls or controls that overlap, hold the Shift key while clicking each control you want to select.

To move a control, first select it, then move the pointer near the border of the control. When the pointer changes into the shape of an outstretched palm, click and drag the control to the desired location. To move a control apart from any attached label, first select the control (or the label) by clicking it. Then, place the pointer on the move handle (it is larger than the sizing handles and is in the upper-left corner of the control), and click and drag the control to the desired location.

Text boxes, combination boxes, and list boxes have labels attached when you create them. You can select the control, the label, or both. When the text box alone (or the combination or list box) is the selected object, it contains both a move handle and a sizing handle, while the attached object contains only a move handle. If the label is the selected object, it contains both the move and sizing handles, while the text box contains a move handle only. You can keep controls aligned if you use the Shift key as you move them. When you hold the Shift key depressed as you move a control, the control moves horizontally or vertically, but never in both directions. Hence, you could keep horizontal alignment of a control while moving it vertically, by selecting the control, holding the Shift key, and dragging the control vertically.

To resize a control, select the control, move the pointer to any of the control's sizing handles (where the pointer changes to a double arrow), and click and drag the control to the desired size.

To delete a control, select the control and press the Del key (or choose Edit/Delete from the menus). If you want to delete only the label, make sure that the label (and not the text box) is the selected object.

Adding Fields

The most common type of controls used in forms are text boxes that are bound to fields. You can add these with the bound Text Box tool in the Toolbox, but it is easier to add them using the Field List. If you use the Text Box tool of the Toolbox, you must modify the text box properties to tell the text box what field is the source of the data. With the Field List, this happens automatically. To create a bound control using the field list, you perform these steps:

1. Open the desired form in Design view, and display the Field List if it is not already visible.

2. In the field list, select the field or fields that you want to add to the form as bound controls. To select a single field, click the field. To select a block of fields, hold down the Shift key and click the names of the first and last fields in the block. When you do so, Access automatically selects all of the field names in between. To select nonadjacent fields, hold down the Ctrl key, and click the name of each field that you want to include. To select all fields, double-click the list's title bar.

3. Drag the selected field or fields from the field list to the form.

4. Place the upper-left corner of the mouse pointer where you want to put the upper-left corner of the first control (not its label), and release the mouse button. Access adds one bound control on the form or report for each field you selected in the field list. Figure 5.16 illustrates the process of adding fields to a form using the Field List.

If, for some reason, you prefer to use the Toolbox to add fields to a form, you can do so by clicking the bound Text Box tool in the Toolbox, and clicking in the form where you want to place the field. When you click in the form, an unbound text box appears, and you must modify its properties to bind the text box to the desired field. With the unbound text box selected, click the Properties icon in the Toolbar (or choose View/Properties) to open the Properties window, click in Control Source, and enter or select a source for the field.

Adding Labels to a Form

Besides the use of fields, you typically will need to include text that's not attached to any object on forms. Such text might be descriptive or explanatory text, such as is used in titles or captions. Unattached text is added to forms with the use of the Label tool. Figure 5.17 shows an example of a label used in a form.

You can create a label with the following steps:

1. Open the form in Design view, and display the Toolbox (if it is not already visible).

2. Click the Label tool.

3. To create a label that is automatically sized as you type, click where you want to start the label, then type the label's text. To create a label of any size, click where you want the label to start, drag the pointer until the label is the size you want, then type its text.

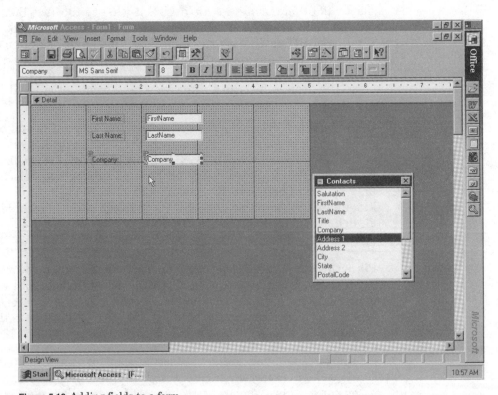

Figure 5.16 Adding fields to a form.

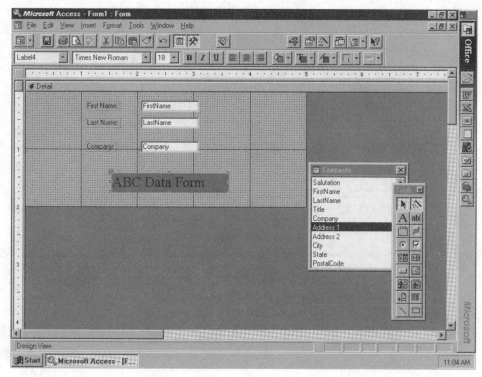

Figure 5.17 An example of a label in a form.

You can display multiple lines of text in a label, by creating the label, entering its text, then resizing it. The existing text in the label automatically wraps to fit the label's new dimensions. You also can press Ctrl–Enter as you reach the desired end of a line when typing the text; the Ctrl–Enter combination forces a new line.

As you design your forms, often the labels will not contain the precise fonts and styles that you desire. You can easily change these by clicking the label to select it and choosing an appropriate font style and font size from the font list boxes in the Toolbar.

Hint: If you change a label's font to a larger size or from plain to bolded text, often the text no longer fits completely in the size allotted for the label. You can drag the box to a new size, but there's a faster way. With the label still selected, choose Format/Size/To Fit from the menus. The label will be sized to fit the enclosed text.

Aligning Controls

When you add fields to a form as a group, Access assumes that you wanted to left-align all of the labels. You might have noticed, however, that the Form Wizards use a style of alignment that right-aligns the labels. You can change

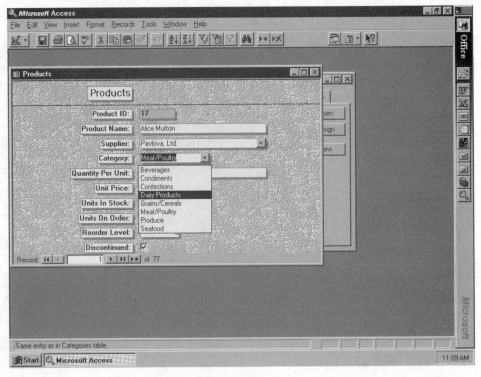

Figure 5.18 An example of a combo box within a form.

the alignment for any selected group of objects, with the Format/Align command. You use the following steps to do so:

1. If the Pointer tool is not already the selected tool in the Toolbox, click it to select it.

2. Click at a point just above and to the left of the first desired field, and drag to a point just below and to the right of the last desired field. When you release the mouse, the fields should all be selected.

3. From the menus, choose Format/Align, then choose Right to right-align all of the fields.

4. Choose Format/Size/To Fit from the menus if you want to automatically expand the controls as necessary to fit the italicized text.

Adding Check Boxes, Option Buttons, and Toggle Buttons

Check boxes, option buttons, and toggle buttons are all used to represent true/false conditions on a form. Typically, these controls are tied to yes/no fields, although they also can be tied to expressions that you define.

Tip: If the check boxes, option buttons, or toggle buttons that you plan to add are part of an *option group* (a group of multiple-choice options), you can use the ControlWizards to help create the option group, with the desired controls in it. The next section provides details on using the ControlWizards to create option groups.

A check box represents a true-or-false situation; if the box is checked, the situation is true, and if the box is not checked, the situation is false. Check boxes can be used separately, or they can be included in an option group.

Option buttons, like check boxes, represent true/false conditions by means of buttons that are darkened in the center when the condition is true. Option buttons can be placed within option groups, in which case only one of the buttons in the group can be used at a time. Option buttons are known to some as *radio buttons*, a term that's popular in the Macintosh environment.

Toggle buttons also represent yes/no choices, but they take on the appearance of a button that is pressed or not pressed. When pressed, the condition is true; when not pressed, the condition is false.

To add check boxes, option buttons, or toggle buttons to a form, you perform these steps:

1. In the Design view of the form, add a check box, option button, or toggle button by clicking the desired tool in the Toolbox and clicking in the form where you want to place the box or button.

2. Bind the control to a field that has a Yes/No data type, or set its ControlSource property to the desired expression. To bind the control to the field, while the control is selected, click the Properties icon to open the Properties window for the control. Click in Control Source, and enter or select a source for the field.

Adding Option Groups

Option groups are groups of check boxes, option buttons, or toggle buttons that are used to select from one of a possible number of options. You can create option groups with the aid of the ControlWizards, or you can create them manually.

Creating Option Groups with the Wizards

To create an option group with the aid of the ControlWizards, you perform these steps:

1. Turn on the ControlWizards if they are not already on (in the Toolbox, click the Control Wizards tool so that it is highlighted).

2. In the toolbox, click the Option Group tool.

3. Click the report where you want to place the upper-left corner of the option group. Access displays the first Wizard dialog box.

4. Follow the directions in the Wizard dialog boxes. (The exact steps will vary, depending on what types of controls you want in the group, and what values you want the buttons, when selected, to store in the fields.)

In the last dialog box to appear, click the Finish button to display the option group in Design view.

Creating Option Groups Manually

You can add an option group manually by performing these steps:

1. In the Design view of the form, turn off the ControlWizards (if on).
2. Click the Option Group tool in the Toolbox, and drag the group to the desired size on the form.
3. Click the desired tool (option button, check box, or toggle button) in the Toolbox, and drag the tool to the desired location within the option group.
4. Repeat step 3 for each option that you want included in the option group.

Remember that, when you create option groups, it is your responsibility to tie those groups to the desired fields or expressions by modifying the Control Source properties for the options that you add. Most option groups can be more easily created with the ControlWizards, which automatically connect the options to the required fields.

Adding a List Box or a Combo Box

List boxes are boxes that present a number of available values from a list. Combo (for "combination") boxes are boxes that you can use to either enter a value by typing it or choose from a list of values. While list and combo boxes can be tied to expressions, they typically are bound to a field of a table or query. Figure 5.18 shows an example of a combo box in a form; the combo box can be used to choose from a desired category in the inventory of products.

The choices shown in a list box or a combo box can come from a number of different sources. The most common are rows of a particular table and predetermined lists of values that you specify. For example, a table might contain the names and abbreviations of valid states, and you could use a list box or a combo box to show the abbreviations for all the valid states. For a field named Ship by, you might use three acceptable options: US mail, UPS, or FedEx. Rather than forcing users to repeatedly type these entries over and over into a text field, you could let them select from a list box that shows only those three values. List or combo boxes that are based on the contents of a table or on a predetermined list of values can be constructed with the aid of the ControlWizards.

In addition to rows of a table and value lists, list boxes and combo boxes also can get the choices from any of the sources that follow. Note that the ControlWizards cannot build these types of list boxes or combo boxes for you; they must be designed manually.

■ You can specify a *field list*, in which case the list box or combo box displays the names of fields of a table or query as the choices.

- You can show values from a SQL statement that you design.
- You can show values that are retrieved from an Access Basic function.

Creating a List or Combo Box with the Wizards

To create a list box or a combo box using the ControlWizards, follow these steps:

1. In the Design view of the form, turn on the ControlWizards if they are not already on (click the ControlWizards tool in the Toolbox until it is highlighted).

2. Click the List Box or Combo Box tool in the Toolbox, as desired.

3. Click in the form where you want to place the control. In a moment, Access displays the first ControlWizard dialog box for a list box or combo box, as shown in Figure 5.19.

4. Follow the steps outlined in the wizard dialog boxes. (These steps will vary, depending on the type of box that you add and which sources you use for the choices in the list.) In the last dialog box that appears, click the `Create` button to display the list box or combo box while in Design view.

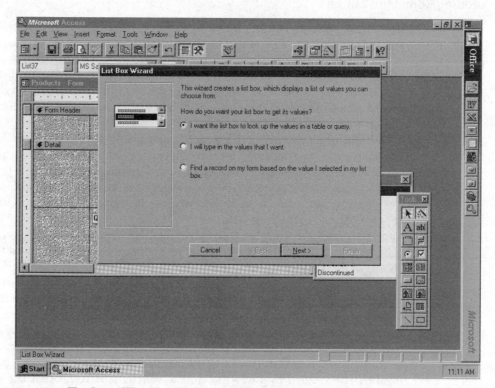

Figure 5.19 The ControlWizard dialog box for adding a list box.

Creating a List or Combo Box Manually

You can manually add a list box or a combo box to a form using the following steps:

1. In the Design view of the form, turn off the ControlWizards (if on).
2. Click the List box or Combo Box tool in the Toolbox.
3. If you want to create a list or combo box that is bound to a field, display the Field List, select the desired field from the list, and drag it to the form. To create a list or combo box that is not bound to a field, click in the form where you want to place the control, then choose `View/Properties` to open the Properties window, and set the RowSource and RowSourceType properties for the list box or combo box.

The RowSource property tells Access where to find the data that appears in the list, and the RowSourceType property tells Access what kind of data source to use (table/query, list of values, list of field names, or an Access Basic function). Typically, the RowSource property is set to the name of a table or query that contains the data used for the list, and the RowSourceType property is set to Table/Query as a data type.

Adding Command Buttons

Command buttons can be added to forms to open other forms, print data, or start other actions. The addition of command buttons to forms has been made much easier with the ControlWizards present in recent versions of Access. Using the wizards, you can add buttons for a variety of standard actions, such as navigating within the underlying table or query, printing the current record, or opening another form. Figure 5.20 shows an example of a form that contains command buttons.

The ability to use a wizard to add command buttons is a significant addition to Access, particularly for developers who must develop complete applications that are easy for others to use. In versions of Access prior to 2.0, many complex tasks could be easily performed with command buttons by designing macros for specific operations (like opening a form or printing a report), then attaching the macro to a command button. While this approach was far simpler than writing lines and lines of program code, it still required a familiarity with Access macro actions and how they would relate to forms and reports. With the Command Button ControlWizard, this process is even less complex; you now can add buttons to your forms for most common operations without needing to design macros. Command buttons designed with the wizard add Access Basic code to the form. When the button is pressed, the Access Basic code carries out the chosen operation. An advantage of this approach over the command-button-and-macro approach is that, if you are familiar with Access Basic, you can modify the code created by the wizard to perform other operations or to protect the users from errors. Table 5.2 shows the types of actions that are possible with the command buttons created by the ControlWizard. While there undoubtedly will

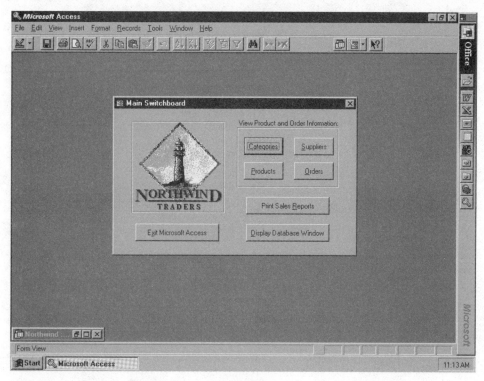

Figure 5.20 An example of a form with command buttons.

be operations that these choices don't cover, you can automate much of the work behind any application by adding command buttons for these choices wherever appropriate. Another advantage of the command buttons placed by the ControlWizard is that they can easily contain text or any of a number of pictures on the face of the button.

You can create a command button by performing the following steps:

1. In the Design view of the form, turn on the ControlWizards if they are not already on (click the ControlWizards tool in the Toolbox until it is highlighted).

2. Click the Command Button tool in the Toolbox.

3. Click in the form where you want to place the command button. In a moment, Access displays the first ControlWizard dialog box for a command button, shown in Figure 5.21.

4. Follow the steps outlined in the wizard dialog boxes. (The exact steps will vary, depending on what action you want the button you place to perform.) In the last dialog box that appears, click the Create button to display the command button while in Design view.

An exercise later in the chapter gives you a chance to work with command buttons by adding a number of them to the form that you created earlier.

Table 5.2

Available categories	When button gets pressed, this happens...
Record navigation	Go to next record Go to previous record Go to first record Go to last record Find record Go to new record Find next
Record operations	Add new record Delete record Duplicate record Print record Save record Undo record
Form operations	Apply form filter Close form Edit form filter Open form Print form Print current form Refresh form data
Report operations	Mail report Print report Preview report Send report to file
Application	Quit application Run application Run MS Excel Run MS Word Run Notepad
Miscellaneous	Auto dialer Print table Run macro Run query

Adding Page Breaks

With forms that will be printed often, you can add page breaks to indicate where one printed page should end and another page should begin. To add a page break, perform these steps:

1. In the Design view of the form, open the Toolbox and the Properties window if they aren't already open.

2. Click the page break tool in the Toolbox, then click the form where you want the new page to begin. The page break appears in the form's design as a small dotted line.

Note that page breaks don't control how much of a form is displayed in a window. If you want each page to be the same size, and each window to show just one page at a time, design the form so that each page break is an equal distance from the other. You can do this by positioning the page break controls with the aid of the vertical ruler.

Working with Multitable Forms

This portion of the chapter details the use of multitable forms, or forms that retrieve data from more than one table at a time. In Access, you create multitable forms by embedding forms within forms. The embedded form is referred to as the subform, and the form that contains it is called the main form. (In database terminology, the main form sometimes is referred to as the *master form*, and the subform as the *child form* or *detail form*.) Multitable forms typically are used to support the common one-to-many relationship that exists between tables in many relational databases. With a multitable form, you can display one record from the master or "one" side of the relationship, along with all the associated records from the detail or "many" side of the relationship. Figure 5.22 shows an example of a multitable form.

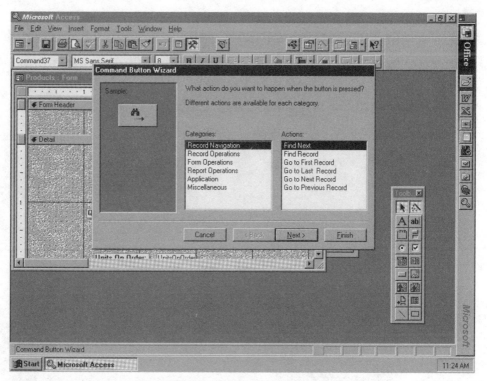

Figure 5.21 The Command Wizard dialog box for control buttons.

In the example, the main portion of the form shows the contact name, address, and phone; these fields are all taken from the Contacts table in the Contacts database. The subform portion displays all phone calls made to a particular contact.

When you create a multitable form, the main form is linked to the subform by means of a common field. (In the example shown below in Figure 5.22, the main form that contains a contact's data gets linked to the subform that contains the phone calls placed by means of the Account Number field.) Once the link has been established, the subform shows only those records that are related to the record in the main form.

As you are designing a multitable form, Access tries to establish the necessary link between the forms. If Access can find two fields of the same name that are compatible data types, it will assume these fields to be the required fields, and it will establish a link between the main form and the subform based on the fields. In some cases, Access guesses wrong, but you can change its assumptions by modifying the subform's properties.

The Available Types of Subforms

Because subforms are a type of form, they can be viewed two ways within a multitable form: as a datasheet or as a form. With one-to-many relationships, the datasheet approach is the most common, as it makes the data from the many side of the relationship easy to view. The multitable forms created by the

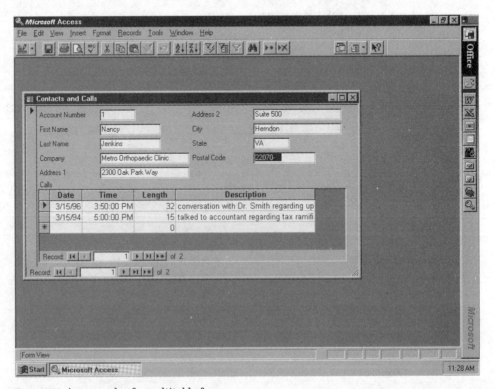

Figure 5.22 An example of a multitable form.

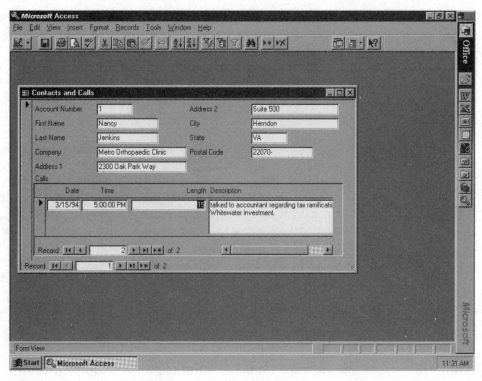

Figure 5.23 Contacts and Calls form from the Contacts database.

Form Wizards display the subform data in datasheet view by default, but this view can be changed to a form view by clicking within the subform and choosing `View/Subform Datasheet` from the menus. Figure 5.23 shows the same form as was shown earlier (in Figure 5.22). In this instance, the subform is visible through the form view.

There are three ways that you can create multitable forms. They are (in order of increasing complexity):

- Use the Main/Subform Form Wizard—The Form Wizards provide a type of form: the Main/Subform form. When you choose this option, the Main/Subform Form Wizard creates a multitable form that contains one master section or main form and one detail section or subform, as detailed earlier in the chapter. The Form Wizards approach is the easiest; however, like all wizards, it does limit your options as far as flexibility in design is concerned.

- Drag and drop a form onto another form—You can create multitable forms by opening a form in Design view and dragging an existing form from the Design window onto the design surface of the first form. The second form that you drag and drop becomes the subform. This method offers more flexibility than the Form Wizards, because you can design the subform in whatever fashion you want before you drop it onto the main form. Unlike the Form Wizards, you're not forced to choose from a few standardized designs.

■ Use the Toolbox Subform tool—Multitable forms can be created by designing the desired subform, then opening the main form in Design view and using the Subform tool of the Toolbox to add the subform. When you use this method, you must open the Properties window for the subform and check to be sure that Access was able to establish the proper link to the main form.

Using a Multitable Form

Because multitable forms are just a collection of Access forms, the techniques used for navigation within single-table forms apply here as well. What's important to remember is that you are simultaneously working with more than one form, so your navigation techniques apply to the form that has the *focus* at any instant in time. (A form is said to have the focus when the insertion pointer or active cursor is somewhere within that form.) The main form and subform each have their own separate navigation buttons, as visible in Figure 5.22. Click in either portion of the form to give it the focus.

Unless you change it, the default view of a subform is always the datasheet view. This is true whether you create the form with a wizard, by using drag-and-drop techniques, or with the Subform tool in the Toolbox. As you work with the form, you can switch between datasheet view and form view in the subform with the following steps:

1. Click anywhere in the subform to give it the focus.

2. From the menus, choose View/Subform Datasheet.

This menu command is a toggle, so repeatedly choosing the same command changes between datasheet view and form view for the subform.

Understanding the Design Behind a Multitable Form

As you work with multitable forms, particularly when creating them manually, it helps to understand the design behind this type of form. If you open a multitable form that uses a subform and switch to Design view (click the Design icon on the Toolbar), it resembles the illustration shown in Figure 5.24.

Like all forms, this form is made up of controls. What's different about a multitable form is the presence of *subform controls* that denote the presence of a subform. The large rectangle titled "Calls Subform" at the bottom of the form's design is the Calls subform, which was created by the wizard during the form-design process. Like other controls, the subform control can be moved and sized as desired within the body of the main form.

When the Form Wizard warns you that a subform must be saved before proceeding and asks you for a name for the subform, it is creating the subform that is shown here. The name given in the Save As dialog box presented by the wizard is the name that's assigned to the subform, and the subform is stored along with all of the other forms. Whether you create multitable forms manually or with the aid of the Form Wizards, the subform must exist before you can create the main form.

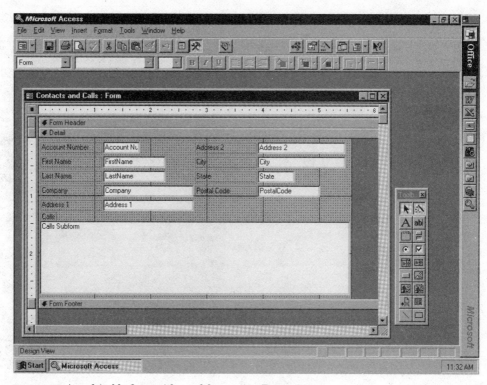

Figure 5.24 A multitable form with a subform using Form view.

You can see the properties used to establish the links between the main form and the subform by opening the Properties window. (You can click the subform to select it and choose View/Properties). The Properties window for the subform opens, as shown in Figure 5.25. (If All Properties does not appear in the list box at the top of the window, click in the list box and choose All Properties.)

Note that the Link Child Fields and Link Master Fields properties have been set to Account Number, which is the common field between the tables. You can use these properties to establish any desired link between tables when you create multitable forms without the aid of the wizards. Even with the wizards, there might be unusual cases where Access does not choose the fields that you wanted for the link; in such cases, you can open the Properties window for any subform and make your own entries in the Link Child Fields and Link Master Fields properties to establish the desired link between the forms.

Opening the Subform in Design View

Because the subform is another form saved under a different name, you can click the subform by name in the Database window and click Design to open it in Design view. However, if you are working with the design of the main form and you also want to make changes to the design of the subform, there is a faster way. Double-click the subform, and it will open in Design view. Figure 5.26 shows the effects of double-clicking the subform from the main form's Design window.

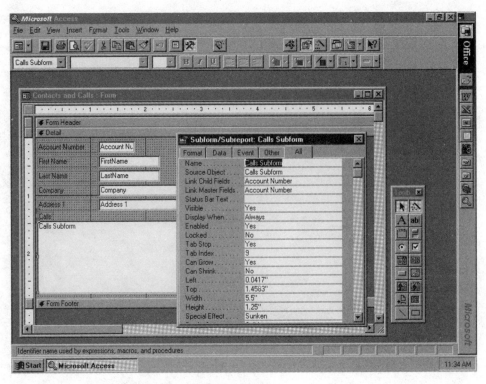

Figure 5.25 An example main/subform in Design view.

The Properties window for the subform (in this case, named "Form" because the subform is open in its own Design view) contains two properties that are of particular interest: the Default View property and the Views Allowed property. In this example, the Default View property is set to Datasheet; this is the setting that the Form Wizard normally gives to a subform. You can click in this property and change it to any of the three available views: single-form, continuous-form, and datasheet view. Single-form displays one record at a time, while Continuous-form displays multiple records (as many as will fit in the current window), each in its own copy of the detail section of the form. The Datasheet view displays the fields as a datasheet with the data arranged in rows and columns.

You can use the Views Allowed property to limit the available views that the user can change to for the subform. Your choices here are Form (which lets the subform be shown only in single-form or continuous-form view), Datasheet (which restricts the viewer to the datasheet view), and Both (no limitations). If you want it to be absolutely clear that the subform contains "many" data in a relationship, you might want to set this property to Datasheet to prevent the user from ever switching the subform to a form view. (In form view, it could be harder to see a many relationship because the form would show only one detail record at a time.)

Design Tips for a Multitable Form

Because all multitable forms are forms within forms, some unique tips apply to the design of these types of forms.

Avoid redundant controls. Controls that exist in one form usually should not be duplicated in the other. In the example form created earlier, the Member ID field exists in both the Members and the Rentals tables, but the field was not added to the subform. Because all of the records displayed by the subform are associated with the member whose name appears in the main form, there was no need to display the Member ID field again in the subform.

Consider size constraints with the subform. In the subform, you should include only those fields that are necessary to accomplish the task at hand. You'll probably want the subform to use a datasheet view, and you can only fit so many fields in the row and column arrangement of a datasheet. Don't hesitate to omit fields that don't serve a useful purpose to the specific form. In the example created earlier, the movie description was purposely omitted from the subform because it really wasn't necessary for this form and would have used up valuable space.

Decide which, if any, fields should be locked. To protect referential integrity, you might want to lock some fields (make them unavailable to editing). The form

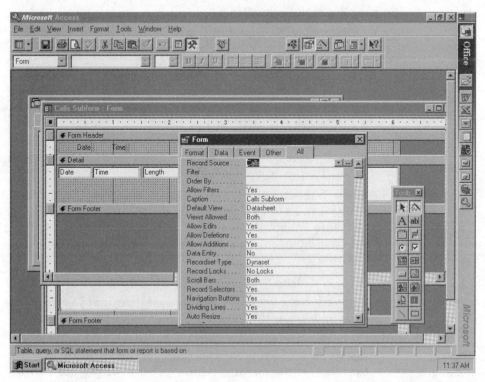

Figure 5.26 The Properties window for subform/subreport.

created in the exercise is an excellent example of the potential problem. If you were to change the member ID for a particular member after contacts had been made under that member's old member ID, you would effectively disconnect the master record in the Members table from the associated child records in the Calls table. The Calls table would contain contacts for which no corresponding member could be found. You could prevent this from happening by opening the Properties window for the Member ID field in the main form and setting the Locked property to Yes. (A better way to protect referential integrity is to do so at the table level, by specifying relationships when you design your tables.)

Solving Possible Problems

If you create a main/subform and it doesn't give you the data that you want, chances are that Access is having a problem with the way the underlying data has been used in the form's design. If you are using the form to show the details of a one-to-many relationship, make sure that the "one" table is the basis for the main form and the "many" table is the basis for the subform, and not the other way around. If, during the form-creation process, the wizard displays an error message like "Unable to link main form to subform," make sure that the tables or queries that you are trying to use have a matching field with the same name or establish default relationships beforehand with the Edit/Relationships command.

Creating Multitable Forms Manually

When manually creating a multitable form, first create and save the subform. You will likely want to design the subform so that it displays as much data as possible in a row-and-column format. Once the subform has been designed, you can create the multitable form by performing these steps:

1. Open the main form in Design view, and add any desired controls (including fields) to the main form. During the design process, be sure to leave sufficient space to place the subform.

2. If the Database window is not visible, click the Database window button on the Toolbar to show the Database window.

3. In the Database window, click Form, then find the name of the subform that you want to add to the main form. Click and drag that form from the Database window onto a blank area of the main form. When you release the mouse button, a subform appears within the main form, as shown in Figure 5.27.

4. Move and size the subform within the main form as desired.

5. Right-click the subform, and choose Properties from the menu that appears to open the Properties window for the subform.

6. Check the entries in the Link Master Fields and Link Child Fields properties (under All Properties or Data Properties in the list box). Make sure that the field name under Link Child Fields is the common field in the table or query that provides data to the subform. In the same manner,

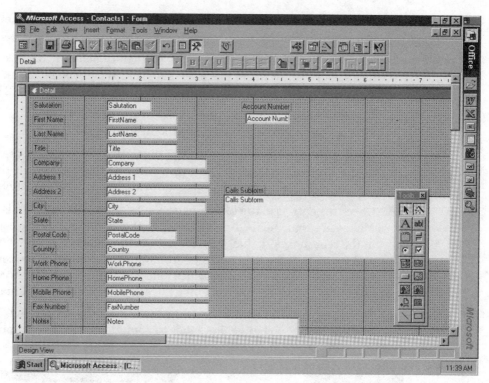

Figure 5.27 A subform open in Design view.

make sure that the field name under Link Master Fields is the common field in the table or query that provides data to the main form. If Access has not established the link, you can enter the names of the fields manually.

7. Save the form by choosing `File/Save` from the menus and assigning the form a name. You can switch to Form view for the form to see the data.

Note that Step 3 of this process recommended the "drag-and-drop" method for placing the subform. Of the two manual methods, this method is recommended because it automatically adds the name of the source object (the query or table supplying the subform with data) and it automatically creates a subform of the minimum size needed to contain the data in Datasheet view.

A third way of creating a multitable form manually is to use the Subform tool on the Toolbox; when you use this method, Access adds a subform control, but you must specify where that control gets its data, and you must size the control. The steps that you can follow with this technique are similar to those of the drop-and-drag technique, but with slightly more complexity. To create a multitable form using the Toolbox, you use these steps:

1. Open the main form in Design view, and add any desired controls (including fields) to the main form. During the design process, leave sufficient space to place the subform.

2. If the Toolbox is not visible, click the Toolbox button on the Toolbar to show the Toolbox.

3. Click the Subform button in the Toolbar to select it, then click in the form where you want to place the subform. When you do so, an embedded control appears within the main form, as shown in Figure 5.28.

4. Right-click the subform, and choose Properties from the menu that appears to open the Properties window for the subform.

5. Click in the Source Object property (under All Properties or Data Properties in the list box), and click the arrow to open the list box. In the list box, choose the table or query that is to provide the data for the subform.

6. Check the entries in the Link Master Fields and Link Child Fields properties. Make sure that the field name under Link Child Fields is the common field in the table or query that provides data to the subform. In the same manner, make sure that the field name under Link Master Fields is the common field in the table or query that provides data to the main form. If Access has not established the link, you can enter the names of the fields manually.

7. Move and size the subform within the main form as desired. You probably will want to change the label to something more appropriate; when

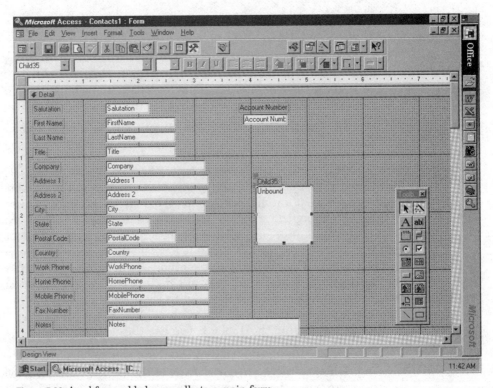

Figure 5.28 A subform added manually to a main form.

using the Toolbox to add a subform, Access assigns rather meaningless names like "Child35" to the subforms.

8. Save the form by choosing File/Save from the menus and assigning the form a name. You can switch to Form view for the form to see the data.

Creating Subforms Within Subforms

One way to create multitable forms that draw data from three (or more) tables is to base some or all of the data on a query. Sometimes, however, what is needed is a form with two complete levels of subforms. This type of multitable form can used to show a one-to-many-to-many type of relationship. You can create a form that supports this type of relationship by embedding a subform within another subform. The subform that contains the subform then can be embedded in the main form. Because there is no Form Wizard designed for this type of form, you must design this form on your own.

An example of the one-to-many-to-many type of relationship exists in the Northwind Traders database. In the query shown in Figure 5.29, three tables show records for customers, their orders, and the details of their orders. A one-to-many relationship exists between the customer and orders tables; for every customer, there are many orders. For each of the orders, there exist many records in the order details table. Hence, when all three tables are considered together, they comprise a one-to-many-to-many relationship.

The basic steps behind creating a multitable form to handle this kind of data are as follows:

1. Create the first and the second subforms, and save them to disk. The Form Wizards can help here; you can use them to quickly create single-column forms based on the underlying tables or queries, then go into the forms in Design view and change the properties so that the forms always display the data in Datasheet view.

2. Open the first subform in Design view.

3. Drag the second subform from the Database window onto a blank area of the first subform.

4. Move and size the second subform as desired.

5. Save the changes to the first subform.

6. Create the main form.

7. While in Design view for the main form, drag the first subform from the Database window onto a blank area of the main form.

8. Move and size the first subform as desired.

9. Save the changes to the main form.

Adding Graphics to Forms

Graphic images as design elements can easily be added to forms using Windows cut-and-paste techniques. While you can use the Image tool of the

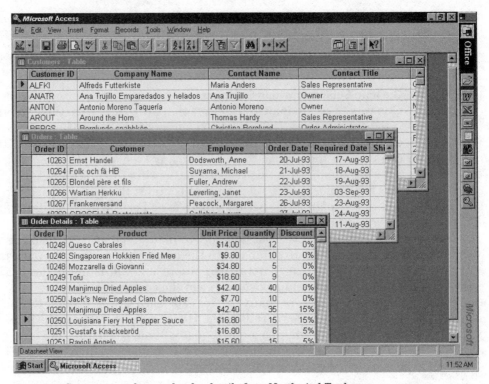

Figure 5.29 Customers, orders, and order details from Northwind Traders.

Toolbox to insert an object, if all you are after is a graphic, it usually is easier to just paste in the graphic from the other Windows application. When you paste in a graphic selection from another Windows program into a form's design, it automatically appears in an unbound object frame, and you can move or size the frame as desired. You use the following steps to paste a graphic into a form as a design element:

1. Open the desired form in Design view.

2. Switch to the graphics program that you are running under Windows, and open the document containing the desired graphic.

3. Using the selection techniques applicable to the graphics program you are using, select the desired portion of the graphic.

4. From the graphics program's menus, choose `Edit/Copy` to copy the graphic to the Windows Clipboard.

5. Use the Windows 95 Taskbar to switch back to Access.

6. Click in the section of the form where you want the graphic to appear, and choose `Edit/Paste`.

7. Use the moving and sizing techniques covered earlier to size the graphic and place it in the desired location in a form.

Figure 5.30 shows a graphic added to a form from a Windows Paintbrush image, using the steps described previously. Note that, once you have placed a graphic in this manner, you can modify it from within Access by double-clicking the graphic (assuming your application used to create the graphic supports Windows OLE). Double-clicking the graphic will switch you back into the original program with the graphic loaded. You can make any desired changes and choose File/Exit from the application's menu to update the graphic that is stored in the Access form.

Summary

This chapter has provided a detailed look at how you can design forms (which is the basis of the user interface for your applications) with the tools provided by Access. You can make use of the Form Wizards, or you can lay out your forms manually to achieve the precise look that you need for a given task. In the next chapter, you'll learn how to further put forms to work by utilizing the event-driven nature of an Access application.

Figure 5.30 A graphic added to a form.

6

Exploring Event-Driven Programming

This chapter details the *event-driven* nature of the Access application and how you can monitor and make use of events in your applications. Before I proceed, it might help to define exactly what an event is. In Access, an *event* is any action that takes place and is recognized by the environment, typically by a form, a report, or a control placed on the form.

As a user works with Access objects (such as the command buttons or menu options on a form), events are generated by the actions that are performed by the user. In fact, by its very nature, Windows is an event-driven environment, as compared to the command-driven nature of the DOS environment that preceded it. With Windows, a user doesn't have to follow some prearranged sequence of events, such as stepping down through layers of menus containing numbered choices. Instead, the user can choose from a variety of options, such as clicking in a dialog box, moving any one of a number of windows, or clicking a button in a custom toolbar. The operating system (in this case, Windows 95) must be prepared to respond to any of these options. The environment is truly modeless, or *event-driven*.

It is the event-driven style of applications design, as demonstrated by Windows and by Apple's Macintosh, that has taken over the personal computer world. Being a Windows application designed to follow the structure of Windows, Access adheres to that event-driven nature. Here's the general event scenario that takes place in an Access application:

1. Access is launched, and the desired database is opened. Typically, there's an autoexec macro that establishes the working environment for the application. This macro also opens the main form that serves as the initial user interface that the user sees, with menus and/or command buttons attached.

2. Some action generally taken by the user, such as selecting a menu option or clicking on a command button, triggers an *event*. In addition to actions taken by the user, a form also can have code or a macro attached to its OnOpen property. When this is the case, the form's opening is the event that triggers the action.

3. The macro or the program code ("event procedure") that is attached to the event runs, and the steps that are assigned to that macro or specified by that code are carried out.

4. Access monitors the environment, waiting for the next event. When that event occurs, the appropriate actions take place.

In getting a better understanding of the event-driven nature of Windows applications, it often helps to compare it to the procedural style of application that preceded it in the DOS world. With DOS-based applications written around a procedural interface, the application would always present the user with an opening screen (or "main menu") that contained a specific set of numbered or lettered choices. Only one choice could be selected at a time, and that choice often led to yet another menu with more lettered or numbered choices. As an example, selecting Reports from a main menu could cause a Reports menu to appear that contains a number of available reports. As a user selects from a specific group of choices, certain actions occur in response to one selection at a time. This was the approach commonly used in database programming languages before the popularity of Windows. Programs written using dBASE for DOS and compatible environments were famous (or infamous, as the case may be) for taking this approach.

By comparison, applications that make use of the event-driven approach to design don't lock the user into a limited series of steps. The application instead monitors the environment for any of a number of events that are triggered by possible user actions, and the application responds accordingly.

One point that is important to realize is that the presence of a mouse, onscreen windows, and pull-down menus alone does not make for a truly event-driven application. Even using Access, you could design and implement an application that is procedural in nature. (You would have to work at it, but it definitely could be done.)

As an example, you might structure an application that, upon being launched, hides the Access menus, the Database Window, and all the toolbars, and opens a switchboard with a limited number of command buttons serving as a main menu. Each command button could take the user to another menu that contains a limited number of buttons or to just one specific task (such as the printing of a report) before returning control to the main menu. If you designed an application like this, it would be largely procedural in nature, in spite of the fact that you implemented it using the event-driven environment that is Access.

Because it takes more than the appearance of windows, menus, and dialog boxes to produce what is truly an event-driven application, as the designer, you must consider the different tasks that the user needs to undertake, keeping in mind the desire of the user to move in any one of a number of different directions. Throughout the rest of this chapter, you'll learn exactly how the different events can occur in Access. Once you know this, you'll be better equipped to implement applications using an event-driven approach.

Linking Events to Visual Basic Code

In Access, events are linked to *event procedures*, and you specify what events call the event procedures. When an event takes place in a form, a report, or a control, the event procedure that you've written gets executed by Access. For Access to know that the event must trigger an event procedure, you must tie the event procedure to the desired event during the design stage. To do this, you open an *event procedure code template* for the event procedure that you want to write, then you add the desired code that must run when the specified event occurs. You can open an event procedure code template by performing the following steps:

1. Use the View/Code menu option to open the module window for the form or report.
2. Click the Object list box, and choose the desired object.
3. Click the Procedure list box, and select the desired event procedure.

Once you do this, the starting and ending lines for a Sub procedure appear in the Module window. Access inserts default names that are used to link the procedure to the added event. To see how you can do this, perform the following steps:

1. Open any form in any database in Design view.
2. From the menus, choose View/Code, or click the Code button on the toolbar, to open a Module window.
3. Click in the Object list box, and choose any of the form's fields.
4. Click in the Procedures list box, then click AfterUpdate.

Figure 6.1 gives you an idea of the results. You'll see a Sub procedure with an appropriate name assigned to it. Access bases the name on the name of the field that you selected earlier, and Access adds a matching End statement two lines below the Sub statement. The insertion pointer gets placed on the blank line between the Sub and End statements. At this point, you could proceed to enter any desired Visual Basic for Applications code.

Because you chose AfterUpdate from the Procedures list box, any statements placed in this Sub procedure would be executed after an update, meaning after data in the field of the form is changed by the user and the changes are accepted within Access.

In Access, there are a number of properties that can call Visual Basic for Applications procedures in response to a specific event. As an example, you might need to execute a certain code sequence when a form is opened, when the focus moves to a certain control within a form, or when the focus moves off the current record. In Access, events can occur for forms, for controls and records on forms, for reports, and for report sections.

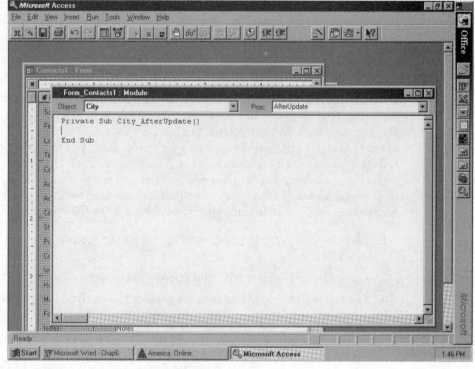

Figure 6.1 An example of an event procedure.

Which events occur depends on how the user interacts with the various elements in the Access form or report that is active. Events are most often triggered by a change in *focus*. As with its close relative, Visual Basic, an object in Access is said to have the focus when the user is interacting with the object. For example, in any form, you can press the Tab key to move between the controls of the form. As you do so, when each control is highlighted by the cursor, it is said to have the focus. Access can respond to a number of different events that are related to controls, forms, and reports.

Whether you are programming with macros, with Visual Basic for Applications code, or with a combination of both, you can use different events to perform an appropriate action when the user takes some action. One example is a `Billing Rate` field in a Time and Billing database. You might have Visual Basic for Applications code that performs a specialized sort of validation; you could run that code by naming the function that contains the code in the BeforeUpdate property for the Salary field.

About the Default Events

In Access, many objects have a *default event*. A common example is the command button, which has a default Click event; in other words, when you mouse click on a button, it appears to depress and release. That visual response is the default event for a command button.

You can define your own responses to the default events by using the Build Event option of the shortcut menu for any object. Right-click the object, and from the shortcut menu that appears, choose Build Event. Doing so causes the Choose Builder dialog box to appear, as shown in Figure 6.2.

Select Code Builder in the dialog box and click OK, and the default event procedure will appear in a window. Figure 6.3 shows the default event procedure for a command button.

In the window, between the Sub and the End sub lines, you can enter the Visual Basic for Applications code that you want to use to change the behavior of the default event. Table 6.1 shows the various default events for all the Access objects that have default events.

Managing an Application's Events

The event-driven nature that defines an Access application means that whatever operations take place will follow some predefined sequence of events. For example, take the common task of opening a form. When a form that contains data initially opens in Access, before any record appears, the Open event occurs for the form. As the form opens and a record or records appear, the Load event occurs. Next, once the form becomes the active window, the Activate event occurs. Finally, for the record that gets the focus, the Current event occurs. As you work with forms and the data that's in them, various other events also occur. You can tie Visual Basic for Applications code or Access macros to these events to run procedures when you need to do so.

In Access, all events can be grouped into a number of different categories. Table 6.2 summarizes the different events and the categories that they fall into.

Managing Events Within Forms

Given that the most common tasks in any Access application involve opening and closing forms and working with the controls placed within forms, it's vital to have a working knowledge of how events occur in forms. Here's the sequence of events that takes place when you initially open a form that contains an active control:

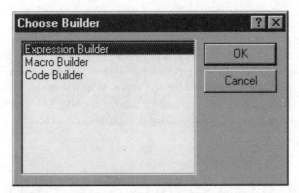

Figure 6.2 The Choose Builder dialog box.

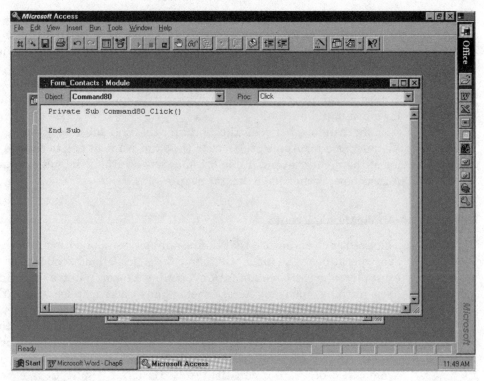

Figure 6.3 The default event procedure for a command button.

Open event > Load event > Resize event > Activate event > Current event

If the form has no active controls, there's also a GotFocus event for the form itself, which is triggered just before the Current event.

When a form that contains an active control is closed, here's the sequence of events that occurs:

Unload event > Deactivate event > Close event

If you switch between two open forms and both forms have active controls, here's the sequence of events that occurs:

Deactivate event (for form A) > Activate event (for form B)

As to the controls that are in the forms, whenever you open a form that has one or more active controls, the Enter event occurs for the control that gets the focus, followed by the GotFocus event for that same control. These events take place after the Activate and Current events for the form. When you leave a control (for example, by clicking on a different control in the form), the Exit event occurs for the control that you are leaving, followed by the LostFocus event for that control.

Events for Controls on Forms

One of the most common uses for events is to have an action occur when the focus moves into a control or when data changes within a control. For controls,

Access provides the Enter, BeforeUpdate, AfterUpdate, and Exit properties. Table 6.3 shows when these properties can call your specified procedures.

Note that the DblClick property can be used with controls. The DblClick property runs a function (or macro) when you double-click the control, but before the result of the double-click action takes place. If you double-click a control that does not yet have the focus, the Enter function or macro runs before any DblClick function or macro runs.

Events for Records on Forms

You might need to tie some events to an overall action concerning an entire record as seen through a form, rather than to a single control. For records that contain existing data, Access provides the Current, BeforeUpdate, and AfterUpdate properties. Table 6.4 shows when these properties can call your specified procedures.

Note that, as you leave a record (but before the focus enters the following record), any Exit macro that's attached to the control that had the last focus runs. Any macro or function that you have assigned to the Exit property runs after any BeforeUpdate and AfterUpdate macros or functions. If you need to

Table 6.1

Object	Default event
Form	Load
Report	Open
Bound object frame	Updated
Unbound object frame	Updated
Image control	Click
Chart	Updated
Check box	Click
Command button	Click
Label	Click
List box	Before update
Option button	Click
Rectangle	Click
Option group	Before update
Toggle button	Click
Subform	Enter
Text box	Before update
Combo box	Before update
Section (report)	Format
Section (form)	Click

Table 6.2

Category	Events	Occurs when...
Window events	Close, Load, Open, Resize, Unload	A user performs an action in a form or on a report
Focus events	Activate, Deactivate, Enter, Exit, GotFocus, LostFocus	Objects get or lose the focus
Data events	AfterDelConfirm, AfterInsert, AfterUpdate, BeforeDelConfirm, BeforeInsert, BeforeUpdate, Change, Current, Delete, NotInList,Updated	Changes occur to data
Mouse events	Click, DblClick, MouseDown, MouseMove, MouseUp	A mouse action occurs
Keyboard events	KeyDown, KeyPress, KeyUp	A keyboard key is pressed, or a key is sent using the SendKeys statement or a SendKeys action
Print events	Format, NoData, Page, Print, Retreat	A report is printed, or a report is formatted for printing
Filter events	Filter, ApplyFilter	A filter is created, or a filter is applied to a form
Error and timing events	Error, Timer	An error is reported by Access, or a timeout results (specific time interval elapses)

Table 6.3

Event property	Runs macro or function...
Enter	As you move into the control, but before it gets the focus
BeforeUpdate	Before the existing data displayed in the control is updated
AfterUpdate	After the existing data displayed in the control is updated
Exit	As you leave the control, but before it loses the focus

Table 6.4

Event property	Runs macro or function...
Current	When you move to the record, but before the record is displayed
BeforeUpdate	Before the data entered in the record is updated
AfterUpdate	After the data entered in the record is updated

run BeforeUpdate or AfterUpdate macros or functions without running any Exit macros of functions, save the record by choosing File/Save Record from the menus.

Also note that the Delete property runs any attached macro or function when you delete an existing record, but before the record actually is deleted. After you delete a record, the focus moves to the record that follows the deleted record. Access then runs any Current macro or function for the record, along with any Enter macro or function for the first control in the record.

If you click the record selector of the current record and have changed any data in the record, Access runs the BeforeUpdate and AfterUpdate macros or functions for the record and the Exit macro or function for the control that has the focus. If you click the record selector of a different record, Access also runs the Current macro or function.

The BeforeUpdate and AfterUpdate macros or functions run only when changes have been made to the data in the record.

Events for Reports and Report Sections

When you open a report to print or preview it, the events in Table 6.5 occur, in the order shown.

Entering Data in a Control, and Moving to Another Control

After you enter new data or change existing data in a control or a form, then move the focus with the Enter, Tab, or arrow keys or by clicking with the mouse, the following sequence of events takes place:

1. Any macro or function that is attached to the BeforeUpdate property for the control runs.

2. The data that has been entered into the control is stored in a temporary record.

3. Any macro or function that is attached to the AfterUpdate property for the control runs.

Table 6.5

Event property	Runs macro or function...
Open	For reports: When you open the report, but before the report is displayed
Format	For report sections: After Access selects the data to be inserted in the section, but before the data is formatted for printing
Print	For report sections: After Access formats the data in the section for printing, but before the section is printed
Close	For reports: When you close the report

As the focus is moved from control to control within the record, this same sequence of events occurs for each control. While the focus remains within a control, you can undo any changes made to the data in the control. To do so, press Esc, or choose Edit/Undo Current Field from the menus. You also can use the CancelEvent action in a BeforeUpdate macro that you've created to cancel the updating of the data. After the focus has been moved to a new control, you can't undo changes to the data in the previous control with the Undo Current Field command. You can use the Edit/Undo Current Record command to undo all changes made to the entire record until you leave the record.

Summary

In this chapter, I've examined the event-driven model and how you work with it in a very different manner than the traditional or "procedural" approach that preceded it. A better understanding of the event-driven model and how you can make use of it should be the primary goal of any developer who makes use of Microsoft Access. The numerous techniques presented in this chapter, including tying events to Visual Basic for Applications code and utilizing events for controls on forms and reports and within report sections, will serve as a guide for the approaches that you can take within your applications. For times when errors occur in your Visual Basic for Applications programs, chapter 11, "Debugging and Handling Errors in Applications," provides techniques that prove useful in the error-handling and debugging processes.

Working with Tables in Access Applications

When you get to the heart of the matter, tables are the very basis of your Access applications. Because this is the case, creating, maintaining, and manipulating table data—and the process of database design that precedes table creation—has to take place early in the process of applications development. This chapter will examine the ways in which you can effectively plan the tables that support your applications and how you can structure and define relationships between those tables in Access.

Database and Table Planning

If you are unfamiliar with the nuances of database design, you should spend some time learning about proper database design and about normalization before you create your tables in Access. Any carefully planned computer database involves three steps in the planning process: *data definition*, *data refinement*, and *normalization* (or the elimination of unnecessary redundancies). With relational databases, this process is important, because it helps you to determine when certain data should be stored in separate tables. When someone is new to database design, there is a tendency to create a single table that contains all of the data associated with a task. This harmful tendency results in tables that are awkward to use, easy to damage, and wasteful in regard to disk space. The planning process using the steps that follow helps avoid the kinds of problems associated with such databases.

Step 1: Data Definition

During the first step, *data definition*, you will want to define the categories, or fields, that will make up your database. As you do so, examine your needs carefully to determine the kinds of information that must be stored in your database. Because you initially do this on paper, it is not necessary to try to separate the fields into different tables, as you will tackle this in Step 3 of the process.

Because attributes are the groups of data that make up a database, any data that you can imagine within a column of a table is an individual attribute, or field. Names, addresses, customer numbers, stock numbers, descriptions, and item costs are common fields that your database might contain. As you plan for the required fields, it often helps to keep in mind what information is needed from the database in the form of reports. Because the information that the reports will provide will be based on the data that's placed in the fields, you will want to be sure that there are sufficient fields to provide the needed data.

One important point to keep in mind is that, during this phase of database design, it is a wise idea to list all of the possible attributes needed by your application. You might later find that some of the categories are unnecessary, but any unneeded categories can be eliminated during the data refinement stage.

Step 2: Data Refinement

During the next step, *data refinement*, you will refine your list of categories so that it more accurately reflects the types of data that will be stored within your database. One tip that can significantly help in avoiding later troubles is to include suggestions from users of the application in the design process. The people who must use the database on a day-in and day-out basis are likely to know what kinds of information they must obtain from the database. In some cases, the refinements will likely be obvious, and others might not be so obvious. One step that will help in identifying possible refinements is to go over your written list of fields that were compiled during the first step of the process.

Step 3: Normalization

The last step, *normalization*, is the vitally needed step whenever you are working with relational databases. In a nutshell, normalization is a process by which data attributes (or fields) are grouped into individual tables. By performing this process, you eliminate any unnecessary redundancies between your tables. Remember that Access is a relational database, so the data stored in one table can be related to the data stored in another. It is important not to lose sight of this fact; it is all too common for users of database-management software to create bulky, nonrelational databases. Such an approach can drastically increase the time involved in working with the data and can make the entire application difficult to use.

Whenever you must have related tables, it helps to have a field that will always contain data that is unique to a record. Employee ID numbers, customer numbers, stock numbers, transaction numbers, and part numbers are examples of fields that commonly are used to establish relationships between tables. If the design of your application does not lend itself to a unique field, remember that Access lets you include a special field type, called *counter fields*, that contain numbers that Access automatically adds as you add new records. The values that Access places in counter fields will be unique. So, in many cases, you can use these as a means of identifying records in a unique fashion.

Remember that, even after you refine your database design and create the tables in Access, no database structure is set in stone. If you later find that additional fields are needed, you can always add them. If you find redundant data that should be placed in multiple tables, you can create queries that will extract the data that you need, then store that data into new tables. However, such steps represent work after-the-fact. The ideal is to take the time to plan your database from the start, so major changes later will not be needed.

Defining Tables in Access

Once you complete the database design process and you know exactly how you want to implement your table structures, you need to approach the table design and implementation process using two steps: *field identification* and *determination of the data types, sizes, and names*. During the process of identifying the fields, you'll need to decide not only what fields you'll need, but also where you plan to store them. Once you've identified your fields, you'll need to decide on the field type, the size of the field in some cases, and the name for the field.

Access lets you design tables in a number of ways, including through the use of the *Table Wizards*, an automated help facility that steps you through the process of table creation by suggesting predefined layouts for your tables. Given that this is a book aimed at developers, I'll skip coverage of the Table Wizards and assume that you prefer to manually create your tables, which offers more control over the table creation process.

Starting the table creation process is fairly simple. To create a new table, perform these steps:

1. In the Database window, click the Tables tab.

2. Click the New button.

3. In the New Table dialog box that appears, select Design View, then click OK.

When you do this, Access displays the Table Design window, shown in Figure 7.1. Access adds a sequential name (such as Table1, Table2, etc.) at the top of the window; this name gets replaced with the name that you give the table when you save it. When designing a table manually, you use the Table Design Window to define the fields in your table.

Access lets you look at tables in one of two views: *Design view* and *Datasheet view*. In Design view, you see the design, or structure, of the table. This is where you design the table; you name the fields, tell Access what types of data should be stored in them, and specify any rules that will govern data entry into the table. You can create new tables, as well as change the structure of existing tables, while in Design view.

The other view, Datasheet view, is used once a table has been created for examining data and adding and editing data in the table.

To open an existing table in Design view, you click the table name in the Database Window to select it, then you click the Design button. (As a shortcut, you also can right-click the table name and choose Open from the shortcut menu that appears.)

The Table Design Window is divided into three columns: Field Name, Data Type, and Description. Under the Field Name column, you type the name for

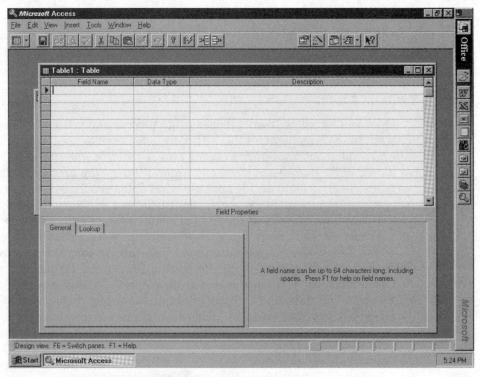

Figure 7.1 The Table Design window.

the field. Field names can be up to 64 characters in length and can include letters, numbers, spaces, or punctuation marks. Considering the flexibility of
Access, it is a good idea to give fields descriptive names; for example, the name
"Weekly Salary" might make more sense than a field name of "Wk.Sal."
However, avoid using field names that are overly long, as these can complicate
matters when you are trying to design columnar reports. The field names might
be so long that it becomes difficult to fit as many columns as you might prefer.

After entering the desired field name, press Tab, and the insertion pointer
will move to the Data Type column. In this column, you specify the data type
for the data that will be stored in the field. By default, Access assigns a data
type of Text. You can change this default by clicking the arrow to cause the
drop down list box of data types to open (Figure 7.2).

Access allows a choice of eight types of fields, along with a choice called
"Lookup Wizard," which helps you define a field that gets its value by looking
up the content of another field in another table. The field types are described
in the following sections.

Text Fields

Use text fields to store any kinds of textual data, such as customer names,
product names, and addresses. Text fields can contain any combination of text

and numbers of up to 255 characters in length. Entries in text fields can include punctuation marks, and you can insert special symbols using the combination of Alt and numeric keypad keys or the Windows Character Map. (To use the Character Map, run it from the Windows Accessories group, double-click the desired special character, then click `Copy`, place the insertion pointer in Access where you want the character to appear, and choose `Edit/Paste`.) Numbers that you don't intend to perform calculations on — such as part numbers, patient ID numbers, or phone numbers — should be stored in text fields. If you need to store more than 255 characters, use a memo field instead.

Tip: While Access allows a 255-character maximum, the default size of a text field is 50 characters. If you want to store more than this, you'll need to change the Field Size property. Click under Field Size in the Field Properties section of the Table Design window, and enter a desired size for the field.

Number Fields

Use number fields to store numeric data (other than money) on which you are likely to perform calculations. You can store integers or fractional values (using decimals), and you can enter negative values. To enter negative values, precede the value with a minus symbol, or enclose the value in parenthesis.

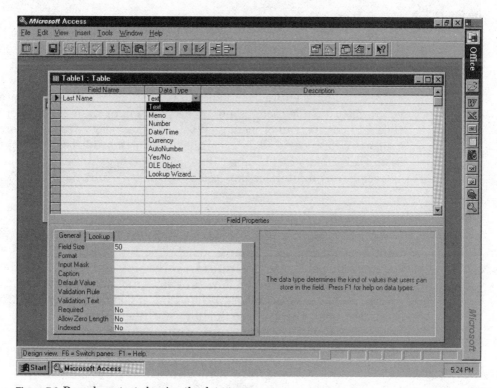

Figure 7.2 Drop-down text showing the data types.

Caution: While you could store monetary amounts in a number field, you should avoid such a practice. Access provides a currency field that provides a more accurate rounding off for currency values. Using the currency type means that the currency symbol (according to your Windows Control Panel settings) will automatically appear where the field appears in forms and reports.

Currency Fields

Use these for numeric values that represent monetary amounts. By default, numbers that you store in a currency field always maintain a fixed number of digits to the right of the decimal point; this prevents rounding errors that could otherwise occur.

Date/Time

Use these for date and/or time entries stored in a table. In Access, validation of existent dates is automatic; you cannot enter invalid dates or times (such as 02/31/93 or 26:17PM). Date/time fields can be useful in calculations, as Access lets you perform date or time-based arithmetic. For example, you could subtract one date field from another in a report to come up with the number of days between both dates.

Memo Fields

Use memo fields to store amounts of text that will be too large to fit in a text field. Memo fields are ideal for items like employee job descriptions, product descriptions, article abstracts, or other long paragraphs of text. In Access, memo fields can be as long as 32,000 characters.

Tip: If you have entire documents stored using a Windows word processor and you want to include them in a database, you might want to consider using OLE Object Fields instead of memo fields. Assuming your Windows word processor supports OLE (nearly all do), you can store an embedded copy of your document in an OLE Object Field. Using Windows' OLE capabilities in this manner also overcomes any limitations imposed by the 32,000 character limit of memo fields.

Counter Fields

If you add a counter field, Access will automatically insert sequential values into the field for each record added. The first record added is assigned a counter value of 1, the next record a value of 2, and so on. (Counter fields are routinely used as primary keys in relational databases, because they are always unique for each record.) Note that, if you delete a record that contains a counter field, the counter fields in the remaining records are not renumbered; Access will not let you change the value of a counter field.

Yes/No Fields

Logical fields contain a Yes/No, True/False, On/Off, or other Boolean entry (such as -1 for yes or 0 for no).

OLE Object

Use these to embed or link objects created in other Windows programs. In Windows, *objects* are any form of information — such as a picture, a graph, or a word processing document — that can be linked or embedded in another application (in this case, Access). OLE Object fields can contain word processing documents, spreadsheets, graphic images or pictures, sound, and even video. In Access, the most common use for OLE Object fields is to display photos or drawings of people or items; as an example, the Employees table of the Northwind Traders database contains an OLE Object field for employee photos. Viewed through a form, the contents of the field for a particular record can be seen in Figure 7.3.

Hyperlink

Use these to store a combination of text and numbers that serves as a hyperlink address, or a path to an Access object, an Office 97 document, or a Web page. Hyperlink fields (which are not available in Access 95) can be addresses to Internet or Intranet Web sites, or file names on a hard disk or a network drive.

After choosing the field's data type, press Tab again to move to the Description column. In this column, you can enter an optional description of the field. Descriptions can be useful for novice users, because they appear in the status bar of a form when you view data through the form.

Figure 7.3 A Northwind Traders form with a photo stored in an OLE Object field.

After entering any desired description for the field, press Tab again, and the insertion pointer will move to the next field. You can continue entering field names, data types, and descriptions for the remaining fields as desired. Figure 7.4 shows the People table of the Sales database in Design view.

As mentioned, when you specify a field as a Text field, Access defaults to a field size (in the Field Properties area of the window) of 50 characters. Note that this value is a maximum value, but Access does not use all of this space for the actual storage of records. Access uses *variable-length fields* to store textual data; therefore, unlike some database managers, if you enter a value that contains 12 characters, Access will use only 12 characters to store the data, and not 50. However, you should realize that the value in the Size properties box is a maximum value; if you leave it set to the default of 50 characters, you will not be able to store more than 50 characters in that field within any given record. If you plan to store larger amounts of text, you might want to increase the size in the Properties box or consider using memo fields to store the text.

Adding a Primary Key

Access lets you define any field as a *primary key*. Simply put, a primary key is one or more fields that uniquely identify every record stored in the table. With primary keys, what is important to remember is that Access will not let you

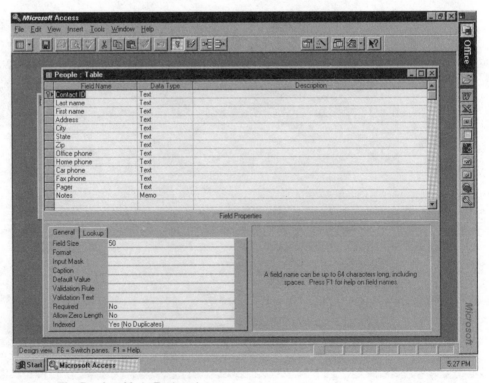

Figure 7.4 The People table in Design view.

place the same data in the primary key (or fields) of more than one record. For example, it would not be a wise idea to designate a "Last name" field as a primary key; if you were to enter a record in the table with the last name of "Johnson," you would never be able to enter another record in that table with the same last name.

Access lets you designate either a single field or a combination of fields as a primary key. So, in cases where no single field will serve as a unique record of data, you can use more than one field. For example, in a mailing list, you might decide to specify a combination of last name, first name, and address as a primary key. This would suffice, assuming that you never have a case of two persons with the same last and first names living at the same address.

Microsoft recommends that you always specify a primary key for the tables that you create. While doing so is not required, it will speed the performance of Access in queries, sorts, and other operations. (A primary key is required if you want to create a default relationship between tables.) Social security numbers, driver's license numbers, or invoice numbers are commonly used as primary keys in business applications. If your application has not previously used ID or account numbers, now might be the time to add such organization to your application, as it will make your work with Access more efficient. When database applications do not lend themselves to the idea of a primary key, you can define a field as a counter field, name it "Record number" or "Record ID" and designate that field as the primary key. As data is added, Access will automatically increment the value in that field.

To set the primary key, perform these steps:

1. Click anywhere in the field that you want to use for the primary key. If you want to create a primary key based on more than one field, hold down the Ctrl key and click the field selector to the left of each field you want to include.

2. Click the Primary Key button in the toolbar, or choose Edit/Set Primary Key. When you do so, Access adds a primary key indicator to the left of the fields you've specified (Figure 7.5).

Keep in mind that, unless you are using a sorted query, Access displays records in your table in primary key order. So, if there is a particular order that you'll use most often when viewing or printing your data, it makes sense to try to design the table so that the primary key keeps the table in the desired order. (You can sort a table using any fields that you want.)

Where possible, it makes sense to specify a single field as a primary key. In some cases, however, this is simply not feasible. There might not be any field in a record that is unique. If you can't convince your organization to add some kind of identifying field (such as a member number, stock number, or a customer identification number), you can create a key based on a combination of fields. As an example, consider the table structure shown in Figure 7.6.

In this table, designed to store records of rented videos from a video store, there are fields for a customer ID number, the title of the video rented, and the date of the rental. None of these fields could be used alone as the primary key,

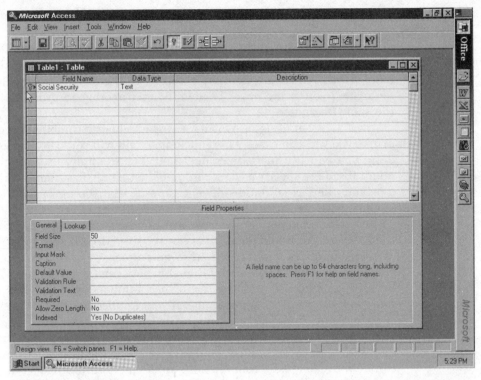

Figure 7.5 The primary key indicator.

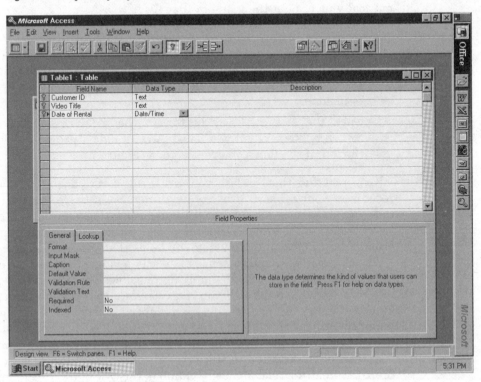

Figure 7.6 A table structure having multiple primary keys.

for there will likely be duplicates in each of these fields. However, you could create a primary key by selecting all three fields (to do so, you would hold the Ctrl key while clicking the Field Selector at the left edge of the fields), then you would click the Primary Key button on the toolbar. As shown in the figure, the key designations that would appear in the Field Selectors would show keys in each field, indicating that the fields combined serve as a primary key. This would suffice for this application, assuming that the same customer never rents the same video twice in the same day.

Rearranging and Deleting Fields

"Nothing in life is permanent save change," the saying goes. You can easily change, rearrange, or delete fields as needed in any of your tables. To change a field, just click where the change is needed and make the desired changes, using the Backspace or Del keys to delete existing characters.

To move a field, first select the field by clicking the Field Selector to the left of the field name, as shown in Figure 7.7. Then, click the Field Selector again, and while holding the mouse button depressed, drag the field to the desired location.

To delete a field, first select the field by clicking the Field Selector. Then, press the Del key, or choose Edit/Delete Row.

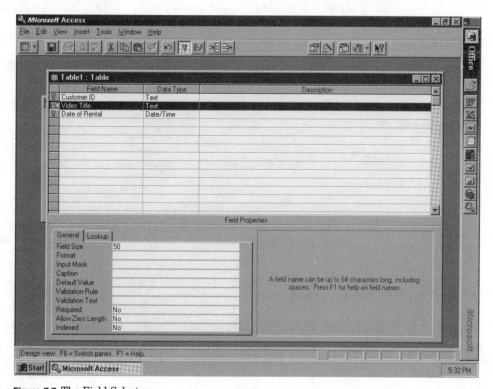

Figure 7.7 The Field Selector.

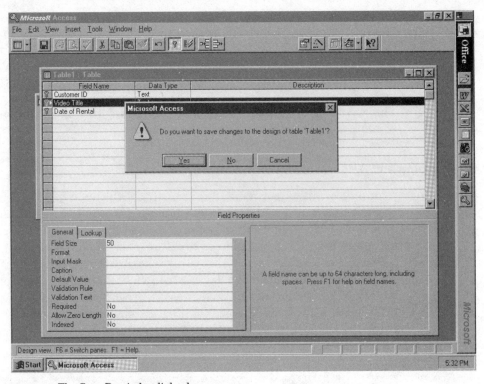

Figure 7.8 The Save Reminder dialog box.

To insert a new field at a specific position in the table, place the insertion pointer anywhere in the desired row and choose `Edit/Insert Row`.

Saving the Table

Once you've completed the process of defining a table's structure, you must save the table before data can be added to it. To save a table, perform the following steps:

1. Choose `File/Close`, or double-click the Control menu icon (it's at the upper-left corner of the Table window). The dialog box shown in Figure 7.8 appears. Click `Yes`. The Save As dialog box appears, as shown in Figure 7.9.

2. Type the desired name for the table. Note that you can use any names up to 64 characters in length for your tables (as well as for the forms, queries, and reports that you create in Access). Table names *cannot* contain periods, exclamation points, brackets, or leading blanks.

3. Click `OK`. If you did not define a primary key for the table, Access will ask if you desire one now by displaying the dialog box shown in Figure 7.10.

If you click Yes and no counter-type field currently exists in the table structure, Access will create a counter field, call it "ID," and make it a primary key. (If a counter field already exists, Access will make that field a primary key.) If you click No, Access will save the table structure without a primary key.

Once the table has been saved, you can view the table using a datasheet view, and you can add, edit, or delete records as desired, as outlined in the following section.

Setting Field Properties

While you are in the process of designing a table, you also can set *field properties* for the table. Field properties are properties assigned to fields that tell Access how you want data stored or displayed. As an example, if you have a text field that will store ZIP codes, it probably is a good idea to change the field size from the default of 50 characters to something more reasonable (such as 10). For a number field, you might want to specify a number of decimal places. For many types of fields, you might want to enter *validation rules*, which identify conditions that entries must meet before the data will be accepted into the table.

During the design process, you can see the field properties for each field in the table window; when you click in any field, the field properties for that field are visible in the bottom half of the Table window, as shown in Figure 7.11.

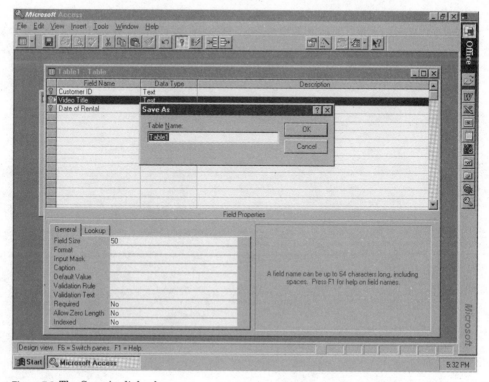

Figure 7.9 The Save As dialog box.

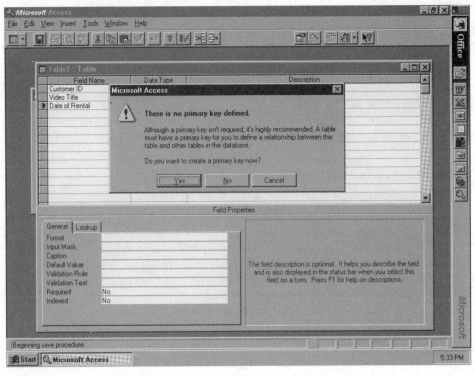

Figure 7.10 A dialog box for including a primary key.

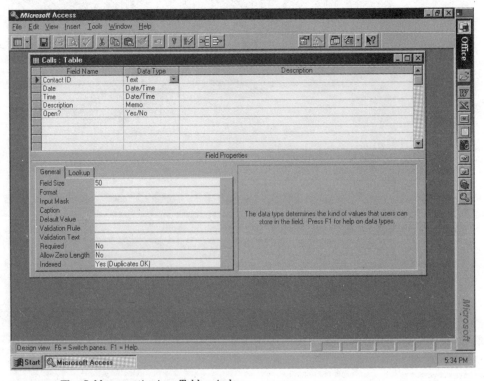

Figure 7.11 The field properties in a Table window.

The properties that you can define will vary, depending on what data type is chosen for the field; for example, number and currency fields let you specify a number of decimal places as a field property. Table 7.1 details the field properties and their uses.

To set any of the field properties, you perform the following steps:

1. Open the desired table in Design view, then click anywhere in the field whose properties that you want to set.

2. Click the property that you want to set in the bottom part of the window.

3. Enter the desired setting for the property. If an arrow appears at the right of the property, click the arrow, then select from a list of available settings, as shown in Figure 7.12.

Tip: If you are unsure about what to enter as a property, you can get help by first clicking the property in the bottom portion of the window, then pressing F1.

The Field Size Property

You can use the Field Size property to set the maximum data size for the field. When you are working with text fields, this limits the number of characters that you can store in the field. With number fields, this setting controls the size of the number you can store by affecting its precision. If the DataType property is set to Text, enter a number from 0 to 255 (the default setting is 50). If the DataType property is set to Number, the FieldSize property settings and their values are related as shown in Table 7.2.

Table 7.1

Field property	Use
FieldSize	Set the maximum length of a text field, or limit the allowable values in a number field
Format	Specifies a desired format for displaying and printing text, numbers, dates, and times
DecimalPlaces	Specifies the number of places that appear to the right of the decimal point
Input Mask	Specify formatting characters for data entry. You can use predefined masks or design your own
Caption	Default field label that appears in forms and reports
DefaultValue	Value automatically appears in a field when new records are added
ValidationRule	Expression used to define data-entry rules
ValidationText	Text that appears if invalid data is entered
Required	Determines whether an entry in the field is required
AllowZeroLength	Determines whether zero-length strings are allowed
Indexed	Single-field indexes added to speed searches

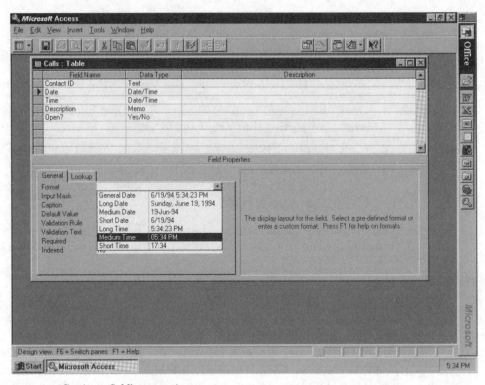

Figure 7.12 Setting a field's properties.

Note that, if you create a table, add data to it, and later reduce the field size, you run the risk of data loss in the case of records where the contents are too long to fit in the new field size. In the case of text fields, Access simply truncates the field contents as necessary. In the case of number fields, you might lose precision, and in some cases, data might be lost when numeric values are concerted to empty fields. (For example, if you were to change a number field's field size from Integer to Byte, any value over 255 would be converted to an empty field.) When you reduce the size of a field for an existing table, Access displays a dialog box warning you that data might be lost.

The Format Property

You can use the Format property to control the appearance of your data onscreen. The Format property applies to all field types with the exception of OLE Object fields. Access offers standard formats for Number, Date/Time, and Yes/No fields. You can select one of the standard formats, or you can create user-defined format using formatting symbols. The standard formats that are available will depend on the country chosen in the International section of the Windows Control Panel. As an example, if the Currency format under Windows is set for the U.S., a value of 167.82 in a currency field appears as $167.82; however, if the format is set for the United Kingdom, it appears as £167.82. Note that, if you make changes to the default Windows formats (through the International settings of the Windows Control Panel), you must exit Access and restart the program before those changes will take effect.

For text and memo fields, you can use certain symbols to create user-defined formats. The available symbols are shown in Table 7.3.

Text and Memo Formatting

With text and memo fields, the Format property is commonly used with entries that must follow a specific layout, such as phone numbers, social security numbers, and part or inventory numbers. Use the symbols shown in Table 7.4 to control the allowable text characters; you also can include other literal characters of your choosing (such as parentheses or hyphens), and they will appear automatically in the data as literal characters. As an example, you could enter a format of (@@@)-@@@-@@@@ to force a phone number to appear as (818)-555-1212. When the user types in the phone number, the parentheses and the hyphens would appear automatically.

Number and Currency Formatting

With number and currency fields, when you click in the Format property and open the list box by clicking on the arrow that appears, you see the list of possible formats shown in Figure 7.13. The types of number formatting that result, depending on the choice you make here, are detailed in Table 7.4.

You also can create user-defined number or currency formats by using any of the codes shown in Table 7.5.

Table 7.2

Setting	Description
Byte	Stores numbers from 0 to 255 (no fractions). Each field occupies 1 byte.
Integer	Stores numbers from -32,768 to 32,767 (no fractions). Each field occupies 2 bytes.
Long Integer	Stores numbers from -2,147,483,648 to 2,147,483,647 (no fractions). Each field occupies 4 bytes.
Single	Stores numbers with 6 digits of precision, from -3.402823E38 to 3.402823E38. Each field occupies 4 bytes.
Double	Stores numbers with 10 digits of precision, from -1.79769313486232E308 to 1.79769313486232E308. Each field occupies 8 bytes.

Table 7.3

Symbol	Meaning
@	Text character (either a character or a space) required
&	Text character not required
<	Force all characters to lowercase (only a single character is required to format the entire field)
>	Force all characters to uppercase (only a single character is required to format the entire field)

Table 7.4

Setting	Description
General Number	Display number as entered (the default). If you enter very large or very small numbers, they might be converted to scientific notation.
Currency	Numbers are preceded by currency symbol, thousands separator is included, and numbers are rounded to 2 decimal places.
Fixed	Displays a fixed number of digits with no currency symbols or comma separators. The default number of decimal places is 2.
Standard	Displays a fixed number of digits with no currency symbols, but includes comma separators. The default number of decimal places is 2.
Percent	Multiplies value by 100, and adds a percent sign. The default number of decimal places is 2.
Scientific	Forces standard scientific notation (the number appears as an exponent) with one digit displayed to the left of the decimal point.

Date and Time Formatting

With Date/Time fields, when you click in the Format property and open the list box by clicking on the arrow that appears, you see the list of possible formats shown in Figure 7.14. The types of number formatting that result, depending on the choice you make here, are detailed in Table 7.6.

Yes/No Formatting

With Yes/No fields, when you click in the Format property and open the list box by clicking on the arrow that appears, you see a choice of three possible formats: Yes/No, True/False, or On/Off. Access actually stores a Boolean value of zero (for no) or -1 (for yes), but the display of the data is according to the formatting that you've chosen.

Table 7.5

Setting	Description
. (period)	Decimal separator
, (comma)	Thousand separator
0	Digit placeholder. Display digit or 0.
#	Digit placeholder. Display a digit or nothing.
$	Display the literal character $.
%	Percentage. The value is multiplied by 100, and the percent sign is appended.
E- or e-	Scientific notation with a minus sign next to negative exponents. It must be combined with other symbols, as in 0.00E-00.
E+ or e+	Scientific notation with a minus sign next to negative exponents and a plus sign next to positive exponents. It must be combined with other symbols, as in 0.00E+00.

The Decimal Places Property

Use the Decimal Places property to determine the number of decimal places that Access uses to display numbers, overriding the Format property setting. (If no entry is made in the Decimal Places property, Access will set decimal places according to the settings in the Format property.) As an example, the default setting for the Currency format displays two decimal places ($9.95). If you wanted to show a currency value using four decimal places ($9.9543), you would need to change the Decimal Places property to a value of 4. Note that the Decimal Places property has no effect if the Format property is set to General Number.

The Input Mask Property

Use the Input Mask property to define input masks that aid in data entry. When all of the values entered in a particular field will have the same format, you can save time by creating a pattern called an *input mask*. The Input Mask property setting controls how data entered in the field appears. As an example, if you set this property to 000-00-0000, hyphens are displayed as shown, and a space is displayed in place of each zero.

The setting can contain up to three parts separated by semicolons; for example, (###) 000-0000!;0;" ". The first part specifies the input mask itself (for example, (###) 000-0000!). The second part specifies whether Access

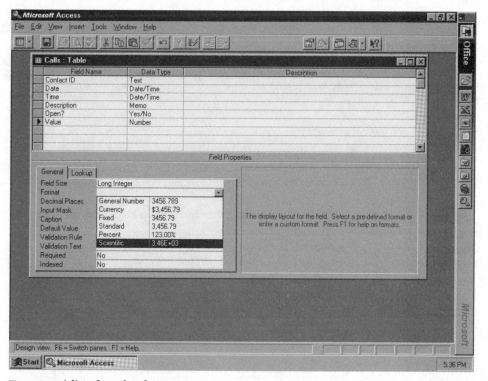

Figure 7.13 A list of number formats.

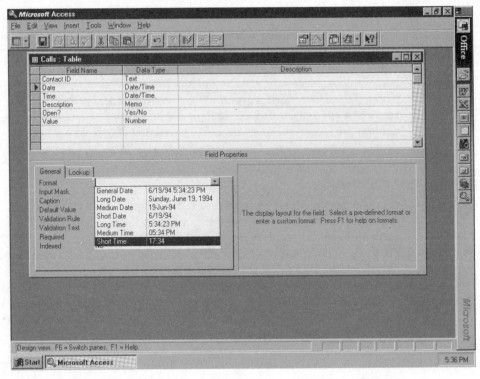

Figure 7.14 A list of date/time formats.

stores the input mask characters in the table when you enter data. If you use 0 for this part, all input mask characters (for example, the parentheses in a

Table 7.6

Setting	Description	Example
General Date	If value is date only, no time is displayed; if the value is time only, no date is displayed (this is the default).	4/3/93 05:34 PM, 4/3/93, and 05:34 PM
Long Date	Same as the Long Date setting in the International section of the Windows Control Panel.	Saturday, April 4, 1993
Medium Date	Same as the Medium Date setting in the International section of the Windows Control Panel.	07-Apr-93
Short Date	Same as the Short Date setting in the International section of the Windows Control Panel.	4/3/93
Long Time	Same as the Time setting in the International section of the Windows Control Panel.	5:34:23 PM
Medium Time		05:34 PM
Short Time		17:34

phone number input mask) are stored with the value; if you enter 1 or leave this part blank, only characters typed into the text box are stored. The third part specifies the character that Access displays for spaces in the input mask. For this part, you can use any ASCII character; to display a space, use a space enclosed in quotation marks (" "). Access interprets characters in the first portion of the Input Mask property setting as shown in Table 7.7.

Table 7.8 offers examples of InputMask settings, the characters that are displayed after data is entered, and the values that actually are stored in the table.

If you need to create a commonly used input mask (such as for a phone number, ZIP code, or social security number), it is probably easier to use the Input Mask Wizard. (The Input Mask Wizard works only with Text or Date/Time fields.) To use the Input Mask Wizard, click anywhere in the Input Mask property, then click the button that appears at the right edge of the property. When you do so, the Input Mask Wizard appears, as shown in Figure 7.15.

From the list of predefined input masks, choose the desired one, and click Next. Answer the remaining questions presented by the wizard about how the data should be stored (you're given the option of storing data with or without the input mask literal characters). When you are done, the wizard automatically enters the proper setting in the Input Mask property.

Table 7.7

Character	Description
0	Digit (0-9, entry required, plus and minus signs not allowed).
#	Digit or space (entry not required, blank positions converted to spaces, plus and minus signs allowed).
9	Digit or space (entry not required, plus and minus signs not allowed).
L	Letter (A-Z, entry required).
?	Letter (A-Z, entry optional).
A	Letter or digit (entry required).
a	Letter or digit (entry optional).
&	Any character or a space (entry required).
C	Any character or a space (entry optional).
. , : ; - /	Decimal placeholder and thousand, date, and time separators. (Character used depends on the settings in the International section of the Windows Control Panel).
<	All characters that follow are converted to lowercase.
>	All characters that follow are converted to uppercase.
!	Causes input mask to fill from right to left, rather than from left to right, when characters on the left side of the input mask are optional. You can include the exclamation point anywhere in the input mask.
\	Causes the character that follows to be displayed as the literal ASCII character (for example, \A is displayed as just A).

Table 7.8

Setting	Displayed	Stored
(000) 000-0000	(703) 555-5952	7035555952
(000) 000-0000; 0	(703) 555-5952	(703) 555-5952
(###) 000-0000!	(703) 555-5952555-5952	70355559525555952
(000) AAA-AAAA	(703) 555-HELP	703555HELP

The Caption Property

Use the Caption property to provide a default label that appears as the name of the field in forms and reports that you create. (If you don't enter any value in the Caption property, Access uses the name of the field as a label in forms and reports.) Captions typically are used to better explain fields to users of an application; you can enter up to 255 characters as a caption.

The Default Value Property

Use the Default Value property to specify a default value for a field. The default value automatically gets placed in the field when a new record is added. As an example, in an address table, you might set the default for the City field to Los Angeles. When new records are added to the table, Los Angeles appears automatically in the City field, and the user can leave this value unchanged or enter the name of a different city. Default values can be set for all field types except for Counter and OLE Object Fields. For Text, Number, and Currency fields, default values will be some arbitrary value depending on the application. For Yes/No fields, Access normally sets the Default Value property to No; you can change this to Yes if most of your records are likely to have a Yes value stored in a Yes/No field.

Tip: You also can use expressions, beginning with an equal sign, as default values. The most common ones are =DATE(), which provides the current date according to the PC's clock, and =NOW(), which provides both the date and time. You can include math calculations in the expression; for example, an expression of =DATE() + 60 would result in a default value 60 days from the current day.

Validation Rule Property

The Validation Rule property defines an expression that is evaluated when data in the field is added or changed. The Validation Text property specifies the text of the message that appears if the field doesn't satisfy the conditions specified in the Validation Rule setting. You enter an expression for the Validation Rule, and you enter text for the Validation Text. (If the Validation Rule is blank, no validation is performed.) The maximum length for both the Validation Rule and the Validation Text properties is 255 characters.

Use the Validation Rule and Validation Text properties to help users enter valid data. As an example, when a record is added for a new order, you can require that the entry in the Ship Date field fall between the current date and the current date plus 30 days. If the date entered isn't in this range, you can display the message: "Must ship products within 30 days." You also could limit numeric fields to a certain range; for example, an Hourly Salary field could be limited to values no less than $3.50 and no greater than $15.00.

You enter Validation Rules using *expressions* that tell Access whether or not the value will be allowed in the field. Table 7.9 shows some common expressions that could be used for various types of validation.

Simple expressions probably are best entered by typing them. However, if you need to enter a complex expression, you can use the Expression Builder. Click anywhere in the Validation Rule property, then click the button that appears at the right edge of the property. When you do so, the Expression Builder appears, shown in Figure 7.16. Use the various available choices in the Expression Builder to build the desired expression, then click OK to close the Expression Builder and insert the expression into the Validation Rule property.

Required Property

Use the Required property to specify whether an entry in a field is required. Your choices here are Yes and No; if you choose Yes, an entry will be required in the specified field for every record added to the table. If you try to add a

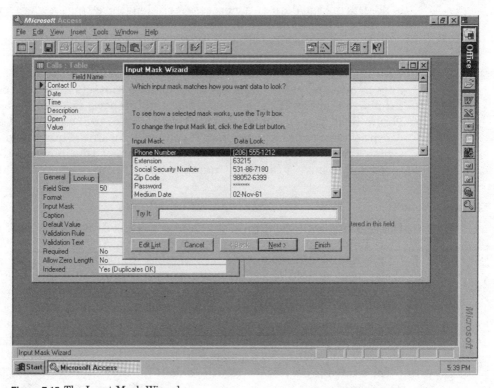

Figure 7.15 The Input Mask Wizard.

Table 7.9

Example	Rule
>0	Value must be greater than zero
="TX"	Value must be "TX"
Between #1/1/96# and #12/31/96#	Value must be a date in 1996
Like 109P####	Value must be 8 characters beginning with "109P"
Is Not Null	Field cannot be empty (have null value)

record without making an entry in the field, Access displays a dialog box like the one shown in Figure 7.17.

Note that, if you set the Required property to Yes in a table that contains existing data, Access will ask whether or not you want to check that the existing data meets the new rule.

Allow Zero-Length Property

Use the Allow Zero-Length Property to indicate whether a zero-length string is a valid entry. Your choices here are Yes (a zero-length string is a valid entry) and No (a zero-length string is an invalid entry). The default for this property is No. During the data-entry process, zero-length settings are entered in fields by typing a pair of quotation marks (" ").

By changing the Allow Zero-Length property to Yes, you can differentiate between a value that doesn't exist (which is a zero-length string) and a value that might exist but is unknown (or a null value). As an example, you might have names and phone numbers in a business contacts table that don't have a car phone number. If the Allow Zero-Length property is set to Yes for the Car Phone field, you can enter two quotation marks to indicate that a customer doesn't have a car phone number. If you leave the Car Phone field null by not typing a number (by deleting the existing number), this indicates that the customer might have a car phone number, but it is unknown.

Indexed Property

Use the Indexed property to find and sort records using a single table field. The field can hold either unique (No duplicates) or non-unique (Duplicates OK) values. As an example, you might create an index on a social security field in a table of employees; because each social security number is unique, the field can be indexed on a no duplicates basis to speed searches and sorts. You also might create an index based on a name field, knowing that some names in the table would be duplicates. When you click on the Indexed property and click the arrow that appears at the right side of the property, you see the menu shown in Figure 7.18.

The available choices are No (the default), Yes (Duplicates OK), and Yes (No Duplicates).

You can create as many indexes as necessary. The indexes are created when you save the table design and are automatically updated when you change or add records. You can add or delete indexes at any time in a table's Design view.

Note that, when the primary key for a table is a single field, Access automatically sets the Indexed property for that field to Yes (No Duplicates). Also keep in mind that you can't index Memo, Yes/No, or OLE Object fields.

Saving the Table

Once you've made all of the desired additions or changes to the table, you can save it by performing the following steps:

1. Choose File/Close, or double-click the Table icon at the upper-left corner of the Table Design Window.

2. In the dialog box that appears asking whether you want to save the changes to the table structure, click Yes. When you do so, the Save As dialog box appears, as shown in Figure 7.19.

3. Enter the desired name for the table, then click OK. Remember that table names can be up to 64 characters long and can include spaces, but they cannot include exclamation points, brackets, periods, or leading spaces.

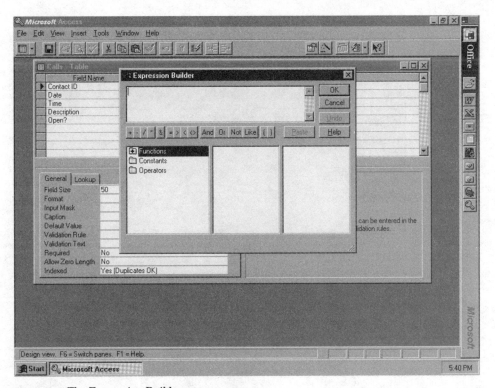

Figure 7.16 The Expression Builder

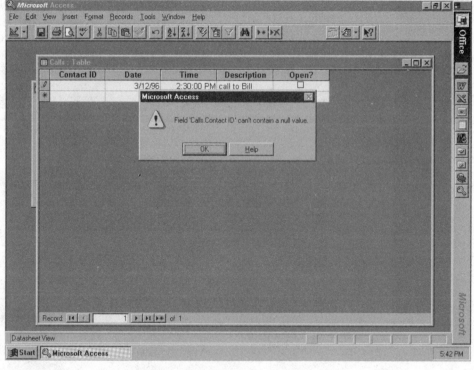

Figure 7.17 The Required Entry dialog box.

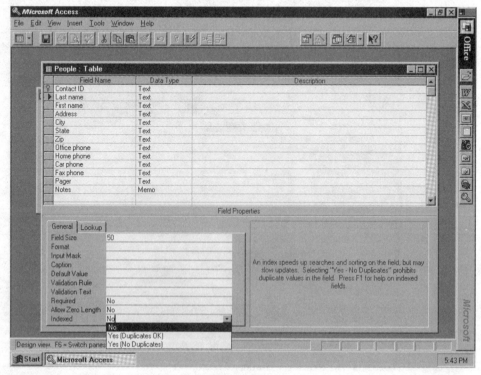

Figure 7.18 A menu of choices for the indexed property.

Adding and Editing Data in a Table

Once a table exists, you can add data to it or edit existing data by typing directly into the table's datasheet. In Access, every table has a blank record, located immediately after the last existing record, as shown in Figure 7.20. In the figure, the empty row marked by the asterisk at the far left is the blank record.

If there are no existing records in a table, the table will contain one blank record. The blank record always contains an asterisk in its record selector (to the immediate left of the record). As soon as you begin to type a record, a new blank record appears beneath your entry. Using the mouse or the tab key, you can move the cursor to any of the fields of the record and type the desired data, using the Del or Backspace keys to correct any errors. As you fill in each field with the desired value, press Tab to move to the next field. When you press Tab from the last field of a table, Access moves you to the next blank record, and you can continue to add data. Note that you can quickly get to the blank record in a large table by choosing Records/GoTo/New from the menus.

Note that there are some fields that, for one reason or another, you won't be able to edit in Access. You cannot edit any of the following types of fields:

- Counter fields—When you specify a counter field, Access automatically stores and increments the value as you add new records. You cannot change the value that Access stores in a counter field.

- Calculated fields—Because calculated fields are based on a calculated value, there is no actual data stored to be edited.

- Locked fields—If a field's Locked property is set to Yes or its Enabled property is set to No, you cannot edit the field.

- Fields in certain kinds of queries—You can't edit totals in select queries, nor can you edit certain fields in queries that draw relationships between multiple tables.

Working with Memo Fields

While you are editing data in a table's datasheet, you cannot see all of the text in a memo field at one time (unless you make the field so wide that you can't see any of the other fields). A quick solution to this problem is to open the Zoom

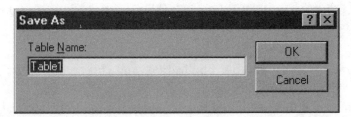

Figure 7.19 The Save As dialog box.

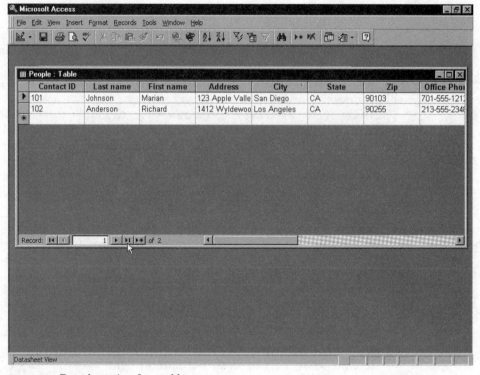

Figure 7.20 Datasheet view for a table.

box for the memo field using the Shift–F2 key combination. Place the insertion pointer anywhere in the memo field, and press Shift–F2. When you do so, a Zoom box into the memo field opens, as shown in Figure 7.21.

You can make any desired changes to the memo field, then click the OK button to accept the changes. You can click Cancel to cancel any changes and return to viewing the datasheet.

Entering Data in OLE Fields

Access supports the use of OLE fields, which are containers that you can use to store data from other Windows applications. The most common use for OLE fields is to store graphics (such as pictures created in a program like Windows Paintbrush), but you can store other types of data, such as part of an Excel spreadsheet, a Word for Windows document, video, or sound. To insert OLE data into an OLE field of a table's datasheet, you perform the following steps:

1. Start the other Windows application in the usual manner. Select the desired data in the other application, and choose Edit/Copy from the application's menus.

2. Switch back to Access, and open the desired table. Tab to or click in the desired field of the table.

3. From the menus, choose Edit/Paste. A copy of the data will appear in the field.

If you are more accustomed to working with word processors and spread-sheets, you might wonder about a command to save your data after you've entered it. There is actually no need to save your data; Access automatically does so when you move to another record or when you close the table (or when you close a form that you might be using to enter or edit the data.)

Deleting Records

To delete a record, place the insertion pointer anywhere in the desired record and click the Record Selector at the left edge of the record, or choose Edit/Select Record. Doing so will cause the entire record to be selected, as shown in Figure 7.22.

Next, press the Del key, or choose Edit/Delete. Access will display a con-firmation box, asking if the deletion should be made permanent. Click Yes if you want to delete the records; if not, click No. Note that, in Access, deletions are permanent. Once you delete a record, there's no way to get it back (short of re-entering the data).

Adding Indexes

Access lets you add an *index* to a field of a table. (You cannot index on Yes/No, OLE, or memo fields.) Adding an index speeds the performance of searches on a given field. (Note that there is a drawback, as indexes slow the performance of Access when it comes to updating records.) You can add an index by per-forming these steps:

1. Get into Design view for the table, and click the field that you want to index to select it.

Figure 7.21 The Zoom box in a memo field.

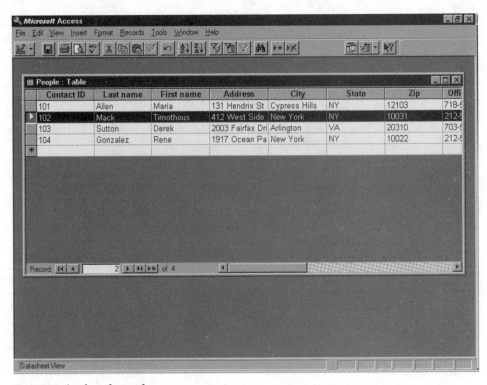

Figure 7.22 A selected record.

2. Click on the General tab at the bottom of the window if it isn't already visible.

3. In the Indexed property box at the bottom of the window, choose Yes (Duplicates OK) or Yes (No Duplicates). If you choose Yes (Duplicates OK), you tell Access that the field can contain more than one record with the same data in this field. Choosing Yes (No Duplicates) prohibits duplicate records.

Note: Users of dBASE and similar products should note that indexes in Access are not added for the purpose of ordering records. If you want to place records in a certain order in Access, you do so by *sorting* the data using the toolbar's Sort buttons, from within a query, or from within a form.

Multiple-Field Indexes

If you routinely search for data based on a combination of fields that aren't part of a primary key, you can speed such searches by adding a multiple-field index. As an example, consider the classic case of last and first names. If users of an application routinely search for records in a table based on a combination of last and first names, it would make sense to add a multiple field index based on a combination of those fields. You can create a multiple-field index with the following steps:

1. Open the table in Design view.

2. From the menus, choose View/Indexes (or click the Indexes button in the toolbar) to open the Indexes window for the table.

3. In a blank row under the Index Name column, enter any desired name for your index.

4. Click in the Field Name column, and choose the first field that you want to base the index on from the list box; then, in the Sort Order column, choose Ascending or Descending, as desired.

5. Click in the Field Name column of the next empty row, and choose the next field that you want to base the index on from the list box. Then, in the Sort Order column, choose Ascending or Descending, as desired. Repeat this step for each field that you want to add as part of the index.

6. From the menus, choose File/Save. This causes the new index to be created.

As an example, the multiple index called "Names" shown in Figure 7.23 is based on a combination of last and first names. Keep in mind that the name for the multiple-field index should be included only in the row of the first field that you choose. In the Indexes dialog box, Access treats all rows as part of the same index until it comes to a row that contains another index name.

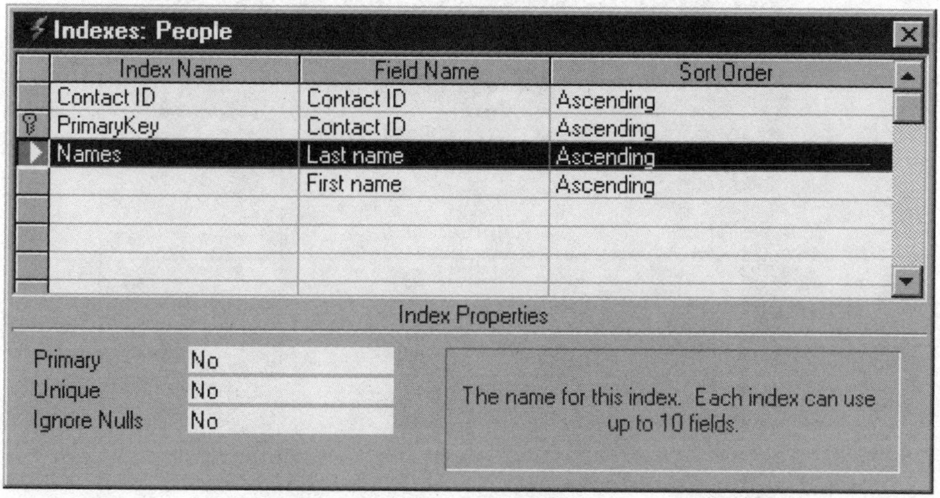

Figure 7.23 A multiple index based on first and last names.

Creating Relationships Between Tables

Once you have more than one table in a database, you often will need to establish relationships between the tables. In Access, there are two ways that you can establish relationships. One way is to do so through queries, which are detailed in Chapter 8. The other way is to choose `Edit/Relationships` from the menus to open the Relationships window and add the tables or queries that you want to relate to the window. Then, to define the relationship, you fill in the options in the Relationships dialog box that appears. To establish a relationship through the Relationships window, you perform these steps:

1. From the menus, choose `Tools/Relationships`, or right-click the `Tables` tab in the Database Window and choose `Relationships` from the shortcut menu that appears. When you do this, the Relationships window appears that contains the Show Table dialog box, as shown in Figure 7.24.

2. Choose the table or query that you want to use as part of the relationship, then click the `Add` button. The table or query will be added to the Relationship window.

3. Repeat Step 2 for each table or query that you want to add to the relationship.

4. Drag the field or fields that you want to use for the link from the primary table or query to the matching field or fields of the related table or query. Once you drag and drop the field or fields, the Relationships dialog box appears, as shown in Figure 7.25.

5. If desired, you can change the suggested field names in the dialog box. Fields used for establishing relationships need not have the same names,

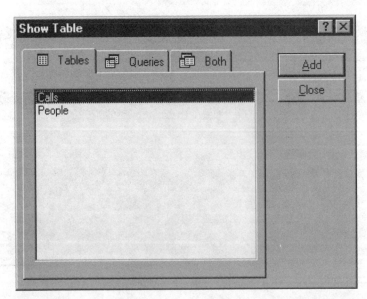

Figure 7.24 The Relationships window with the Show Table dialog box.

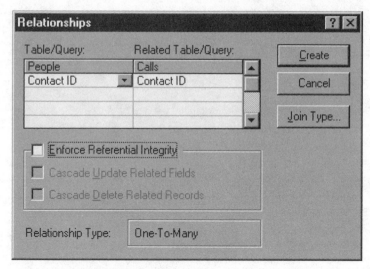

Figure 7.25 The Relationships dialog box.

but they must be of the same type (with the exception of Counter fields, which can be related to Number fields.)

6. If referential integrity is desired, turn on the Referential Integrity check box. Once the box has been turned on, you then can choose whether to enable the other options of Cascade Update Related Fields and Cascade Delete Related Records. If the Cascade Update Related Fields option is on, any changes made to the field used as the link in the first table are updated automatically in all fields of a related table having the same data. If the Cascade Delete Related Records option is turned on, any deletion of records in the first table will cause an automatic deletion of all associated records in the linked table.

7. At the bottom of the dialog box, select the desired type of relationship (one-to-one or one-to-many).

8. Click the Create button in the dialog box to create the relationship.

9. Repeat these steps for each relationship that must be added between tables. When you are done adding relationships, close the Relationships window by double-clicking the Control icon in the window's upper-left corner. When Access asks if you want to save the changes, answer Yes.

Summary

In this chapter, you learned how to create and work with tables, which is a primary component of your Access applications. In the chapter that follows, you'll learn how you can access specific data for use in your applications by means of queries.

Chapter

8

Designing Queries to Support Applications

Chapter 7 detailed how data could be stored in Access tables and also demonstrated how you could perform quick searches to find desired records. This chapter details how you can use a major building block of Access applications, *queries*, to retrieve the specific data needed to perform any given task.

Access makes use of *graphical query-by-example*, or *graphical QBE*, to describe what data you're looking for and quickly obtain results. (Query-by-example is a term for a method of obtaining data that was pioneered by IBM in the 1970s, and graphical QBE is the method of query-by-example implemented in Microsoft Access.) With graphical QBE, you can perform most of the aspects of designing the query by dragging objects around a query form.

Most queries that you'll need to design for your Access applications are likely to be *select queries*; these queries select desired information, based on how you structure the query. Select queries can display all fields in a table, certain fields, all records, certain records, or even a combination of selected portions of records from more than one table. Queries also can be used to sort your data, to ask questions about data stored in other file formats (such as Paradox or dBASE files), and to calculate totals of numeric fields. You can base forms, reports, and even other queries on the results of queries. Figure 8.1 shows an example of a query's design and a table produced as a result of the query.

Once you run a select query, Access presents your data as a set of records in something called a *dynaset*. A dynaset strongly resembles a table, but it isn't. Instead, it is a *dynamic* set of records from the table or tables that the query is based on—hence the name, dynaset. For users of other PC-based databases, this is an important distinction to appreciate, because dynasets offer flexibilities that are not available in many other database managers. Some other database managers that use a form of query-by-example produce sets of data that are static, meaning that they are a copy of the data in the original tables. If you make changes to the data in the answer provided by the query, you are not changing the data in the original tables.

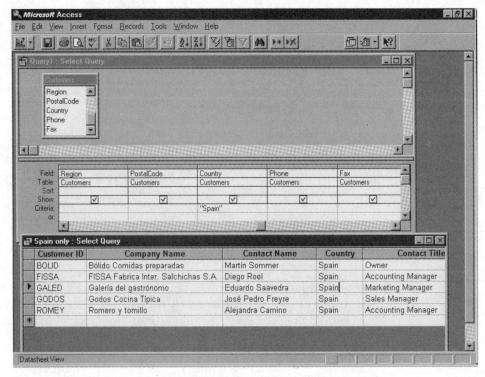

Figure 8.1 An example of a query's design and the results of the query.

In Access, because the answers to a table are dynamic and not static, you see the actual data in the answer to the query. If you make a change to the data in the dynaset, you are changing the data in the original table. An important plus for network users is that, because the data is dynamic, any changes made by others to the same table will be immediately apparent. Another significant plus of Access is that it lets you easily use queries as the basis for data shown in your forms or printed in your reports.

Select queries aren't the only type of query that you can perform in Access; you also can design and use *action queries*, which make changes to a group of records in a single operation. For example, in a moment of insane generosity, you might decide to give every employee in a personnel database a 15% raise. You could update the salary field in the employees table by performing an action query. Access also lets you perform *crosstab queries*, which present numeric data in a spreadsheet format.

Queries as a Data Source

In Access, queries can (and often do) serve as a data source for other objects, usually forms and reports. This is an important concept to grasp, particularly if you are accustomed to working with query-by-example in earlier PC-based database managers.

In most other products, query-by-example served as an easy way for users to obtain *ad hoc* data without knowledge of complex commands, but that was about as far as it went. In Access, queries meet this need, but they can provide far more. You can use Access queries as the basis for forms and reports. This greatly reduces the time involved in the development of complex applications.

As an example, if you are designing a database system to manage a large mailing list, you might need to generate mailing labels by city, customer income, or ZIP code group. In Access, you could design a single report to produce the mailing labels, use the Edit/Copy command to make multiple copies of that report, and base each report on a different query to provide the desired labels.

The same concept applies to forms; you might want to use a form to edit all employees in a particular department. You could create a query that retrieves all employee records for a particular department and base a form on that query. A major advantage to basing your forms and reports on queries is that each time that you open the form or print the report, the query runs automatically, and you get the most up-to-date data in the form or report. New forms and reports can be based on queries by choosing the query by name in the New Form or New Report dialog box that appears when the form or report is created. Existing forms and reports can be based on queries by setting the Record Source property for the form or the report to the name of the query. (For specifics on how to change the Record Source property, see the chapters on form design and report design.)

Creating a Query

In Access, you can create a query in either of two ways: manually or with the assistance of the Query Wizards. The Query Wizards help you quickly structure queries for specialized tasks, such as providing a crosstab view of the data or finding all duplicate records in a table. However, for designing the types of queries commonly used in your Access applications, the manual method of query design is what you'll want to use, The basic process is this: You open a new query, add the fields from the desired table or tables to the query, and ask any questions that you need to ask about the data. You can save the query as part of the database. Later the query can be run independently in your application, or it can be named as the data source for a report or a form so that, when the report runs or when the form opens, the query automatically executes and provides the needed data. Here are the steps involved in creating a new query manually:

1. Click the Queries tab in the Database Window.

2. Click New. When you do this, the New Query dialog box appears.

3. In the New Query dialog box, select New Query or, in Access 97, Design View then click OK. Once you do this, a new query appears in a window, and the Show Table dialog box appears above it, as shown in Figure 8.2.

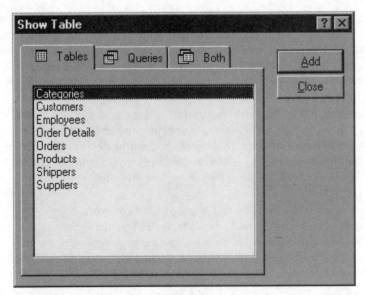

Figure 8.2 A new query window that contains the Show Table dialog box.

In the Show Table dialog box, you click the Tables tab to see all tables, the Queries tab to see all existing queries, or the Both tab to see both tables and queries. You then click the table or query that you want to base the new query on. After clicking a table or query, click Add, and a list box of the fields appears in the Query window. (If you are designing a relational query to access multiple tables, you can repeat this step for all of the tables that are to be used in the query.) When you are done adding tables to the query, click Close to put away the Show Table dialog box.

The Query window is divided into two portions. The upper portion displays the field lists for all tables that you included in the query, and the lower portion displays the query form itself, where you will indicate which fields will be included in the query, how the records should be sorted, and any criteria that will select certain records from the tables.

Adding Fields to the Query

There are a number of ways that you can add fields to the query, depending on whether you want to add selected fields or want to add all fields to the query. To add selected fields to a query, you can click and drag each desired field from the Field List to the desired cell within the field row of the query. As an example, you might create a query based on the People table detailed in Chapter 3. To create a query that contains the Last name, First name, City, and Region fields, you would drag each of these fields to the Field row of the query form. Figure 8.3 illustrates this process.

You also can double-click a field name in the Field List. When you do this, it is added to the next blank column of the query grid. You also can just type the name of any field directly into the field row of the query grid, although the click-and-drag methods generally are faster, and less error-prone, as you reduce the chances of typos using click-and-drag.

To add all fields to a query, you can either select them as a group and drag them all to the query grid or drag the asterisk at the top of the Field List to the query grid. To select the fields as a group, just double-click the Title Bar at the top of the Field List. When you do this, Access selects all of the fields. Then, click and drag any of the selected fields to the query grid.

To add all of the fields using the asterisk, drag the asterisk at the top of the Field List to the query grid or just double-click the asterisk. When you do this, the name of the table appears in the column of the query grid followed by an asterisk, indicating that all fields in the table will be included in the query, as shown in Figure 8.4.

There are advantages and disadvantages to using the asterisk to indicate all fields. An advantage is that, even if you later change the fields in the table that the query is based on, the query still will include all of the fields. A disadvantage is that you cannot directly sort or specify criteria with a query that uses the asterisk.

Rearranging, Inserting, and Deleting Fields

Once a query exists, you can easily rearrange the fields in the query grid; you also can delete or insert new fields. To move a field, simply click the *field selector*

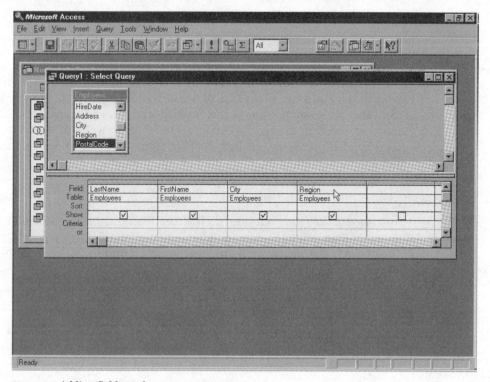

Figure 8.3 Adding fields to the query.

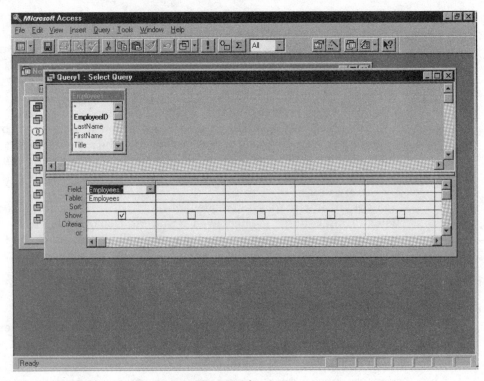

Figure 8.4 All fields added by dragging the asterisk.

(it is the narrow bar located directly above the field's name). Then, click the selector again and drag the column to the desired position in the gird. To insert a field, first click within the Field List to select the field that you want to insert, then drag the field from the list to the desired column in the query grid. Any existing fields will shift to the right to make room for the new field. To delete a field, first click the field selector to select the field that you want to delete, then press the Del key (or choose Edit/Delete from the menus).

Viewing the Dynaset

To view the answer to a query, click the Run button in the toolbar, or choose Query/Run from the menus. Using either method, a dynaset that contains the records that match the query appears, similar to the example shown in Figure 8.5.

Using Criteria

You will rarely want to obtain a query that contains every record in a table. The reason for most queries is to obtain specific information. By entering specific criteria in the Criteria row of the query grid, you can tell Access precisely what data you're looking for. As an example, assume you are using the Customers table in the Northwind Traders database supplied with Access. You could perform the following steps to experiment with the use of criteria in Access queries:

1. Click the Queries tab in the Database Window, click New, then select Design View in the list box, and click OK. In the Show Tables dialog box that appears over the new Query window, click Customers, then Add, then Close. The resultant query contains the Field List for the Customers table.

2. In the Field List, click Customer ID, scroll down in the list to the end, then hold the Shift key and click Fax to highlight all of the fields, then click and drag any of the highlighted fields to the Field row of the query grid. Doing so causes all fields in the Fields List to be added to the query grid, as shown in Figure 8.6.

3. In this case, you want to see all customers in Germany, so click in the Country field within the Criteria row, and type Germany. Once you move out of the field, Access will automatically add quotation marks around the information, indicating that it is a text value.

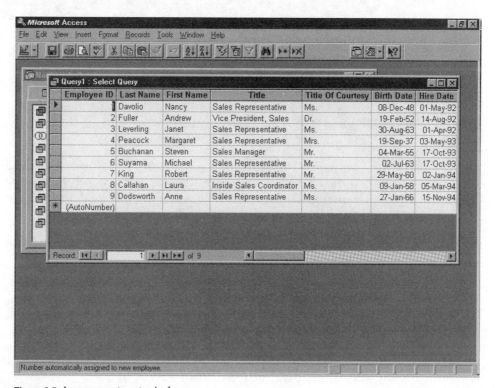

Figure 8.5 A response to a typical query.

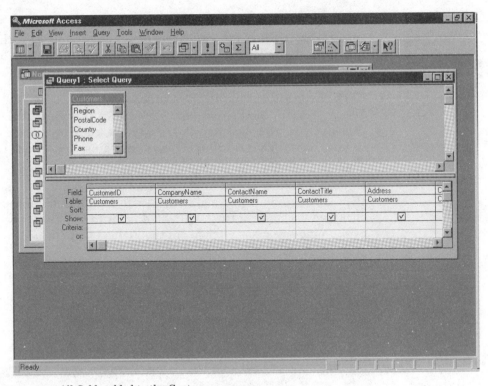

Figure 8.6 All fields added to the Customers query.

4. Click the Run button in the toolbar. The dynaset that appears as a result shows the records in the table for those customers based in Germany (Figure 8.7). When done, choose View/Query Design to switch back from the dynaset to design view for the query.

You can select records that meet criteria in two or more fields by simply entering the criteria in the desired format within each field of the query grid. As an example, if you wanted to see all of the customers based in Madrid, Spain, the following steps would suffice:

1. Click in the Country field within the Criteria row, and replace the previous entry of "Germany" with Spain.

2. Click in the City field within the Criteria row, and enter Madrid.

3. Click the Run button in the toolbar. The dynaset that appears as a result shows the records in the table for those customers based in Madrid, Spain (Figure 8.8). When done, choose View/Query Design to switch back from the dynaset to design view for the query.

When you are using criteria in a query, as in the case of the previous example, you are entering *expressions* that tell Access precisely how it should limit the data that's retrieved by the query. As an example, entering `Chicago` in a Criteria row underneath a `City` column would tell Access to retrieve all of the records that contain the word "Chicago" in the `City` field of a table. Also, entering `>12  and  <18` in a Criteria row under a `Cost` column would tell Access to retrieve all of the records that have values greater than 12 and less than 18 in a `Cost` column of a table.

In Access, you can specify multiple conditions for queries in either of two ways: by including OR statements within the expression or by entering the desired criteria in more than one column of the query grid. As an example, in a table of customers, you could enter `Smith` in the criteria row underneath the `Last` name column, and you could enter `Chicago` in the criteria row underneath the `City` column. This would tell Access to retrieve all records that contain the name "Smith" in the `Last` name field of the table, and the name "Chicago" in the `City` field of the table. On the other hand, you could enter `Chicago` in the first criteria row underneath the `City` column, and `New York` in the second criteria row underneath the `City` column. This would tell Access to retrieve all records with either the word "Chicago" or the words "New York" in the `City` field of the table.

The true power behind the use of queries in Access lies with being able to construct the different types of criteria needed to get at the data that you

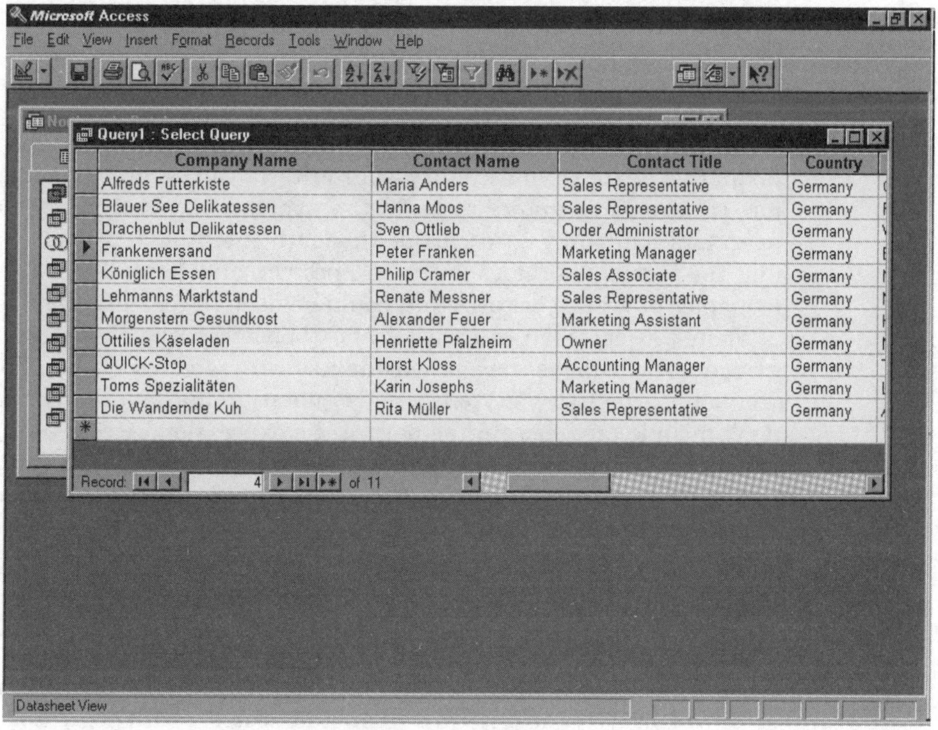

Figure 8.7 The results of a query that contains a criteria.

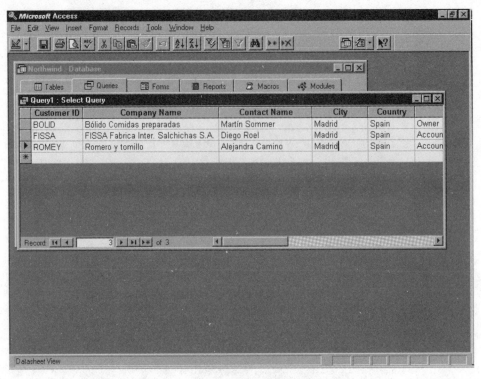

Figure 8.8 The results of a query for customers based in Madrid, Spain.

want. You certainly aren't limited to the simple kinds of criteria described so far in this chapter; in actuality, your criteria can be quite complex. You make use of various *operators* to build the expressions used in your criteria. The operators commonly used include the math operators (such as >, <, >=, <=, <>) and the logical operators (such as And, Or, and Not). Table 8.1 shows some examples of typical criteria that could be used in formulating queries.

When you enter an expression and then move out of the cell of the query grid, Access displays the entry using its own preferred syntax. For example, if you enter a text string, Access adds quotation marks around the text. If you don't include any operator as part of the expression, Access assumes that the expression begins with an equal (=) symbol. Hence, if Chicago were entered in the Criteria row underneath a City column, Access would interpret the expression to mean "City = Chicago."

Building Queries Based on OR Criteria

The types of queries described so far either have been queries that select records based on a single criteria or have been "AND" queries, where data is selected based on one criteria *and* another criteria both being true. In the database world, this is commonly known as AND logic. In many cases, however, you will need another kind of logic, known as OR logic. In this case, records are qualified if any one of a group of conditions is met. As an example, perhaps you want to display all of the records of customers based in Madrid or Barcelona. With the visual query-by-example nature of Access, OR logic is simple; you can just add additional criteria on the lines below your first criteria, using as many lines as are necessary. As an example, consider the query shown in Figure 8.9.

In this query, three criteria cells have been filled in underneath the City field. Because the entries are London, Paris, and Madrid, the query will extract records where the entries in the City field is London, Paris, or Madrid.

Combining AND and OR Criteria

You can combine AND and OR logic in the same query as needed to obtain the results that you need. As an example, take the case of the Customers table in the Northwind Traders database. If you need to see all of the customers where the entry in the Contact Title field is "Sales Representative" and the customer is based in either France or Spain, you would need to enter Sales Representative in the criteria rows under the Contact Title field, and you would enter Spain and France in separate rows of the Country field, as shown in the example in Figure 8.10.

Note that the criteria of "Sales Representative" exists in both criteria rows of the query grid. This is what is needed to obtain all sales representatives of companies based in either France or Spain. If the Sales Representative

Table 8.1

Field	Criteria expression	Results of criteria
City	"New York"	Records with New York in the City field
City	"New York" or "Washington"	Records with New York or Washington in the City field
City	NOT "Denver"	Records with anything but Denver in the City field
Last Name	Like "D*"	Records with last names starting with the letter D
Last Name	Like "[A-L]*"	Records with last names that start with any letter from A to L
Last Name	Like "Jon*"	Records with last names that start with the letters "Jon"
Cost	<= 17.50	Records with amounts of 17.50 or more in the Cost field
Cost	between 40.00 and 65.00	Records with amounts from 40.00 to 65.00 in the Cost field
When Sold	< Date( ) - 60	Sales older than 60 days
When Sold	Year([When Sold]) = 1996	Sales in calendar year 1996

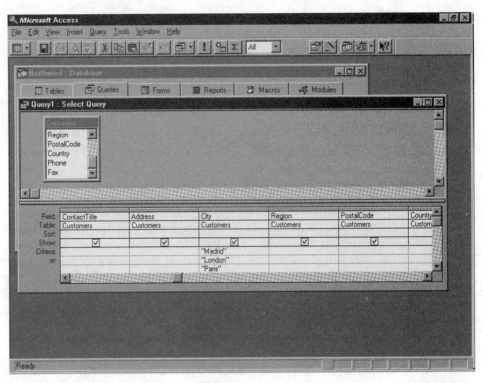

Figure 8.9 An example of a query using OR logic.

criteria were omitted from the second row, the query would interpret this as all sales representatives from customers based in France or all of the customers based in Spain.

Using Query Symbols and Operators

You can use any of the symbols and operators in Table 8.2 to construct your queries. By combining these symbols within your expressions, you can select records based on a wide variety of numeric conditions, ranges, and pattern matches.

On occasion, you might need to locate a set of records in which characters match a given pattern. Access permits the use of certain "wildcards" as part of an expression in a query. The valid wildcard operators are the question mark, which represents a single character, and the asterisk, which represents any number of characters. As an example, for a date field, you could enter the expression:

```
LIKE * / * / 96
```

to query a date field for any dates in the year 1996. In a text field that contains last names, you could use the expression:

```
LIKE "J*n"
```

to query a last name field for names that might include Joyton, Johnson, and James-Anderson.

You can use the asterisk wildcard character to look for text that is embedded in a field by including an asterisk both before and after the desired search text. As an example, perhaps someone wants to find a member who lives "somewhere on Columbia Pike." In the Address field of the query, you could enter an expression like "*Columbia Pike*", and Access would include the desired records in the results. Note that you can use this technique with memo fields to find a text string that is somewhere in the memo text.

Querying for Today's Date

You can easily query a date field for records matching the current date or for records that match a calculation based on the current date. Simply use the date function in Access, which is `date()`. As an example, if you were to enter the expression:

```
date( )
```

within the criteria cell for a date field, the query would select records where the entry in that field matches the current date (according to the computer's clock). You also could use an expression like:

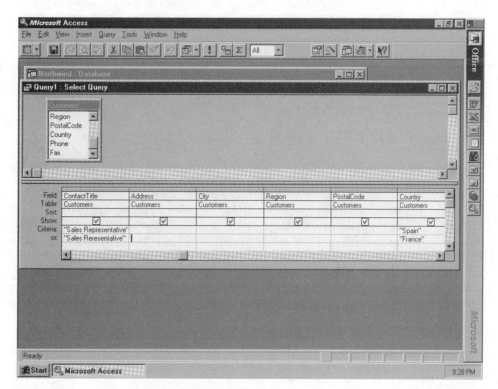

Figure 8.10 A query that contains AND and OR logic.

Table 8.2

Symbol	Means	Example
=	Equals	= Smith
>	Greater than	> 10.00
<	Less than	< 3000
>=	Greater than or equal to	>= 2/15/96
<=	Less than or equal to	<= 4500
<>	Not equal to	<> Miami
between	Between two values, including the values	between 10 and 80
in	Within a set of values	in (USA Mexico Canada)
is null	Field contains no data	is null
is not null	Field contains data	is not null
like	Pattern matching	like Jon*
and	Both expressions are true	>2/15/96 and <4/30/96
or	Either expression is true	USA or CANADA
not	Expression is not true	not Jon*
?	Pattern matching for any one character	=(212) 555-????
*	Pattern matching for any characters	Jon*

```
Between #1/1/96# and date( )
```

to retrieve all records with a date falling between January 1, 1996 and the current date. You could retrieve all records falling within the past 30 days with an expression like:

```
Between date( ) and date( ) - 30
```

Entering Expressions

The query-by-example used by some database products (such as earlier variations of dBASE) requires that you enter expressions using a fairly precise syntax, particularly when working with dates. Access, on the other hand, offers quite a bit of flexibility in the manner in which you can enter expressions. Text can be entered with or without quotes and preceded or not preceded by an equal symbol. (When you move out of the criteria cell or when the query is run, Access automatically adds quotes around text.) As an example, all four of the following expressions would mean the same thing in a text field of an Access query:

```
Texas
"Texas"
=Texas
="Texas"
```

Dates can be entered in nearly any date format. The # symbol that surrounds dates is optional, but Access automatically will add the date symbol around a date value that you enter into a query. As an example of dates, any of the following entries would be acceptable:

```
Apr 30 96
#4/30/96#
30 April 1996
4/30/96
30-Apr-96
```

Logical (yes/no) values can be entered as Yes or No, True or False, On or Off or as numeric values of -1 (for yes) and 0 (for no).

If you need to locate a set of records where there is no entry in a specific field, you can use the term Is Null as an expression that tells Access to find records where there is no data in the field. Note that this is not the same as simply leaving a field in the query grid empty. An empty field in the query grid tells Access that it does not matter what is in that field in a given record. The term Is Null indicates that the field must be blank (contain no data) before the record will appear in the dynaset in response to the query. The opposite expression, Is Not Null, can be used to indicate that the field must contain some kind of data.

Using the NOT Operator

At times, you might want to query your database for records that do not match a particular value. For example, you might want to see all customers who do not live in Atlanta. You can do so by including the NOT operator within a query expression. For example, in a City field, you could enter the expression Not "Atlanta" to find all records from cities other than Atlanta.

Using Ranges

The range operators (which are shown in Table 8.2) can be used to select records that fall within a certain range of values. Database users often think of numeric and currency values as falling within certain ranges, but you can use the range operators with text as well as with date values. You could design a query to select all records with last names from the letters *A* through *M*, or you could use a date field in a table of customer orders to show all orders processed between the first day and the last day of a certain month. As an example, entering the following expression:

```
Between "M" and "Zz"
```

in the Last name criteria column of a query grid would result in the retrieval of all last names beginning with the letters *M* through *Z*. In this example, note the inclusion of the second letter *z*. It is important in this case, because if it were omitted, Access would retrieve all names up to *Z*, but none following the letter *Z* alone. This would have the effect of omitting all last names containing more than one character and beginning with the letter Z. Another example of a criteria involving ranges would be with a date field, with a criteria entry like the following:

```
Between 1/1/94 and 12/31/96
```

In this case, the query would include all records with dates in the field falling between January 1, 1994 and December 31, 1996.

Omitting Fields from the Dynaset

Access gives you the ability to omit fields from the dynaset that results from your queries. As an example, you might want to display only those customers based in Canada, but you do not want the data from the Country field included in the results of the query. To omit a field from the results, click the Show check box for that field to remove the X in the box. (By default, an X appears in the Show check box for any field included in the query, indicating that the field will be shown in the results.) As an example, in Figure 8.11, the Country field contains a criteria limiting the records to Canada, but the X has been removed from the Show box in the field column; hence, the dynaset that results from the query will not include the data from the Country field.

Note that you cannot omit any fields that you plan to use in forms or reports based on the query.

Including Calculations in Queries

Often, you might need to perform calculations on groups of records. While you can easily obtain totals in reports, you also can do so in queries. You can obtain other calculations besides totals:

- Averages
- Maximum or minimum values
- A count of the numbers of values
- Standard deviation
- Variance (which is the square of standard deviation)
- First value in a field
- Last value in a field

Because you obtain calculations based on groups of records, you need to decide how you want to group the records in your query and include those fields that will be necessary to group the records in the query. To perform calculations in the query, open the query in Design view and choose View/Totals (or click the Totals button on the toolbar). When you do so, the Totals row appears in the query grid, and the designation "Group By" appears in every field of the query. Click the down arrow to open the list box of possible calculation types, and choose the desired type, as shown in Figure

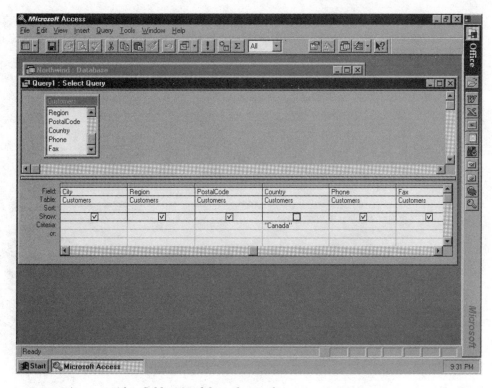

Figure 8.11 A query with a field omitted from the results.

8.12. Once you've chosen the desired type of calculation, you can run the query, and the calculation will appear in the result. Table 8.3 shows the types of calculations that you can choose from in query totals.

Adding Calculated Fields to Queries

Besides having the fields that are a normal part of a table's design, you also can include *calculated fields* in an Access query. You use calculated fields to show the results of calculations, which usually are based on numeric fields that are in the table. You can create a calculated field within a query by entering the expression that will perform the calculation in an empty cell in the Field row. You can precede the expression with a name and a colon; if you do so, that name will be used for the field name in the query's dynaset. If you omit a name and colon, Access will name the field Expr**N**, where **N** is a numeric value starting with 1 for the first calculated field used and incrementing by 1 for each calculated field in the query.

As an example, if a query contained fields for Sale Price and Quantity Sold, you could create a calculated field named Total Cost by entering an expression like this one in an empty cell of the Field row:

```
Total Cost: [Sale Price]*[Quantity Sold]
```

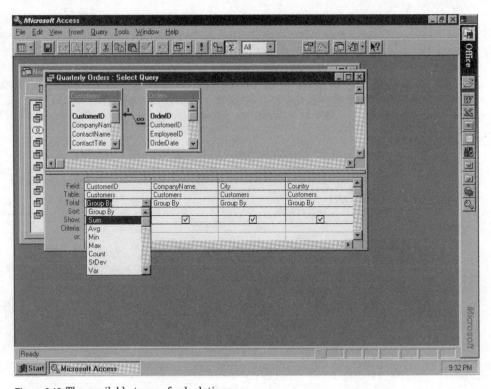

Figure 8.12 The available types of calculations.

When the query runs, Access would multiply each of the values in the `Sale Price` field by the corresponding values in the `Quantity Sold` field to produce the new values, which would be stored in the field named `Total Cost`. Table 8.4 shows examples of expressions that could be used to create calculated fields within a query.

Calculated fields also can be used to *concatenate*, or combine, text strings. To do so, use the concatenation operator (&) as a part of the expression. As an example, you could create a calculated field in a query that would combine the `Last name`, `First name`, and `Middle Initial` fields into a single name using an expression like this one:

```
[First name] & " " & [Middle Initial] & "." & [Last name]
```

Tip: When you enter long text expressions to perform calculations, you can see an entire expression without scrolling, by pressing Shift–F2 to show the Zoom box.

Sorting Records

Another important use for queries is the sorting, or arranging, of your data in the desired order. (By default, Access sorts tables in the order of the primary key; if you create a table that has no primary key, by default, Access displays the data in the order in which the records were entered into the table.) Your data can be sorted alphabetically or numerically, in either ascending (A to Z, 0 to 9) or descending (Z to A, 9 to 0) order. You can sort on a single field (such as a Last name field) or on a combination of fields (up to a maximum of 10 fields). To sort the records in a query, you perform the following steps:

1. Open the query in Design view. Click in the Sort cell in the query grid for the field that you want to sort.

2. Click the down arrow and select ascending or descending, as desired (see Figure 8.13).

3. To sort on additional fields, repeat Steps 1 and 2.

When you are sorting on a combination of fields, note that the order in which the fields are shown in the query grid determines the priority of the sort, with the leftmost field being sorted first and the rightmost field being sorted last. You can change the priority to what you desire by rearranging the fields in the query.

As an example of a multiple-field sort, consider Figure 8.14. In this example, the query will sort the records in the Customers table by Country first. Where the countries are the same, the records will be sorted by Region, then by City.

Saving Queries

To save a query, choose File/Save from the menus. If you are saving a query for the first time, Access will display a dialog box asking for a name for the new query. Enter the desired name (up to 64 characters in length, and spaces are allowed), then click OK.

Table 8.3

Calculation type	Result
Sum	Total of values in a field
Avg	Average of values in a field
Min	Lowest value in a field
Max	Highest value in a field
Count	Number of values in a field (null values are not counted)
StDev	Standard deviation of values in a field
Var	Statistical variance of values in a field
First	Value from the first record in the underlying table or query
Last	Value from the last record in the underlying table or query

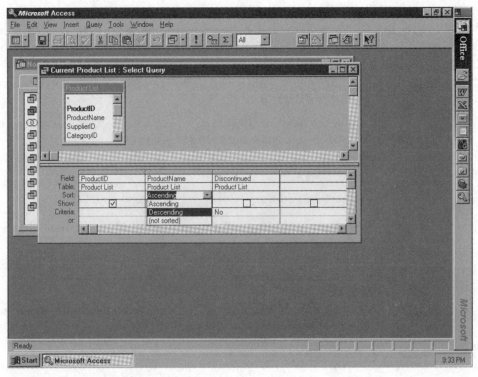

Figure 8.13 The Sort Order list box.

You also can press Ctrl–F4, or double-click the Control icon in the upper-left corner of the Query window. If you have made any changes since opening the Query window, Access will ask if you want to save the changes. Click Yes in the dialog box, and the query will be saved.

Table 8.4

Expression	Results
[Sale Price] * 1.05	The sale price plus 5%
New Price:[Sale Price] * 1.1	The sale price plus 10%, to be stored in a field labeled New Price
Total Stock:[Warehouse A] + [Warehouse B]	The sum of the fields Warehouse A and Warehouse B, to be stored in a field labeled Total Stock
Name:[First Name] & " " & [Last Name]	The values in the First Name and Last Name fields, separated by a space and stored in a field to be labeled Name

Printing Queries

You can easily print the contents of your queries. This capability of Access provides an excellent way to get a fast report, although such a report will not contain the fancy formatting offered by reports that you design in Access. You can print a query by performing the following steps.

1. Open the query in Datasheet view.
2. If you desire only certain records within the query, select those records.
3. Choose File/Print from the menus, or click the Print icon in the toolbar.
4. When the Print dialog box appears, if you selected certain records, click the Selection button in the dialog box. Choose any other desired options in the dialog box, then click OK.

Tip: To obtain a fast, formatted report of your query data, use the Report Wizard to create a report and base it on your query. Create a new report using the Report Wizard (see Chapter 9 for more details). In the Select A Table/Query list box (in the New Report dialog box), choose your query by name as the source of the records, then answer the remaining questions asked by the Report Wizard and save the report.

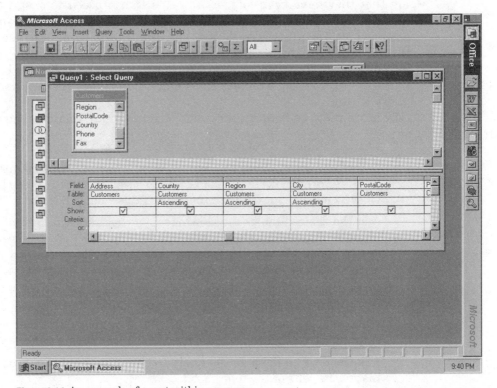

Figure 8.14 An example of a sort within a query.

Getting the Latest Data on a Network

When you run a query while on a network, Access gives you the latest data based on the underlying tables at the time the query runs. It's always possible that, if the query is open for some time, others might change the underlying data, and your query will no longer reflect reality. You can display the most current data at any time by pressing Shift–F9.

Using Queries to Draw Relationships

Access lets you draw relationships between tables using either of two methods. One way is to set the relationships at the table level using the Edit/Relationships command from the menus. (This technique was covered in the previous chapter.) The other method is to use queries to draw relationships between more than one table.

To build a relational query, open a new query, and add the desired tables using the techniques detailed earlier in the chapter. If the tables share a common field name and field type, Access automatically will join them (a join line appears between the field lists for the tables).

You can manually join tables in the Query window. To join two tables, you simply click a field in one table and drag it to the equivalent field in the other table. (When you do this a *join line* appears between the tables, indicating that they have been joined.) You then can proceed to drag the desired fields into the query grid as detailed earlier in the chapter, add any desired selection or sorting criteria, and run the query to obtain your desired results. Figure 8.15 shows a query based on two tables, with a join established between the Product ID field of both tables. Fields have been added to the query from both tables, and Figure 8.16 shows the results when the query is run.

Here are the specific steps that you'll need to create relational queries:

1. In the Database Window, click the Queries tab, then click New.

2. In the New Query dialog box that appears, select New Query (or, in Access 97, Design View) in the list box, then click OK. When you do this, a new Query window appears, with the Show Tables dialog box above it.

3. Add the desired tables to the window by clicking each desired table, followed by the Add button. (Alternately, you can just double-click each desired table.) When done adding the needed tables, click Close to put away the Show Tables dialog box.

4. Add the needed relational joins by dragging the common field or fields from one table to the other. As you do so, lines will appear between the tables, indicating the presence of the joins. (If you already established relationships at the table level, Access will add the join lines automatically.)

5. Add the desired fields to the query by dragging the fields from the Field List to the cells of the query grid.

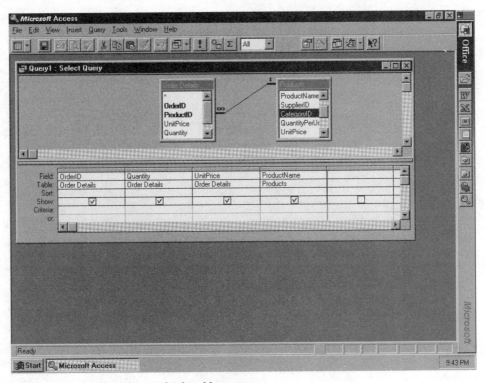

Figure 8.15 A query based on multiple tables.

6. Add any desired criteria and sorting order.

7. Save the query, and run it as needed.

Adding Multiple Tables

During the first part of the process, you open a new query and add multiple tables to that query. You can add multiple tables by selecting each in the Show Table dialog box and clicking the Add button. Each time you add a table (or existing query) to the Query window, a Field List appears in the Query window for that table or query. Note that you also can add tables or queries using drag-and-drop; you can click and drag any table or query from the Show Tables dialog box to the upper portion of the Query window.

Creating the Relational Joins

Once you've added the multiple tables to the Query window, the next step outlined involves linking the common fields by means of join lines. When you do this, you are establishing a link between the primary key of one table and the foreign key of another. (A *foreign key* is always the key field or fields that provide a link in a related table back to the primary table.) Figure 8.17 shows a

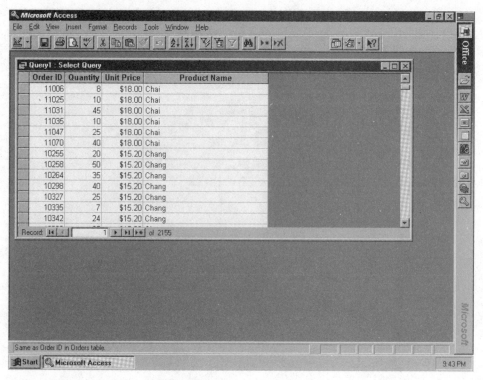

Figure 8.16 The results of the relational query.

join line between the Customers table and the Orders table of the Northwind Traders database.

In many cases, Access makes its best guess and tries to automatically determine where join lines should be placed. If you've already established relationships using the Edit/Relationships command, Access will add join lines based on those relationships. Also, if two tables that you add have a field with the same field name and the same data type, Access will add a join line between those fields. (You can always delete any line that you don't want by clicking it to select it, then pressing the Del key.)

If Access is unable to determine where the join lines should appear, you'll need to add them manually. To do this, just click the desired field in the Field List for one of the tables, drag the field over the desired linking field in the other Field List, and drop it. When you drop the field over the matching field in the other table, the join line appears between the two tables. You can repeat these steps for as many relationships as are needed. As an example, Figure 8.18 shows a database with three relationships between four tables.

Once you've established the relationships, the remaining steps (numbers 5 through 7 in the prior list of steps) are identical to those for a nonrelational query. You just add the desired fields to the query, add any necessary criteria, and establish any desired sorting order. Figure 8.19 shows the results of the query shown in Design view earlier in Figure 8.18.

Deleting Joins and Tables

When Access adds a join line that you don't want, you can easily get rid of it. To delete the unwanted line, click it to select it, then press the Del key. If you want to remove a table that you've added to a query's design, just click anywhere within the Field List for the table, then press the Del key.

There's a Catch...

Relational queries have certain limitations that you'll need to keep in mind when working with them. The limitations apply to editing data in the resulting dynasets and to deleting records. Data in relational queries that are based on one-to-one relationships can be updated as long as there are no totals or crosstabs and as long as the Unique Values Only query property isn't turned on. If your relational query is dealing with a one-to-many relationship, you can only edit records on the "many" side of the relationship. When the query

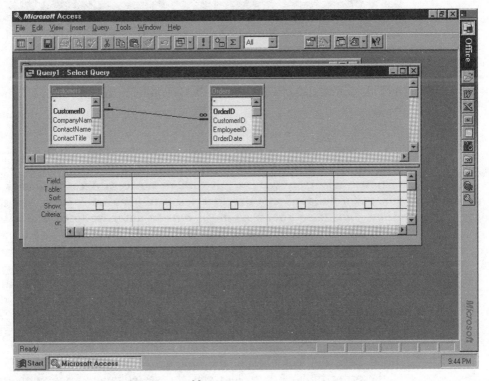

Figure 8.17 A join line between two tables.

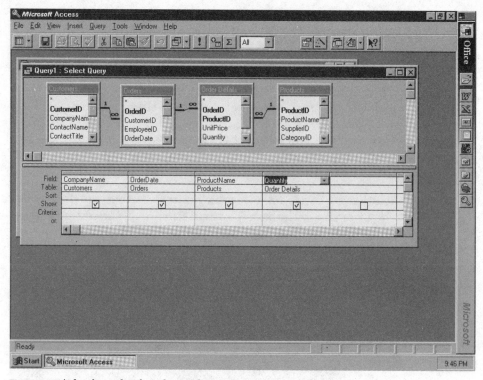

Figure 8.18 A database that has three relationships between four tables.

includes more than two tables, only the table at the end of the "many" side can be updated.

About the Join Types

The join types covered until now are *equi-joins*. The equi-join is the most common type of join, but you can have others in Access. Access supports three types of joins for building relational queries: equi-joins, outer joins, and self-joins.

Equi-joins (also known as *inner joins* in database lingo) are joins in which records will be retrieved if data in the linked field of one table is equal to data in the linked field of the other table. In most cases, equi-joins are used with one- to-many relationships, where the primary key in one table contains unique values that match multiple entries in the foreign key of the other table. If any records in the table that's on the "many" side of the relationship don't match any entries on the "one" side, those records don't appear in the query's dynaset. Any default relationship that Access creates automatically will be an equi-join.

Outer joins are joins where records are always included from one of the tables, regardless of whether there's a match between the linked field or fields of the other table. Access lets you choose *left outer joins*, which include all records from the first table regardless of whether they match records in the second table, or *right outer joins*, which include all records from the second table regardless of whether they match records in the first table. Note that outer joins can be useful in locating orphan records, which are records in one table that have no matching records in a related table.

Self-joins are joins where a field of a table is related to another field in the same table. Access lets you create self-joins by adding the same table to a query window twice, then dragging the desired field from one Field List to the related field in the other Field List.

Choosing the Desired Join

Once you create a join between tables, you can change the type of join by double-clicking the join line. When you do this, the Join Properties dialog box appears, as shown in Figure 8.20.

In the dialog box, the default choice is 1, "Only include rows where the joined fields from both tables are equal." This type of join is an equi-join. Choice 2, "Include all records from Customers and only those records from Products where the joined fields are equal," is a left outer join. Choice 3, "Include all records from Products and only those records from Customers where the joined fields are equal," is a right outer join.

Once you click the desired option and click OK, the join line takes on an appearance that indicates the type of join chosen. With left outer joins, the join

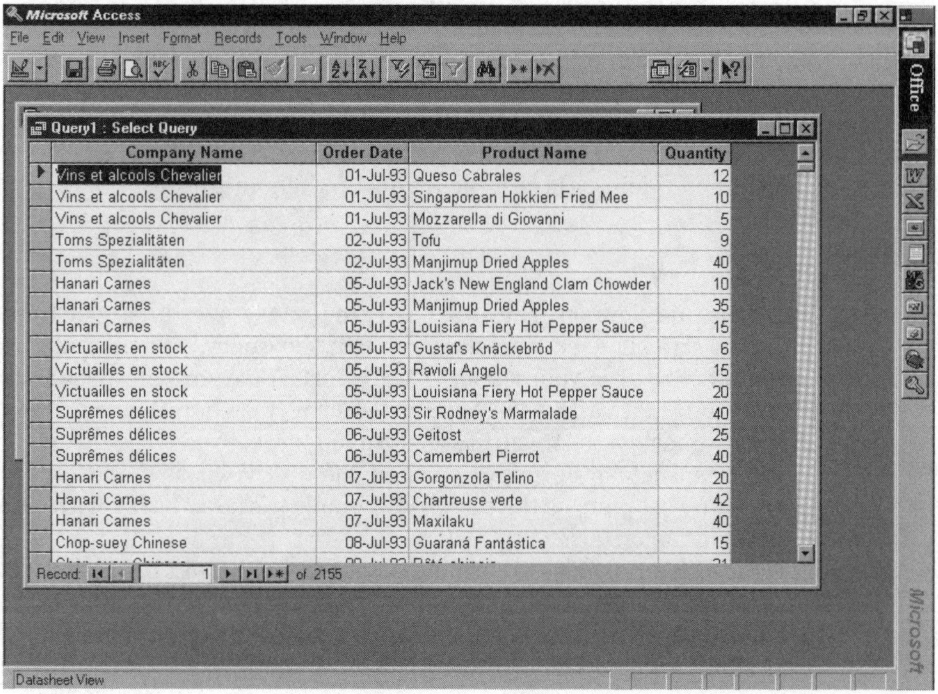

Figure 8.19 The results of relational query using three join lines.

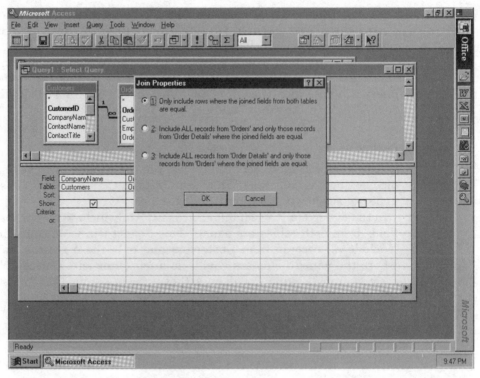

Figure 8.20 The Join Properties dialog box.

line has an arrow that points to the table that is considered to be on the "left" side of the relationship. With right outer joins, the join line has an arrow that points to the table that is considered to be the "right" side of the relationship. (With equi-joins, there is no arrow on the join line.)

Using Parameter Queries

If you find yourself running the same query over and over and entering different criteria each time that you run the query, you should create a *parameter query* to save yourself time and effort. A parameter query is simply a query that automatically asks for needed criteria when it is run. You can use the same queries that you have already created as the basis for parameter queries. Instead of having to open the query window and type the new criteria into the query grid, Access will display dialog boxes with prompts, asking you for the criteria.

Parameter queries are an important tool in designing complete applications, as they provide an easy way to prompt users of the application for needed information to obtain selective data. You can create a parameter query with the following steps.

1. Create a query with the tables and the fields that you want.

2. In the Criteria cells underneath the fields that you want to use as parameters, enter your parameter text, enclosed in square brackets. (This text will be used as a prompt in the dialog box that Access displays when the query runs.) As an example, if you wanted a parameter in a `Country` field to ask for the name of the desired country when the query runs, you could enter an expression like `[Enter the desired country name:]` in the `Country` field. Be careful to use text that is different than your field names. Figure 8.21 shows parameter text entered into the `Country` field of a table.

3. Save the query (choose `File/Save` from the menus, or press Ctrl–F4 and answer `Yes` to the prompt that appears).

When you run the query, Access displays a dialog box like that shown in Figure 8.22, asking for the parameter value. When you type in the data and click OK, the query runs and provides the data according to your criteria.

While the previous example made use of a parameter with only a single value, you are not limited to a single value in a parameter. One common use of multiple values in the same parameter is to prompt for a range of acceptable values, usually done with numbers, currency amounts, or dates. For example, consider a query based on a table that contains a `Date` field for the date of hire

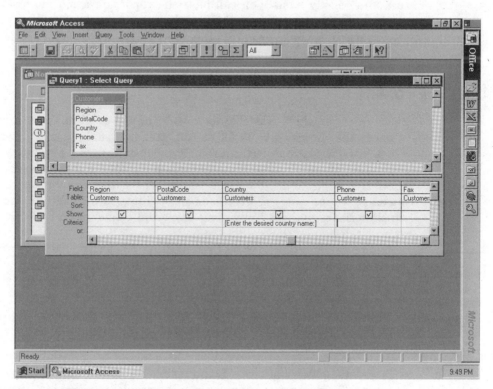

Figure 8.21 The parameter text entered into the Country field of a table.

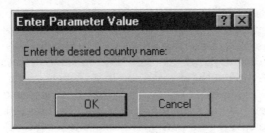

Figure 8.22 A dialog box produced by a parameter query.

of employees. If you want a parameter query that prompts for all employees hired between two dates, you could enter:

```
between [Enter the starting date:] and [Enter the ending date:]
```

in the criteria cell for the Date field. When you run the query, Access first would ask for the starting date, then for the ending date. The resulting records shown in the query would contain only those records falling between the two dates.

Tip: Parameter queries are excellent for use as data sources for reports that require different, selective sets of data each time the report runs. As an example, if your application has a sales report and that report needs to be run on a weekly basis, you can base the report on a parameter query that asks for the starting date and the ending date of sales. That way each time the report runs, the user enters the appropriate dates for that week, and the resulting report contains records from the desired week's sales.

Using Action Queries

Select queries, which this chapter has examined until now, are just one type of query that Access can perform. You often will make use of *action queries*, which are queries that perform some type of task, such as updating a table or appending records to a table. Access lets you create any of four types of action queries. They are *make-table queries*, which create new tables based on existing data; *append queries*, which add records to existing tables; *update queries*, which perform changes to existing data; and *delete queries*, which delete the records selected by the query.

You create action queries by first creating a select query and running it to make sure that the records that it will contain are the records that you want to perform the action on. Then, while in Design view, you change it to an action query by clicking the appropriate toolbar button or by opening the Query menu and choosing one of the four options for action queries (Make Table, Update, Append, or Delete). Action queries have a number of uses in Access applications:

- Processing batch updates—Some tasks call for the mass updating of large groups of records; a good example is the problem caused by the proliferation of new telephone area codes in many parts of the world. If a city gets assigned a new area code by the phone company, it would be a thankless task to update a large batch of customer records manually. Instead, an update query can be designed to change the area code for all customers based in that city.

- Mass deletions or archives of records—If you need to delete a group of records or *archive* the records (move them from one table that's used on a daily basis to another, backup table), you can do so with a combination of append queries and delete queries.

- Creating temporary tables for reporting needs on a network—With any network database application, reporting needs are one area that can slow performance of the application, because sizable tables are often accessed to process the reports. You can use make-table queries to build temporary tables and use those tables for reporting needs to speed up overall performance.

Using Append Queries

Append queries can be used to append data from one table to another. The tables need not have the same structure, but the fields that you use as you append the data must be the same types of fields. Append queries are commonly used when you have data in one Access database and you want to add that data to a table in a different Access database. You can even append data from foreign tables that have been attached to your database. To perform an append query, you use the following steps:

1. Design and test a select query that retrieves the records that you want appended to the table. (If the records are to come from an attached database, you must attach to the database first.) Get into Design view if you are not there already.

2. From the menus, choose Query/Append or click the Append Query button in the toolbar to change the query into an Append query. When you do so, the Queries Properties dialog box appears, as shown in Figure 8.23.

3. In the Table Name box, type the name of the table that you want to append the records to, or click the down arrow and choose a table name from the list. If you want to append to a table in a different database, click the Another Database button in the dialog box and enter the name of the database in the File Name text box. When you are done with the options in the dialog box, click OK. Access will add an Append To row to the query grid.

4. Enter the field names from the table that you are appending records to in the Append To row, matching them to the existing fields in the Field row. (Where the field names are the same, Access automatically displays the field names in the Append To row.) *Note:* The Append To row and the Field row of your append queries must contain the same number of fields.

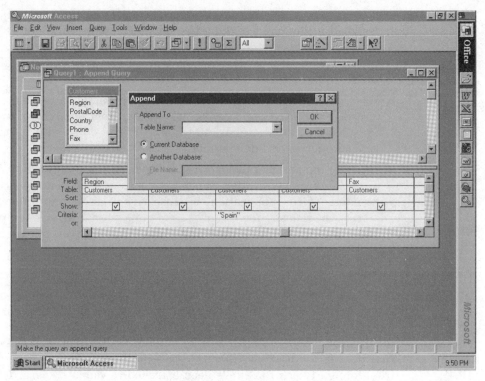

Figure 8.23 The Queries Properties dialog box for the append query.

5. Run the query by choosing Query/Run from the menus, or by clicking the Run button in the toolbar. Access displays a confirmation dialog, telling you how many records will be added to the table. Click OK to run the query and append the records.

A Note About Counter Fields

If a table includes counter fields and you use append queries to add data to the end of that table, you can handle the addition in either of two ways: You can have Access add new counter values that automatically increment from the existing values for each new record added, or you can retain the values in the counter fields of the original table. To have Access add new counter values automatically, omit the counter field from the Query Grid when you design the query. Because the table receiving the records has counter fields, Access automatically adds a value that is one more than that of the previous record in the counter fields. To maintain the counter values that were stored in the records of the original (source) table, drag the counter field of the original table to the Query Grid when you design the query.

Deleting Records

You can compose delete queries, which are action queries that delete all records meeting a specified criteria. As with other action queries, you first design a select query that obtains the records that you want to delete. While in Design view, you choose Query/Delete from the menus or click the Delete Query button on the toolbar to change the type of query from a select query into a delete query. When you run the query, Access will warn you how many rows will be deleted. Once you click OK in the confirmation dialog box, the deletions will occur. You can use the following steps to perform a delete query:

1. Design and test a select query that retrieves the records that you want deleted from the table.

2. From the menus, choose Query/Delete, or click the Delete Query button in the toolbar. The Query window's title will change to "Delete query," indicating that the query, when run, will delete the records.

3. Run the query by choosing Query/Run or by clicking the Run button on the toolbar. Access displays a confirmation dialog, telling you how many records will be deleted from the table.

4. If you do not want to delete the records, click Cancel. Otherwise, click OK to run the query and delete the records.

Updating Records

You can compose update queries, which are action queries that update (or make specified changes to) all records meeting a certain criteria. Update queries are a very handy tool to have when you need to change data in a global fashion. For example, you might need to give a new telephone area code to all residents living in a particular city. In an employee table, you might want to increase all salaries of a given type of worker by $.50 an hour.

As with other action queries, you first design a select query that obtains the records that you want to update. While in Design view, you choose Query/Update from the menus or click the Update Query button on the toolbar to change the type of query from a select query into an update query. Access adds an Update To row to the query, and you enter criteria in this row that specifies how you want to update the data. You can use the following steps to perform an update query:

1. Design and test a select query that retrieves the records that you want to update.

2. From the menus, choose Query/Update, or click the Update Query button in the toolbar. Access adds the Update To row to the query grid.

3. In the Update To cell for the field that you want to update, enter a desired expression or a value that will change the data. As an example, you could

increase salaries by $.50 in a Salary field by entering [Salary] + .50. If you wanted to change all area codes for residents of Fredricksburg, Virginia from 703 to 540, you would enter Fredricksburg in the criteria cell of the City field, and 540 in the Update To cell for the Area Code field.

4. Run the query by choosing Query/Run or by clicking the Run button on the toolbar. Access displays a confirmation dialog, telling you how many records will be updated. Click OK to run the query and update the records.

Creating New Tables

Access lets you create new tables with make-table queries. This type of query creates a new table that contains all of the records selected by the query. Make-table queries can be useful for creating backup tables of your data or for storing data in tables that are contained in other Access databases. Make-table queries are also useful for exporting selective data to a foreign file format (such as FoxPro, Paradox, or dBASE). Here are the steps you can follow to create a make-table query:

1. Design and test a select query that retrieves the records that you want to insert in the new table.

2. From the menus, choose Query/Make Table, or click the Make Table Query button in the toolbar. When you do so, the Queries Properties dialog box for a make-table query appears, as shown in Figure 8.24.

3. In the Table Name box, type the name for the new table, or click the down arrow and choose a table name from the list if you want to replace an existing table with the results of the make-table query. If you want to create a new table in a different database, click the Another Database button in the dialog box and enter the name of the database in the File Name text box. When you are done with the options in the dialog box, click OK.

4. Run the query by choosing Query/Run or by clicking the Run button on the toolbar. Access displays a confirmation dialog, telling you how many records will be added to the new table. Click OK to run the query and create the new table.

Note: When Access creates a new table based on a make-table query, it does not transfer any key field specifications, nor does it transfer any field properties to the new table. If you had specific field properties or key fields designated in the original table, you will probably want to designate the same information in the newly-created table.

Problems with Action Queries

In some cases, action queries might present problems because incompatibilities arise between new and existing data or records are locked on the

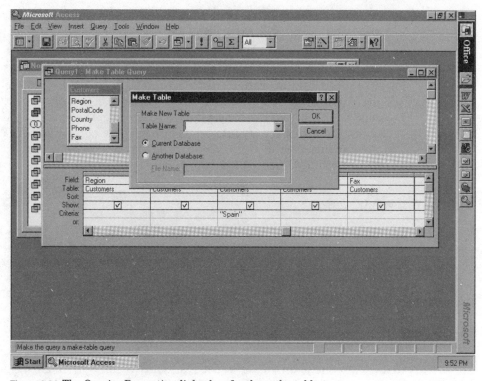

Figure 8.24 The Queries Properties dialog box for the make-table query.

network. When Access encounters a problem in running an action query, it will let you know by presenting a dialog box that clearly defines the source of the problem. The dialog box will offer an OK button and a Cancel button. You can choose Cancel to cancel the query and try to resolve the problem before running the query, or you can choose OK to proceed with as much of the operation as Access can perform given the circumstances. The most common problems with action queries include key violations, data type mismatches, and records locked on a network.

Key Violations
Access will not allow an append query to cause changes that would create duplicate values in the key fields of records. Nor will Access permit any changes that attempt to create null (or empty) values in key fields. When update or append queries attempt to create records that violate these guidelines, the results are *key violations*. You must change the values in the incoming records or in some other manner omit the new records or the changes that are causing the problem.

Data Type Mismatches
Access won't append a value if the data types between the fields do not match. As an example, if you design and run an append query that tries to move data from a text field to a number field of the same name, any text that

is not composed entirely of numbers does not get appended to the table, and Access inserts null values in its place.

Records Locked

If records are locked by other users on a network, Access will not perform an update or append operation involving the locked records. In such cases, the dialog box that appears gives you the options of Proceed or Cancel. Be warned that the Proceed option is rather dangerous because, if you choose it, Access performs the update on the unlocked records but not on the locked ones. You then are likely to have a hideous time figuring out which records were successfully updated and which ones weren't.

Creating Crosstab Queries

Access lets you create *crosstab queries*, which are queries that let you analyze (or cross-tabulate) numeric data in a spreadsheet-like row-and-column format. Crosstab queries are easily handled with the aid of the Query Wizards, a feature of Access that assists you in quickly designing this complex query type. Crosstab queries let you show your data with row and column headings, similar to the layout of a spreadsheet. Crosstab queries can be quite useful for summarizing large amounts of numeric data. To create a crosstab query using the Query Wizards, you perform these steps:

1. Click the Queries tab in the Database Window, then click New.

2. In the New Query dialog box which appears, select Crosstab Query Wizard in the list box, then click OK. When you do this, you will see the first Crosstab Query Wizard dialog box, as shown in Figure 8.25.

3. In the View portion of the dialog box, choose Tables to show all available tables, Queries to show all available queries, or Both to show both tables and queries. Click the table or query desired as the basis for the crosstab, then click Next.

4. The next dialog box that appears (Figure 8.26) will ask you which fields should be used as row headings in the crosstab. Choose the fields that should serve as the row headings, then click Next.

5. The next dialog box that appears (Figure 8.27) will ask which fields should be used as column headings in the crosstab. Choose the desired field or fields, and click the right arrow button in the dialog box to add the fields to the Selected Fields list, then click Next. As you choose the fields, they appear as headings in the Sample portion of the dialog box.

6. The next dialog box that appears (Figure 8.28) will ask which fields should be used for the crosstab calculation, and what type of calculation should be made. First choose a desired field, then select the desired type of calculation from the list of functions at the right side of the dialog box. Note that the dialog box also has an option titled Yes, include row sums. If you turn this option on, each row of the

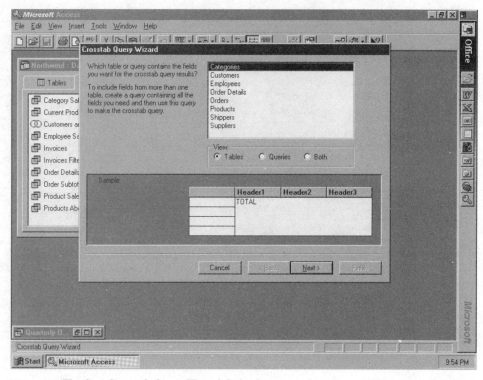

Figure 8.25 The first Crosstab Query Wizard dialog box.

crosstab will include a summary. When done with the options in this dialog box, click Next.

7. The final dialog box that appears asks for a name for the query. You can accept the default name provided by Access or enter a name of your own choosing. You then can click the View button in the dialog box to run the query and see the results, or you can click the Modify button to open the query in Design view, where you can make additional changes to the query's design.

About SQL and Your Queries

If you are familiar with the database language known as SQL, you should know that Access interprets the queries that you design visually into SQL statements (SQL is a database language originally developed by IBM in the 1970s for use with mainframe computers). You can view and edit the SQL statements used by Access to process your queries. Open any query in Design view, and choose View/SQL from the menus (or click the SQL button in the toolbar), and you will see the SQL statement in a window. An example of this window is shown in Figure 8.29.

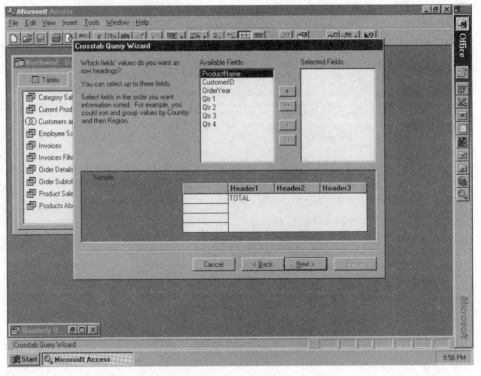

Figure 8.26 The second Crosstab Query Wizard dialog box.

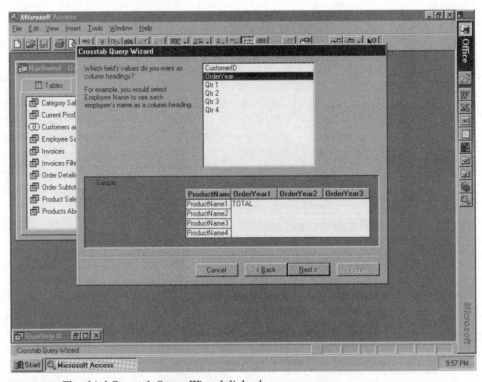

Figure 8.27 The third Crosstab Query Wizard dialog box.

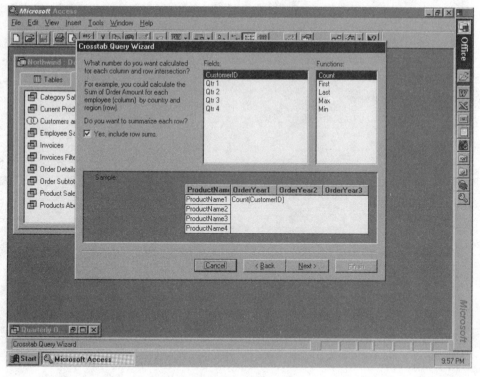

Figure 8.28 The fourth Crosstab Query Wizard dialog box.

The window contains the SQL statement that is responsible for providing the results of your query. You can manually edit the SQL statement, if desired (assuming that you are familiar with the SQL language of database manipulation). Any changes that you make will be reflected in the query grid.

One useful application for the SQL statements created behind every query is their possible use in forms and reports. You can use the text of the SQL statement directly in the RecordSource property for any form or report. The end result is the same as if you had based the form or report on the query, but there is the advantage of having less objects cluttering up your database.

As an example, if you had 6 different reports, and each report was based on a different query, you would have 12 objects stored in your database, all necessary to produce the reports. However, if you were to open each query and copy its SQL statement into the RecordSource property of the corresponding report, you could then delete the queries. The reports would no longer need to access the queries, as they would use the SQL statements contained in the RecordSource properties to obtain the data.

The easy way to base a form or report directly on a SQL statement is to use the cut-and-paste capabilities of Windows to copy the SQL statement from an existing query design and paste the copy into the appropriate property of the form or report. You can use the following steps to accomplish this task:

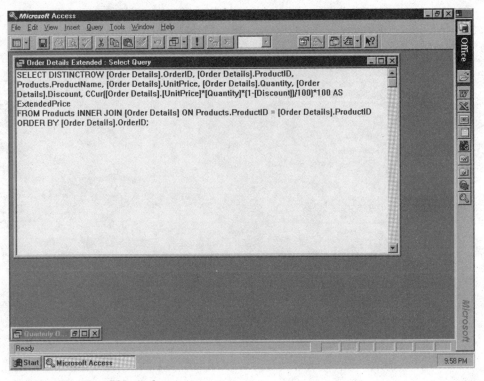

Figure 8.29 The View SQL window.

1. Get into the Query Design window, and create the query that you want to use to generate the SQL statement.

2. Click the SQL button in the Toolbar, or choose View/SQL from the menus. The SQL window that opens shows the SQL equivalent of the existing query.

3. In the dialog box, select all or part of the SQL statement, then press Ctrl–C to copy the selected text onto the Windows Clipboard.

4. Close the dialog box.

5. Place the insertion pointer in the form or report's property where you want to insert the SQL statement.

6. Press Ctrl–V.

Another advantage of adding the needed SQL statement directly to the form or the report is speed; forms and reports might open faster when there is no need to go to disk for a stored query.

Setting a Query's Properties

You can customize your select queries by changing the available options in the Queries Properties window. To change the properties, open the query in

Design view. Click in any blank area of the query (outside of the Query Grid and away from any open Field Lists), then choose View/Properties from the menus, or click the Properties button in the Toolbar. When you do so, a Properties window opens for the query, similar to the example shown in Figure 8.30. Set the properties as desired, then press Alt–F4 or double-click the Close icon at the upper-left corner of the Properties window to close it. The options are detailed in Table 8.5.

Summary

This chapter has provided you with the mechanics that you'll need to effectively design queries for use throughout your Access applications. Effective query design is pivotal to meeting the reporting needs that are so common to any database application. With your queries as a suitable data source, you can use the techniques presented in the following chapter to produce the reports needed by your applications.

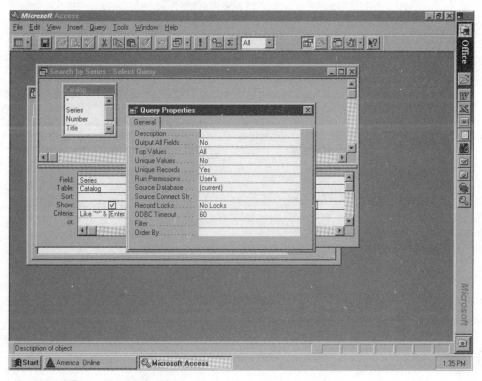

Figure 8.30 A Properties window for a query.

Table 8.5

Property	Use
Description	Enter an optional description that appears when the query is selected in the Database window.
Output all fields	Determines whether all fields in the query will be made available to the dynaset.
Top values	Indicates a number of rows (or a percentage of rows) that the query will return.
Unique values	Indicates whether unique values will be included in the query results.
Unique records	Indicates whether unique records will be included in the query results.
Run permissions	Set to users to run query with any users' permissions or to owner to run query only with owner permissions.
Source database	Source database name for input tables and queries (by default, this is set to "current").
Source connect string	An optional connection string for a source database.
Record locks	Determines whether and how records in underlying table or query are locked.
ODBC timeout	Number of seconds to time out if requests for data from an ODBC server are ignored.
Filter	Expression denoting a filter that is loaded automatically with the query.
Order by	Expression denoting a sort order that is loaded automatically with the query.

Designing Access Reports for the Object-Based Development Environment

For many users of database applications, creating reports is what database management is all about. You can readily perform queries to gain immediate answers to specific questions, but much of your work with Access will probably involve generating reports. Detailed reports are easy to produce with Access thanks to the Report Wizards, which can quickly produce many different styles of reports. You can combine the reports produced by the wizards with selective queries to obtain reports of specific data.

Access provides several ways to design and print reports. You can design and print plain reports by opening a table in Datasheet view and choosing File/Print from the menus. As mentioned, you can use the Report Wizards to quickly design a report. You can use the sophisticated report design options present in Access to create customized reports. You can print form letters of mailing labels.

Reports that you design in Access can be divided into two overall groups: reports that use the wizards and custom reports. As with forms, reports that are created with the wizards require you to answer a few questions about the fields to be used and the style desired for the report. Once you answer these questions, Access creates the report, and you can save it or further modify it manually. The field names supplied during the table or query design phase are used as headings or labels for the fields in the report.

Custom reports, by comparison, are reports that you create or modify to better fit your specific needs. Custom reports that you design can contain any data that you desire from the fields of the database. They can include numeric information, such as totals or other calculations based on numeric fields. Reports can also include headings that contain the specified title of the report, the date (as determined by the system clock), and the page number for each page. Such headings are commonly used with group-oriented

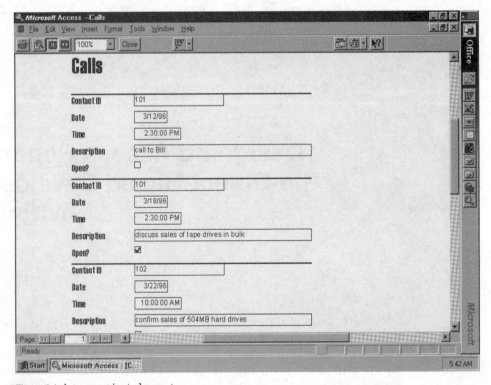

Figure 9.1 A group-oriented report.

reports. Figure 9.1 shows an example of a *group-oriented report*. Group-oriented reports (also known as *tabular reports*) contain the data arranged in groups of columns. Figure 9.2 shows an example of a report using a *single-column layout*. Reports that make use of the single-column layout often resemble paper-based forms.

As with forms, you also can save time when designing reports by combining the two methods. You can use the Report Wizards to create the report initially, then proceed to modify that design as you want, deleting fields, moving the location of fields, changing headings, or adding other text or graphics.

Designing and Implementing Reports

All too often, there's a tendency to jump right into the process of designing a report, with little attention paid to planning beforehand. A little effective planning can save a lot of wasted effort, sparing users the annoyance of reports that don't provide the information in the format that's really needed. If you examine report design as a total process, you could break that process down into the following four steps:

- Define the report's layout manually
- Isolate the source of the necessary data

- Design the report
- Preview or print the report

Define the Report's Layout Manually

Before you start to work in the Report Design window or with the Report Wizards, it's a good idea to have a definite description of what the report should provide, preferably on paper as opposed to just being in someone's mind. Circulating hand-drawn sketches of reports around the department where the reports are needed often provides excellent feedback from users, which helps refine a report's design before it leaves the pen-and-paper stage of the design process.

If you are downsizing from an existing mainframe- or mini-based application, you likely have existing reports that can be used as a model for the new system that you are implementing under Access. This can be a mixed blessing; in such cases, you need to determine whether the existing reports fully met the needs of the users. If the existing reports had their shortfalls and you duplicate them in Access, your new reports will bear the same flaws. The tried-and-proven step of "talking to the users" helps avoid problems during this step of the planning process.

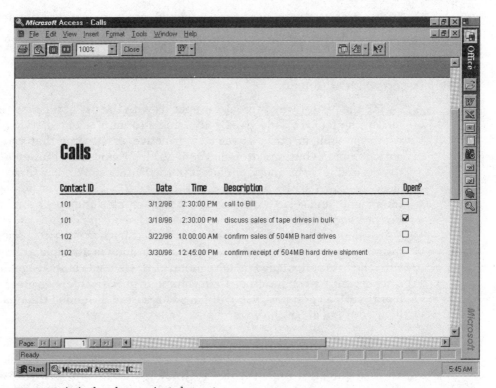

Figure 9.2 A single-column oriented report.

Isolate the Source of the Necessary Data

All reports in Access have a data source, and that data source typically is a query of some kind. Rarely will you want a report that's based on every iota of data in a table (unless the table was created by running a query), so you probably will need to design and save queries that will act as the data sources for your reports. If the reports are relational in nature, you'll need relational queries to support those reports. The queries can provide the needed fields from the needed tables with the desired sort order and the criteria in place to select the specific records that you want included in the reports. You also might want to use *parameter queries* to provide reports that can respond to changing needs of data retrieval at different times. (Chapter 8 provides full details on how you can design queries for your Access applications.)

Design the Report

Once you have a preliminary paper-based design and the needed queries saved, you can move on to the process of laying out the report manually, using the Report Wizards, or using a combination of both techniques. When you design the report manually, you place your desired fields, text boxes, and other controls at the desired locations within the report.

Preview or Print the Report

Once a report's design has been completed, you can print it or preview what the report will look like when printed by choosing `File/Print` or `File/Print Preview` from the menus or by using the appropriate toolbar buttons.

Creating Reports with AutoReport

By far, the fastest way to create a report is with the use of the `New Object` button on the toolbar. This gives you a single-column oriented style of report for whatever table or query is selected or active at the time that you choose the option from the button's drop-down menu. To produce an AutoReport, first open the desired table or query, or click it in the Database Window to select it. Then, click the down arrow to the right of the `New Object` button to open the button's menu, and select `AutoReport`. Access creates and opens a report in Print Preview mode without asking any questions about its design.

An example of such a report was shown earlier in Figure 9.2. As you can see from the figure, what you get with this technique is a simple, columnar report with the fields all aligned in one column at the left side of the page. If you desire a report with a format other than columnar or with totals or other design elements such as graphics, you will have to resort to designing the report manually or with the aid of the wizards.

Creating Reports Using the Report Wizards

You can quickly design a report with the use of the Report Wizards. This feature of Access helps you create a report by asking you questions about the report (such as the type of report that you desire and which fields should appear on the report). Once you answer the questions, the Report Wizard automatically creates the report. You can use the Report Wizards to create single-column reports, group reports, summary reports, tabular reports, and mailing labels. To create a report using the Report Wizards, you use these steps:

1. In the Database Window, click the Reports tab, then click New. Once you do this, the New Report dialog box appears, as shown in Figure 9.3.

2. Select Report Wizard in the list box shown at the upper-right side of the dialog box.

3. In the list box that appears near the bottom of the dialog box, choose the report's *data source* (the table or the query that will provide the data for the report). In cases where the data is to come from more than one table or query, click the primary table or query. Then, click OK. When you do this, the first of the Report Wizard dialog boxes appears, as shown in Figure 9.4.

4. The primary table or query that you chose in Step 3 appears by name in the Tables/Queries list box and all of the fields from that table or query appear in the Available Fields list box. Click each field desired to select it,

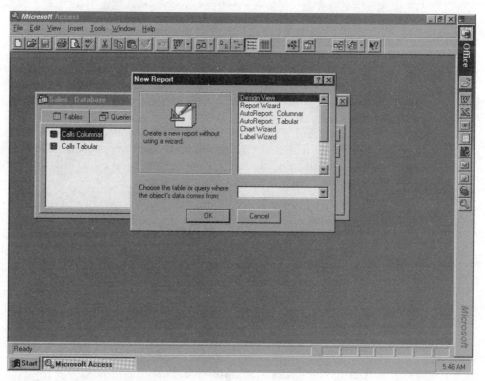

Figure 9.3 The New Report dialog box.

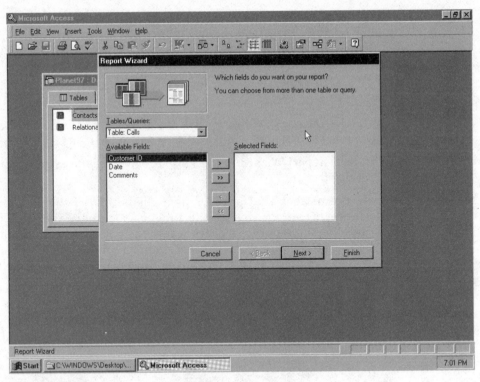

Figure 9.4 The first Report Wizard dialog box.

then click the right-arrow button to add the field to the Selected Fields list box at the right side of the dialog box. Also, note that the dialog box has a double-right-arrow button; you can use this button to add all the fields in the Available Fields list box to the Selected Fields list box. If you make a mistake and want to remove a field, you can choose that field in the Selected Fields list box, then use the left-arrow button to remove it, or you can use the double-left-arrow button to remove all the fields from the Selected Fields list box.

5. In cases where you are basing the report on more than one table or query, after adding all desired fields from the first table or query, select another table or query in the Table/Queries list box, then add the desired fields from that table or query. Once you finish adding all the fields that the report will need, click Next.

Which dialog box appears next will depend on whether your report is based on a single table or query, or on multiple tables or queries. If the report is a relational report (using fields from multiple tables or queries), you'll see the dialog box shown in Figure 9.5. Finish creating the report using the following steps:

1. Using the options contained in this dialog box, you tell Access which of the multiple tables or queries should be used to group the data in the

report. Select the desired table in the list box, then click Next. Once you do this (or if you originally selected fields from only one table or query), you will see the Report Wizard dialog box shown in Figure 9.6.

2. If you want to specify fields that should be used for grouping the records in the report, you can select each field, then click the right-arrow button to add a group band for that field. (Each group band denotes a section of the report in which records will appear by groups.) Once you select any desired grouping, click Next to proceed. If you don't want any grouping in the report, don't select any fields, and click Next.

3. The next dialog box to appear, shown in Figure 9.7, asks you to choose a vertical (columnar) or a tabular layout for the report (or a justified one, with Access 97). It lets you select a desired orientation (portrait or landscape). You can also turn on an option that lets Access automatically adjust field widths to fit all fields on a single page. Choose the desired options in the dialog box, then click Next.

4. The next dialog box to appear, shown in Figure 9.8, lets you select a style for the report. A number of different styles are available. As you select a style, you'll see a representative sample of how that style will appear at the left side of the dialog box. Choose the desired style, then click Next.

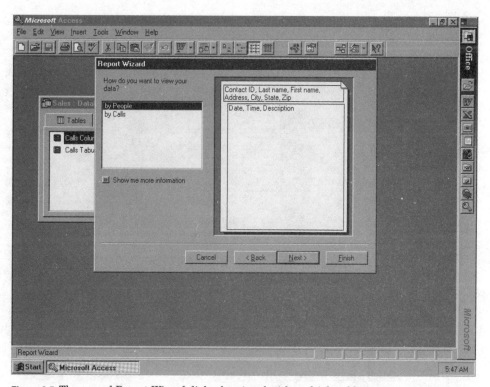

Figure 9.5 The second Report Wizard dialog box (used with multiple tables).

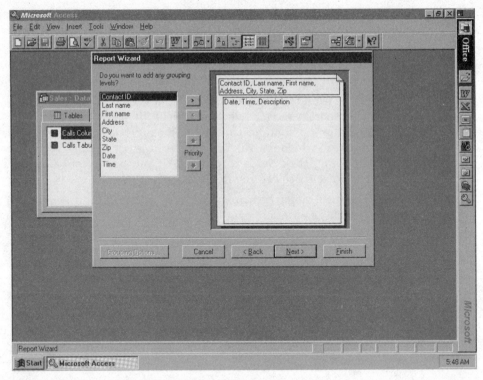

Figure 9.6 The Report Wizard dialog box used for grouping.

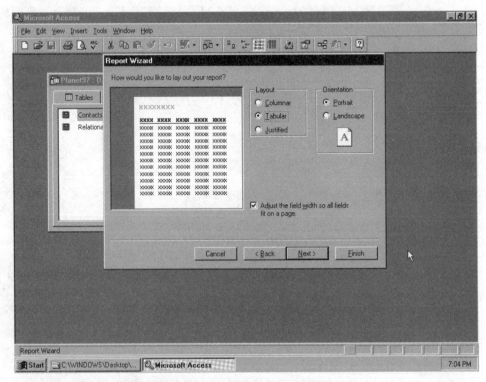

Figure 9.7 The Report Wizard dialog box used for layout and orientation.

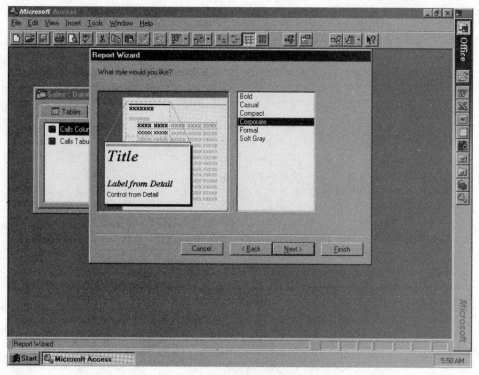

Figure 9.8 The Report Wizard dialog box used for a choice of styles.

5. The last Report Wizard dialog box that now appears will ask you for a title for the report. You can enter a title, and using the options shown in the dialog box, you can choose to open the report (in preview mode) with existing data in it or open the report in Design view, where you can make further changes to the report's design. Once you close an unsaved report, Access will ask if you want to save it. Answer Yes, and you'll be prompted for a name for the report. Report names, like names of other Access objects, can be up to 64 characters in length and can contain spaces.

Printing the Report

You can print any report by selecting it in the Database Window and choosing File/Print from the menus. If the report is already open in preview mode, you can choose File/Print or click the Print button in the toolbar. Whenever you print a report, Access displays the Print dialog box shown in Figure 9.9.

You can use the options in the Print Range portion of the dialog box to specify a range of pages to print or to print all of the pages of a report. To print all of the pages, click the All button if it is not already selected (this is the default). To specify a range of pages, click the Pages button.

To print a range of pages, enter a starting page number in the From text box and an ending page number in the To text box. To print from the first page to a specific page of a report, you can leave the From box empty and just enter a number in the To box. To print a single page, just enter the same page

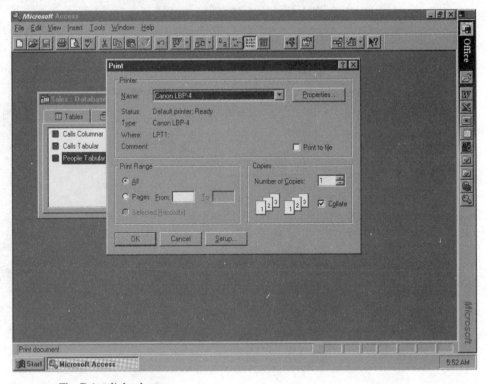

Figure 9.9 The Print dialog box.

number in both boxes. The Print Range options can be useful for reprinting part of a large report after a paper jam where the printer's electronics couldn't recover on its own. You can specify just those pages of the report that you need and avoid reprinting the entire report.

In the Printer portion of the dialog box, you can change the default printer to any other printer installed under Windows. You can use the Copies portion of the dialog box to change the selected number of copies for the report. Leaving the `Collate` option turned on causes multiple copies of a report to be printed in collated order.

Once you've set all the desired options in the Print dialog box, click OK. A status message appears in a dialog box labeled "Printing" while Access sends the report to the Windows Print Manager. You can choose `Cancel` from this dialog box at any time to stop sending the report.

Designing Custom Reports

When you prefer to place fields in various locations, add custom headers and footers, add graphics, and change formatting attributes, you can design custom reports. Depending on how complex your needs are, the precise steps involved in the report's design will vary in complexity. The description that follows illustrates the basic process in creating a custom report:

1. In the Database Window, click the Reports tab, then click New. The New Report dialog box appears, as shown earlier in Figure 9.3.

2. Leave Design view selected in the list box, and click the down arrow beside the Choose a Table or Query list box to open the list box. Then, select the name of the table or query that will provide the data for the report. (If the data that you need is stored in more than one table or query, you'll need to design a relational query and use it as the basis for the report. You can find details on creating relational queries in Chapter 8.)

3. Click OK. Access displays a new report in Design view, as shown in Figure 9.10. Place the desired objects (fields, text, and any graphics) on the report, and add any necessary bands for sorting or grouping. Then, save the report by choosing File/Save from the menus. The placement of objects on a report is covered in more detail in the pages that follow.

Keep in mind that you often can save time by using a wizard to create a report that is close to what you desire. Then, open the report in Design view, and make any additional changes desired to the report.

When you begin designing a report, you are placed in the Design view window, shown in Figure 9.10. You can think of this window as a drawing canvas where you can lay out your desired report. When you are designing a

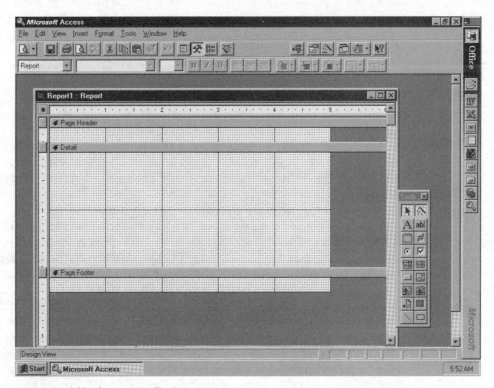

Figure 9.10 A blank report in Design view.

report, the toolbar takes on the appearance shown in Figure 9.10. Note that the toolbar contains a Preview button near the far left; you can click this button to leave Design view and see what your printed report will look like.

In addition to the Preview button, the toolbar also contains buttons for adding, deleting, or changing levels of grouping, viewing properties of a selected object, displaying a list of fields that you can drag to your report, and applying automatic formatting to a report.

Tip: Before you begin designing reports, remember the use of Edit/Undo from the menus. If you make a change or an addition to a report and you don't like the change, in most cases you can choose Edit/Undo to reverse the action.

The Report's Layout

The report's layout is made up of several parts, as illustrated in Figure 9.11. Different portions of the report appear in horizontal areas known as *report bands*. Every report contains a Page Header band, a Page Footer band, and a Detail band. There can also be an optional Report Header band or Report Footer band, and there can be optional Group bands. In the figure, the band that contains the name of a field, Country, is a Group band.

The Page Header band appears once for each page of the report. In many cases, you'll place such information as the date or time of the report and a report title in this area. The Page Footer band at the bottom of the report layout has the same purpose as the header but is for footers: contains the information that typically appears at the bottom of each page.

Report Header bands, when used, contain any information that should appear only at the start of the report (as opposed to at the start of each page). Report Footer bands, when used, contain information that should appear at the end of the report. You usually will use Report Footer bands for totals of numeric fields.

The Detail band is used to define the actual information (usually fields) that will appear in the body of the report. The values in the Detail band are represented by controls (shown as rectangular frames) that contain the names of the field or the expression. While fields are most common, expressions can also be used. Such expressions might contain a function that represents the current date or a calculated value based on a number field.

Group bands, which are optional, are printed once for each group of records in a report. Group bands provide a means of grouping records in a report. Such grouping often includes some type of header identifying the group, along with subtotals of numeric data. You might or might not want to group records in a report. As an example of grouping, you might decide to print a list of members in a membership table by state. The report would be sorted on the State field, and each time that the contents of the State field changed, a new group would begin within the report. If you decide to include groups, Access lets you add an unlimited number of groups to a report. The various bands within a report can be resized at will by placing the mouse pointer above the band's border until the pointer changes shape to a double-headed arrow and clicking and dragging the border up or down as needed.

Using Controls Within Reports

Once the report layout appears in the window, you can use the toolbar, the Toolbox, and various options of the menus to add, rearrange, or remove fields; to add lines, text, or graphics; to increase or decrease spacing between bands; and to change the layout or format of the report in general. As with forms, you place controls throughout your report as desired. Much of the information that follows also is detailed in Chapter 5, which deals with designing forms, because the design surfaces for forms and reports in Access are similar. The information is provided in summarized form in this chapter as a convenience (so you don't need to flip back to that chapter for information). However, if you have not yet become familiar with how you can manipulate controls in forms, you might want to consider Chapter 5.

Placing Controls Bound to Fields

You place *bound controls* or controls that are bound to a field in a table or query to display data in your reports. To add bound controls to a report, you drag them from the *Field List* to the desired location on the form. To add a field to the report, first click the Field List button in the toolbar. (Doing so causes the Field List to appear.) Then, click the desired field within the list, and drag it to the desired location on the report. Figure 9.12 shows a blank report after five

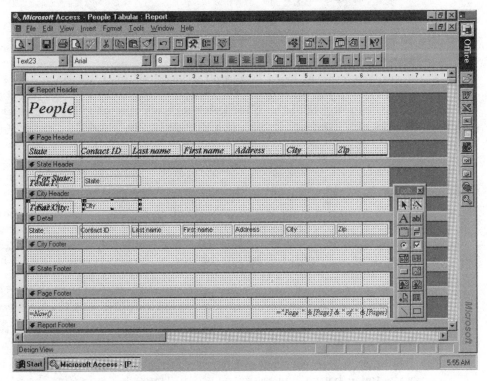

Figure 9.11 Parts of a report layout.

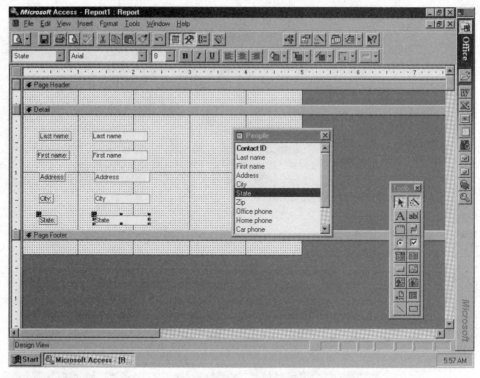

Figure 9.12 A blank report with controls added from the Field List.

fields (First name, Last name, Address, City, and State) were dragged from the Field List into the Detail band of the report.

To select and place multiple adjacent fields at one time, click the first field in the group, hold the Shift key, and click the last field in the group. Then, click and drag the fields (as a group) to the desired location on the report and release the mouse button to place the fields. To select all of the fields in the list at once, double-click the title bar of the Field List.

Selecting Controls

Before you can make changes to a control, such as resizing it or moving it, you must first select the control. To select a control, click anywhere in the control. When you do so, the control becomes surrounded by handles, indicating that it has been selected, as shown in the case of the Last Name field in Figure 9.13.

Note that, with many controls (such as the text box shown here), the handles include *move handles* and *sizing handles*. Most controls, including text boxes, also have two parts, as shown here: a *label* and the text box itself.

Selecting Adjacent Controls

To select a group of adjacent controls, first place the pointer at any point outside the top or bottom control in the group. Then, click and drag the pointer around or through the desired controls.

Selecting Nonadjacent or Overlapping Controls

To select nonadjacent controls (ones that are not next to each other) or controls that overlap, hold the Shift key, while clicking each control that you want to select.

Selecting All Controls

You can quickly select every control on a report by choosing Edit/Select All from the menus. (Note that you can deselect all selected controls by just clicking anywhere outside of a control.)

Moving and Sizing Controls

To move a control, first select it as detailed earlier, then move the pointer to the border of the control. When the pointer changes to the shape of a palm, click and drag the control to the desired location.

To resize a control, first select the control. Then, move the pointer to any of the control's sizing handles and click and drag the control to the desired size.

Aligning Controls

You can maintain the alignment of controls as you move them with the use of the Shift key. Whenever you hold the Shift key while moving a control, the control

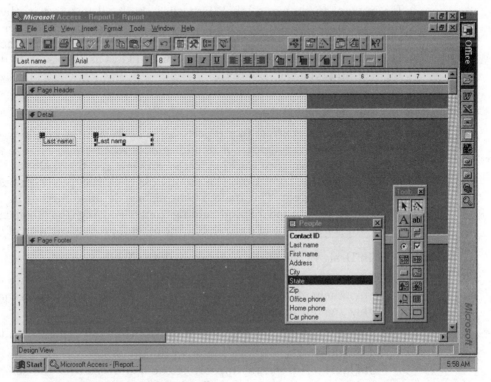

Figure 9.13 A control with selection handles.

moves either horizontally or vertically in whatever direction you started, but not in both directions. Hence, if you wanted to maintain vertical alignment of a control while moving it horizontally, you would select the control, hold the Shift key, and click and drag the control horizontally.

Copying Controls

At times, you might find it helpful to make duplicates of a control for use elsewhere in a report. To copy a control, first select the desired control. (If the control consists of a label attached to a text box, make sure you select the text box; otherwise, you will copy only the label.) With the control selected, choose Edit/Duplicate from the menus. Access will create a duplicate of the control, and you can use the movement methods described earlier to move the copy of the control to the desired location in the report.

Deleting Controls

To delete a control, first select the control, then press the Del key (or choose Edit/Delete from the menus). If you want to delete only the label, make sure that you have the label selected, and not the text box (click on the label to select it).

Changing Labels

If you want to change a label, first click the label to select it, then click the label again. When you click for the second time, the mouse pointer changes to the shape of an I-beam and an insertion pointer appears within the text of the label. You can then use the Backspace or Del keys as necessary to delete existing text and type the new text.

Creating Controls with the Toolbox

To add *unbound controls* to a report—such as decorative graphics, descriptive text, lines, and rectangles—or to add *calculated controls*, you use the Toolbox (Figure 9.14). If you are working in Design view and the Toolbox is not visible, choose View/Toolbox from the menus (or click the Toolbox button in the toolbar) to display it. The Toolbox controls are detailed further in Table 9.1.

The precise method behind adding controls using the Toolbox will vary depending on the type of control, but the overall process consists of these steps:

1. In Design view of the form, display the Toolbox.
2. If you do not want to use the Control Wizards to help create the control, turn them off by clicking the Control Wizards button in the toolbox so that the button is up (not active).
3. In the Toolbox, click the type of control that you want to create.
4. Click in the form where you want the upper-left corner of the control (not its label). The control appears in the default size for the selected type of

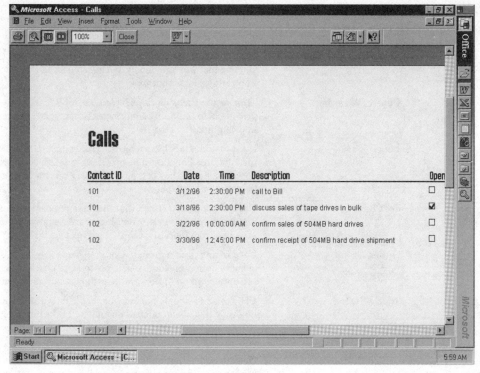

Figure 9.14 An example of Print Preview.

control. Drag the pointer to size the control as desired. If the Control Wizards are on and apply to the type of control you selected, you will see the first of the Control Wizard dialog boxes, which will assist in the creation of the control.

Adding Fields

The most common type of controls used in forms are text boxes that are bound to fields. You can add these with the bound Text Box tool in the Toolbox, but it is easier to add them using the Field List. If you use the Text Box tool of the Toolbox, you must modify the text box properties to tell the text box what field is the source of the data. With the Field List, this happens automatically. To create a bound control using the field list, you perform these steps:

1. Open the desired form in Design view, and display the Field List if it is not already visible.

2. In the field list, select the field or fields that you want to add to the form as bound controls. To select a single field, click the field. To select a block of fields, hold down the Shift key and click the names of the first and last fields in the block. When you do so, Access automatically selects all of the field names in between. To select nonadjacent fields, hold down the Ctrl

Table 9.1

Control	Description
Select Objects Pointer	Used to select, move, or size objects within the report. If another Toolbox tool was previously selected, clicking the Select Objects Pointer deselects that tool.
Control Wizards	This button turns on (or off) the Control Wizards. (Control Wizards provide help in adding some types of controls, such as list boxes and combination boxes.)
Label	Used to add a label, such as descriptive text, titles, captions, or instructions. Labels can be attached to text box controls to serve as descriptions, or they can be completely unattached, used only for informational purposes.
Text Box	Used to create a text box that displays the contents of a field or the results of an expression. Text boxes are usually *bound* (or attached) to a field in a table or a dynaset.
Option Group	Used to add option groups. Option groups are used to display two or more option buttons, toggle buttons, or check boxes; only one of the options in an option group is shown as selected at a time.
Toggle Button	Used to add a toggle button. Toggle buttons are buttons that look like they have been pushed down when selected. They are used within option groups to display one choice from many, or they can be used individually to indicate a yes/no choice.
Option Button	Used to add an option button. Option buttons are circles that are darkened in the center when selected. You can use option buttons (also called *radio buttons)* within an option group to indicate one choice from many, or you can used them individually to specify a yes/no choice.
Check Box	Used to add a check box. Check boxes are small squares that contain an "X" when selected. You can use check boxes within an option group to indicate one choice from many, or you can used them individually to specify a yes/no choice.
Combo Box	Used to create a combination box. Combination boxes display one choice from a list of choices.
List Box	Used to create a list box. You use list boxes to display values from a predetermined list.
Command Button	Used to add a command button. (In reports, a command button that you place will appear but cannot be used for any purpose, because a user cannot interact with a report. Command buttons are normally used in forms, not in reports.)
Image	Used to add a frame that you can use to display a static (graphic) image.
Unbound Object Frame	Used to add an OLE object created by another Windows application to the report. Unbound object frames are routinely used to display graphic elements (such as a corporate logo) in reports.
Bound Object Frame	Used to display the contents of an OLE field from the underlying table or query in the report.

Table 9.1 *(continued)*

Control	Description
Page Break	Used to insert a page break into the report. Page breaks force the beginning of a new page when a report is printed.
Subform	Used to add a subreport to a report. For example, if a report displayed the names of members of a video club, you could use a subreport to display a detail table of all video rentals in a given month for that member.
Line	Used to draw lines in a report.
Rectangle	Used to add rectangles or squares to a report.

key and click the name of each field that you want to include. To select all fields, double-click the list's title bar.

3. Drag the selected field or fields from the field list to the form.

4. Place the upper-left corner of the mouse pointer where you want to put the upper-left corner of the first control (not its label), and release the mouse button. Access adds one bound control on the form or report for each field you selected in the field list.

If, for some reason, you prefer to use the Toolbox to add fields to a form, you can do so by clicking the bound Text Box tool in the Toolbox and clicking in the form where you want to place the field. When you click in the form, an unbound text box appears, and you must modify its properties to bind the text box to the desired field. With the unbound text box selected, click the Properties icon in the Toolbar (or choose `View/Properties`) to open the Properties window, click in Control Source, and enter or select a source for the field.

Adding Labels

Besides the use of fields, you will typically need to include text that's not attached to any field on reports. Such text might be descriptive or explanatory text, such as is used in titles or captions. Unattached text is added to reports with the use of the Label tool. You can create a label with the following steps:

1. Open the report in Design view, and display the Toolbox (if it is not already visible).

2. Click the Label tool.

3. To create a label that is automatically sized as you type, click where you want to start the label, then type the label's text. To create a label of any size, click where you want the label to start, drag the pointer until the label is the size you want, then type its text.

You can display multiple lines of text in a label by creating the label, entering its text, then resizing it. The existing text in the label automatically wraps to fit the label's new dimensions. You can also press Ctrl–Enter as you reach the desired end of a line when typing the text; the Ctrl–Enter combination forces a new line.

As you design your reports, often the labels will not contain the precise fonts and styles that you desire. You can easily change these by clicking the label to select it and choosing an appropriate font style and font size from the font list boxes in the toolbar.

Hint: If you change a label's font to a larger size or from plain to bolded text, often the text no longer fits completely in the size allotted for the label. You can drag the box to a new size, but there's a faster way. With the label still selected, choose `Format/Size/To Fit` from the menus. The label will be sized to fit the enclosed text.

Aligning Controls

When you add fields to a form as a group, Access assumes that you wanted to left-align all of the labels, and this might or might not be the alignment that you desire in your reports. You can change the alignment for any selected group of objects with the `Format/Align` command. You use the following steps to do so:

1. If the Pointer tool is not already the selected tool in the Toolbox, click it to select it.

2. Click at a point just above and to the left of the first desired field, and drag to a point just below and to the right of the last desired field. When you release the mouse, the fields should all be selected.

3. From the menus, choose `Format/Align`, then choose `Right` to right-align all of the fields.

4. Choose `Format/Size/To Fit` from the menus if you want to automatically expand the controls as necessary to fit the italicized text.

Adding Page Breaks

With forms that will be printed often, you can add page breaks to indicate where one printed page should end and another page should begin. To add a page break, perform these steps:

1. In the Design view of the form, open the Toolbox and the Properties window if they aren't already open.

2. Click the page break tool in the Toolbox, then click the form where you want the new page to begin.

The page break appears in the report's design as a small dotted line. Note that page breaks don't control how much of a form is displayed in a window. If you want each page to be the same size and each window to show just one page at a time, design the form so that each page break is an equal distance from the other. You can do this by positioning the page break controls with the aid of the vertical ruler.

Changing a Control's Properties

Every control that you place in a report has its own properties, which you can change to modify the behavior of the control. In addition to control properties, the sections of a report also have properties that can be modified for specific needs, and you can set properties for the entire report. To modify any of the properties used by the report, you perform these steps:

1. In Design view for the report, choose the control, section, or entire report whose properties you want to set. Click the desired control to select it, or click in the section to select a section. To select an entire report, choose Edit/Select Report from the menus.
2. Open the Properties window by choosing View/Properties or clicking on the Properties button in the Toolbar.

Once you do these steps and the Property window opens for the selected object, you first click on the desired tab in the window (Format, Data, Event, Other, or All), then you change the appropriate property as desired.

In particular, two useful properties that you should be aware of when working with text box controls in reports are the Can Grow and Can Shrink properties. These properties permit text box controls to grow or to shrink vertically. When the Can Grow property for a text box is set to Yes, the text box can grow vertically in size as needed in the report to accommodate any text in the record that cannot fit within the size of the text box. When the Can Shrink property for a text box is set to Yes, the text box can shrink vertically whenever text in the record does not fill the area allocated for the text box.

Previewing the Report

You can preview the report at any time during the design process. To do so, choose File/Print Preview, or click the Print Preview button on the toolbar. With either method, you see a window that contains the report as it will look when printed, similar to the example shown in Figure 9.14.

Use the scroll bars or the PgUp and PgDn keys to view additional portions of the report. You can click the arrows at the bottom of the window to view other pages in the report. Click the left-pointing arrow to view the previous page, and click the right-pointing arrow to view the next page. While in Print Preview mode, you can also use the Two Pages button of the toolbar to view two pages simultaneously (both in a reduced size format), and you can use the Zoom button to alternately zoom in or out in the preview. Finally, when you are done previewing the report, click the Close button on the toolbar to return to Design view.

Saving the Report

Saving a report is much like saving any other object in Access. You can choose File/Save from the menus and supply a name (if asked) for the report, then you can close the report by pressing Ctrl–F4 or clicking on the window's Close icon. You also can first click the Close icon (or press Ctrl–F4) to close the window, then answer Yes to the prompt that asks if you want to save the changes. If you are saving a report for the first time, Access will also ask you to supply a name for the report. With either method, the report is saved to the current database.

Modifying a Saved Report

To modify a saved report, click the Reports tab in the Database Window, then click the desired report to select it, and click Design. The report will open in a Design view window, and you can make the necessary changes.

Changing a Report's Data Source

When you design and save a report (whether it is with the aid of the wizards or not), Access stores the source of the data for the report as part of the report's design. The RecordSource property, stored within the report, tells the report where to go to find the data. At times, you might find it helpful to change the source of the data; for example, perhaps you've created and saved a detailed custom report that is based on a particular table. You later design a query that extracts selected records from the table, and you want to use the same report created earlier with the results of the query. One way to handle this need is to change the RecordSource property for the report. Changing the RecordSource property, in effect, changes the underlying table or query used for the report. To change a report's RecordSource property, you perform the following steps:

1. While in Design view for the report, choose Edit/Select Report from the menus.
2. Open the property window by choosing View/Properties or by clicking on the Properties button in the toolbar.
3. Click the Data tab of the Properties window that opens.
4. In the RecordSource property box, select or type the name of the table or query that you want to use as the source of data for the report.
5. Press Alt–F4 to close the Properties window for the report.

Those who are experienced with the SQL language should note that you also can type SQL statements directly into the RecordSource property box. The SQL statement will then be used as the basis for record selection when the report runs.

Adding Sorting to a Report

You can add levels of sorting to your reports. (Keep in mind that there are other ways to sort data. If you base your reports on queries that include sorting, there is no need to sort the report as well.) To specify a sort order for a report, perform the following steps:

1. While in Design view for the report, choose View/Sorting and Grouping from the menus (or click the Sorting and Grouping button on the toolbar). This causes the Sorting and Grouping dialog box to appear (Figure 9.15).

2. Click the Field/Expression box, then click the down arrow to open the list box. Select the desired field to sort on from the list box. If desired, click in the Sort Order box, and choose Descending (ascending is the default sort order).

3. Repeat Step 2 for any additional fields that you want to sort by.

As an example, if you wanted to sort a report that produces mailing labels by State, then by City, then by Last Name, you would place the State field in the first row of the dialog box, the City field in the second row, and

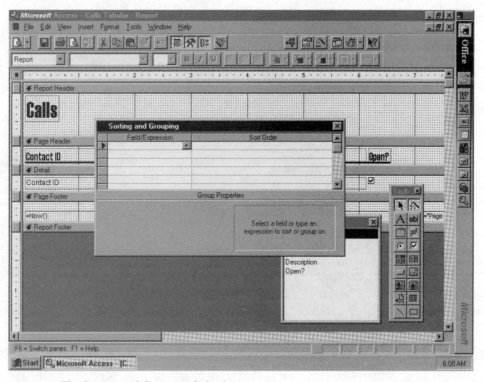

Figure 9.15 The Sorting and Grouping dialog box.

the Last Name field in the third row, as shown in Figure 9.16. When you print the report, Access sorts the data in the order requested.

It's a wise idea to add sorting to mailing labels that you create, because mailings often are grouped by postal codes to save on mailing costs.

Adding Grouping

Access also lets you add groupings of records to a report. You probably will need to arrange your reports to be broken down by groups. For example, you might need to see all customers of a mailing list divided into groups by state of residence. Using the Sorting and Grouping dialog box shown earlier, you can define multiple levels of grouping. While much more than two or three levels of groups might seem like overkill to some, it is nice to know that Access is accommodating when you must base a complex report on a large number of subgroups; up to 10 levels of grouping can be included in a single report.

Because any grouping of data implies sorting, you must tell Access to sort the data that the group will be based on. For example, if you print a report of customers in groups by state and, within each state, in groups by city, you must sort the report by state and, where the state is the same, by city. You use the same technique as described previously in choosing the fields to use for the

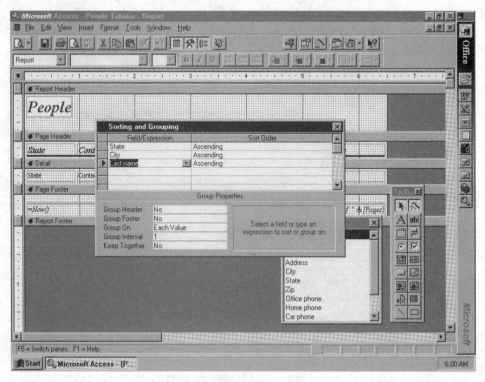

Figure 9.16 A dialog box with the levels of sorting added.

sort from the Sorting and Grouping dialog box. The only difference is that, with grouping, you also must turn on the group header and group footer options, as desired, in the Sorting and Grouping dialog box. To add grouping to a report, you would perform the following steps:

1. While in Design view for the report, choose View/Sorting and Grouping from the menus (or click the Sorting and Grouping button on the toolbar). This causes the Sorting and Grouping dialog box to appear, as shown previously.

2. Click the Field/Expression box, then click the down arrow to open the list box. Select the desired field to sort (and base the group on) from the list box.

3. If desired, click in the Sort Order box, and choose Descending (ascending is the default sort order).

4. To add a group header, click in the Group Header text box at the bottom of the dialog box, then click the arrow and choose Yes from the list.

5. To add a group footer, click the Group Footer text box, then click the arrow at the bottom of the dialog box and choose Yes from the list.

6. If you want to add additional subgroups to the report, repeat Steps 2 and 3 for the additional fields that you want to base the groups on, and repeat Steps 4 and 5 for each group that you add.

By way of example, if you wanted to add grouping for a report of customers by state, you would place the State field in the Field/Expression column of the dialog box. In the Group Properties portion of the dialog box, you would choose Yes for a Group Header if you wanted a header and Yes for Group Footer if you wanted a footer, as shown in Figure 9.17.

After choosing these options and putting away the dialog box, the report's design would contain the new header and footer bands, and you could then proceed to add any desired fields or other design elements to the new bands. In most cases, you will want to add the field that identifies the group to the header band. Calculated objects that contain numeric totals often are placed in group footer bands. Once you've placed the desired groups, you can check to see if the results are what you wanted by choosing File/Print Preview or by clicking the Print Preview button in the toolbar.

Changing the Sorting or Grouping Order

Access lets you change the way the data in a report is sorted and grouped. You do this by changing the order in which your fields (or expressions) appear within the Sorting and Grouping dialog box. To change sorting and grouping order, perform these steps:

1. In the report's Design view, choose View/Sorting and Grouping from the menus.

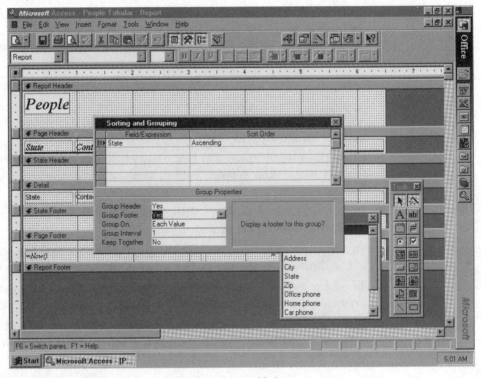

Figure 9.17 A dialog box with the level of grouping added.

2. In the Sorting and Grouping box, click the selector of the field or expression that you want to move.

3. Click the selector again, and drag the row to a new location in the list.

If headers and footers have been assigned to the groups that you rearrange, Access automatically moves the headers, footers, and controls within them to the new positions.

Adding Headers and Footers

The Report Wizards automatically add various types of headers and footers to a report, depending on the options that you choose while using the wizards. If you design your own reports manually, you'll need the ability to add headers and footers on your own. Once in Design view for any report, you can add or remove report, page, or group headers or footers. Note that, when you remove a header and footer, you also remove all of the controls associated with that header and footer. To add or remove a report header and footer, choose Report Header/Footer from the View menu. To add or remove a page header and footer, choose Page Header/Footer from the View menu.

To add or remove a group header or footer, choose Sorting and Grouping from the View menu, or click the Sorting and Grouping button in the toolbar. In the Sorting and Grouping dialog box that appears, click the field name, or type the expression that you want to use to create the header or footer. Finally, to add the group header or footer, set the GroupHeader or GroupFooter property to Yes. Note that you can remove a group header or footer by setting these properties to No.

Adding the Current Date or Time to a Report

You can easily add the current date or time, as measured by the system clock, to a report. You do this by creating a text box, then defining (within the text box) an expression that provides the date or the time. To add the current date or time to a report, perform these steps:

1. Open the report in Design view, and add a text box to the section where you want the date or time to appear.

2. With the text box selected, choose View/Properties to open the Property window for the text box.

3. In the ControlSource property, type an equal sign followed by an expression using the Now function or the Date function. As an example, you would enter =Date( ) to display the current date, or you would enter =Now( ) to display the current date and time.

4. As an option, you can use the Format property to display a date in a predefined format. For example, to show the date using a format like 5-May-96, you would change the Format property to Medium Date.

Adding Page Numbers to a Report

You can include the current page number or the total number of pages in a report by using the Page and Pages properties. Use the Page property to show the current page number, and use the Pages property to show the total number of pages in a report. To add page numbers to a report, perform these steps:

1. In Design view, add a text box to the section (usually the page header or footer) where you want the page number to appear.

2. Open the Property window for the text box.

3. In the ControlSource property, type a page number expression. As an example, =Page in a text box would give the current page number. The expression =" Page " & Page would give the page number preceded by the word "Page," as in "Page 1," "Page 2," and so on.

The following expression:

```
="Page " & Page & " of " & Pages
```

would provide the text "Page 13 of 16" on page 13 of a 16-page report.

Specifying a Custom Starting Page Number

One occasional need with a report is the need to have numbering on the first page begin with a number other than 1. As an example, you might have a report that will be preceded by a three-page Excel spreadsheet, and you want the report's first page to be numbered as page 4, with each successive page numbered one higher. You can handle this task by including a parameter that prompts the user, within the Page property in a control. Add a page header to the report (if one doesn't already exist), and add a text box control to that header. Enter the following expression in that text box control:

```
=Page + [Enter a Starting Page Number] -1
```

Whenever the report runs or is previewed, the user will see a dialog box with a title bar that reads "Enter a Starting Page Number." The page number that appears on the first page of that report will be the number entered in the dialog box.

Adding Expressions to Count Yes/No Responses in a Yes/No Field

Another unusual need that does arise from time to time is the need to include a sum total of responses of a Yes/No field. You can use expressions in text boxes to calculate the number of yes or no responses and include the SUM() function to produce a sum total. The following expressions can be used in a report's Group Footers or in the Report Footer to count the actual number of Yes's and No's in a field whose DataType is Yes/No and whose field name is MyField. Use the same expression, and substitute the actual name of your field for the example TheField in the expressions shown.

Use the following expression to count the Yes responses:

```
=Sum(IIF([TheField],1,0))
```

Use the following expression to count the No responses:

```
=Sum(IIF([TheField],0,1))
```

Adding Line Controls

One type of control that is more common to reports than to forms is the *line control*. The line control lets you add straight lines to a report. The lines can be horizontal, vertical, or at any desired angle. To add a line control to a form, use these steps:

1. Open the desired report in Design view. Click the Line tool in the Toolbox.

2. Place the mouse pointer where the line is to begin, and click and drag to where you want the line to end. *Note:* If you hold the Shift key while you drag, you will force the line to be perfectly horizontal or vertical.

As with other controls added to reports, where you place the line control determines where the lines appear. If a line control is added to a group header, the line will appear within the report's group header. A line placed in a group footer will appear once at the end of each group.

Combining Text Values from Multiple Fields

At times, you will need to combine text values from multiple fields into a single expression within a report. A common example is that of a person's name. Rather than displaying the contents of a last name field, followed by the contents of a first name field, you might prefer to have a single field in a report that shows the first name, followed by a space, then the last name. This type of task can be accomplished by combining values from multiple fields through the use of expressions. To combine text values using an expression, perform these steps:

1. Open the report in Design view, and add a text box to the section where you want the expression to appear.

2. With the text box selected, choose View/Properties to open the Property window for the text box.

3. In the ControlSource property, type an equal sign followed by an expression that combines the fields. As an example, assuming you had fields in the table named Last Name and First Name, you could enter an expression like =[First Name] & " " & [Last Name] to provide the desired results.

As with forms, you can add text boxes to reports that display data based on a calculation. You can include any of the Access functions in expressions that you place in calculations. Some of the functions commonly used in reports are listed in Table 9.2.

As an example, you might want to display a calculation that represents the amount in a Quantity field, multiplied by the amount in a Price field. To create a text box that displays a calculation, you perform the following steps:

1. Click the Text Box tool in the Toolbox to select it. Click in the report at the upper-left corner of where you want the text box to begin, and drag to the lower-right corner.

2. Click in the text box, and type the desired expression, starting with an equal symbol. For example, if you want the text box to display the contents of a field named Quantity multiplied by a field named Price, you would enter =[Quantity] * [Price] in the text box.

Table 9.2

Function	Use
Date()	Provides current date
Time()	Provides current time
Now()	Provides current date and time
Avg *(value)*	Provides average of the values
Min *(value)*	Provides minimum value in the set of records
Max *(value)*	Provides maximum value in the set of records
Sum *(value)*	Provides a sum (total) of the values

As another example, you could use the Access SUM() function to display the total of a numeric or currency field in a report. This function is commonly used in the Group Footer or Report Footer bands of a report. When placed in a Group Footer, it provides a sum for all of the records in a group. When placed in the Report Footer, it provides a sum for all the records in the report. If, for example, you wanted to display the sum of a field called Sales, you could place a text box in the Group Footer or the Report Footer band, and you would enter =Sum([Sales]) in the text box.

Calculating Running Sums

A very common use for calculated fields in reports is to calculate running sums, which are sums that keep a running total of numeric amounts.

You can calculate a running total in a report by using a text box that contains an expression that forms the basis for the calculation. As an example, in the Report Footer section of a report, you might include an expression such as =Count([Order ID]) or =Sum([Salary]). In the first case, a running count is kept of the number of orders; in the second case, a running sum total is kept of the Salary field. The running total can be for the records in each group or for all of the records in a report, depending on where you place the text box (in the group header or footer or in the report header or footer). To calculate running sums, perform these steps:

1. In the report's Design view, add a bound text box or a calculated text box. Place the text box in the detail section to calculate a record-by-record total, or place the text box in a group footer to calculate a group-by-group total.

2. Open the Property window for the text box, and set the text box's RunningSum property according to the type of total that you want. Choose Over Group to create a running total that resets to 0 at the beginning of each higher group level, or choose Over All to create a running total that accumulates until the end of the report.

Adding Graphics or Pictures

You can easily add graphics or pictures as design elements in a report. Any graphics that are stored in OLE fields of a table can be used as fields of the report, and you can place and size those fields just as you would place or size any other type of field. In addition, pictures or graphics can be inserted as design elements from your favorite graphics or photo package (such as Corel Draw or Harvard Graphics for Windows) or from Windows Paintbrush. Figure 9.18 shows an example of a report containing a graphic.

You can perform the following steps to use graphics as design elements within reports:

1. Open the desired report in Access, and get into Design view.

2. Start your graphics program under Windows, and design and load the graphics image that you want to use.

3. Using Windows selection techniques applicable to your package, select the portion of the graphic that you want to place in the report in Access. Choose `Edit/Copy` from the application's menus.

4. Use the Windows 95 Taskbar to switch back to Access.

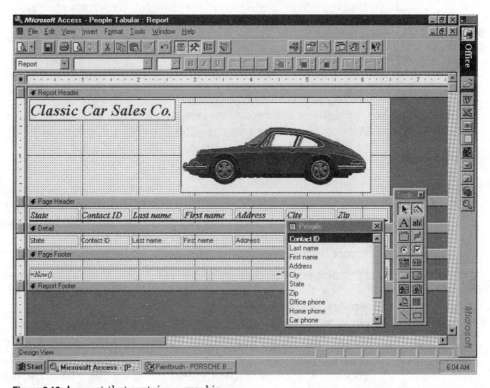

Figure 9.18 A report that contains a graphic.

5. Click in the report in the area where you want to place the graphic, then choose Edit/Paste from the menus. When you do this, the graphic appears in the report.

6. Using the moving and sizing techniques detailed earlier, place the graphic in the desired location on the report.

Tip: Once a graphic has been placed in a report, you can modify it in the original application by double-clicking the graphic, assuming the original application that you used to create the graphic supports Windows OLE (object linking and embedding).

Creating Multitable Reports with Subreports

Access lets you design reports within reports. A common use for this technique is in the creation of multitable reports, which are reports with records from more than one table. Multitable reports use the same design techniques as multitable forms, which were covered in detail in Chapter 5. As with multitable forms, multitable reports use a subreport bound to the main report. The relationship between the underlying tables can either be a one-to-many relationship (in which one record in the main report relates to one or more records in the subreport) or a one-to-one relationship (in which one record in the main report matches only one record in the subreport).

When manually creating a multitable report, you must create and save the subreport before designing the main report. Use the techniques for report design described earlier in this chapter to create the subreport, then use the following instructions to create the multitable report:

1. Open the main report in Design view. (If necessary, move the Report Window so that you can see the Database Window. Also, size the report so that it contains sufficient room to place the subreport.)

2. In the Database Window, click the Reports tab to display all available reports in the database.

3. Find the report that you want to use as a subreport, and click and drag it from the Database Window to the main report. When you release the mouse button, a subreport control appears within the main report, as shown in Figure 9.19. Move the subreport as desired to its location in the main report.

4. With the subreport selected, choose View/Properties from the menus (or click the Properties button in the toolbar) to open the Properties window for the subreport.

5. Click the LinkMasterFields property. If it contains an entry already, verify that Access has created the relational link on the fields that you had in mind. If Access has not established a link, you must type into the property box the name of the field in the main report that will be used as a link to the records shown in the subreport.

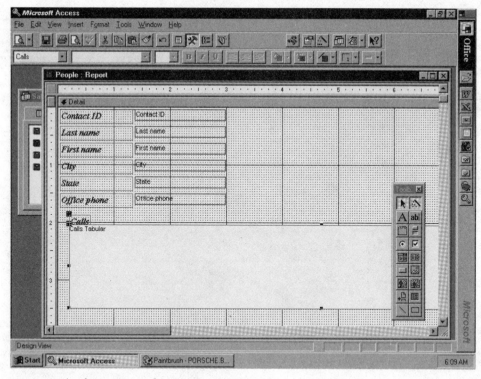

Figure 9.19 A subreport control in a main report.

6. Close the report and save it when prompted, using the methods described earlier in the chapter. When you open the report in print preview, the records for the table that you've used for the main report appear, and the associated records from the related table appear within in the subreport. Figure 9.20 shows a print preview of a report designed using these steps.

Keep in mind that the manual method described earlier is just one way to create a relational report. You can also design a report that's based on a relational query (relational queries are detailed in Chapter 8). You also can use the Report Wizards to create a report that retrieves data from multiple tables or queries, as described earlier in this chapter.

Creating Mailing Labels

A common use for database software is the creation and management of a mailing list. With most mailing lists, the need for mailing labels quickly arises. Access makes this a simple task by providing a Report Wizard designed specifically for the printing of mailing labels. If you want to print labels for a specific selection of records, you might want to create a query first and save it so

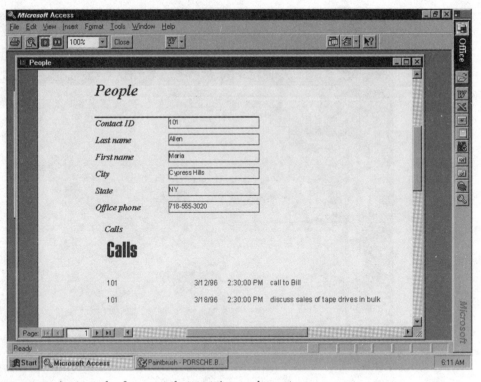

Figure 9.20 An example of a report that contains a subreport.

that you can later create the report that generates the mailing labels. You can create mailing labels by performing the following steps:

1. In the Database Window, click the `Reports` tab, then click `New` to start designing a new report.

2. In the New Report dialog box that appears choose Label Wizard in the list box, then select the desired table or query that contains the fields that you want to use in the mailing labels. Click `OK`, and in a moment, the first Mailing Label Wizard dialog box will appear, as shown in Figure 9.21.

3. The first dialog box to appear asks for the desired label size. Scroll down the list and find the size that you want, click it to select it, then click `Next`. Note that this dialog box has buttons for `English` and `Metric`. With the default of `English` selected, you see labels that are measured in inches. If you click `Metric`, you will see common metric label sizes. Under Label Type, choose `Sheet Feed` or `Continuous` as desired. Then, click `Next`.

4. The next dialog box to appear, as shown in Figure 9.22, lets you choose a font size, weight, and color for the text used for the labels. Check boxes are also included for italics and underlining. Make your desired selections, then click `Next`.

5. The next dialog box to appear, as shown in Figure 9.23, provides a list of the available fields in the underlying table or query. You add the desired fields to your label by clicking the field name in the list of fields to select it, followed by the right-arrow button. To add punctuation, such as a space or a comma, type the needed punctuation at the desired location. When you want to move to a new line of the label, click below the existing line. After adding all of the needed fields and any desired punctuation, click Next.

6. The dialog box that now appears, as shown in Figure 9.24, asks you to select a sort order. You can click Next to bypass this dialog box, or you can use the options in the dialog box to choose a sort order for the labels. Click the desired field or fields that will determine the sort order followed by the right-arrow button, then click Next. For example, to sort on a field called Zip Code, you would click the Zip Code field, then click the right arrow. (You also could just double-click the Zip Code field.) Then, you would click Next to proceed. To sort on a combination of Last Name and First Name fields with the Last Name field being the first field to sort, you would click the Last Name field, then click the right arrow, then click the First Name field, then click the right arrow, then click Next to proceed.

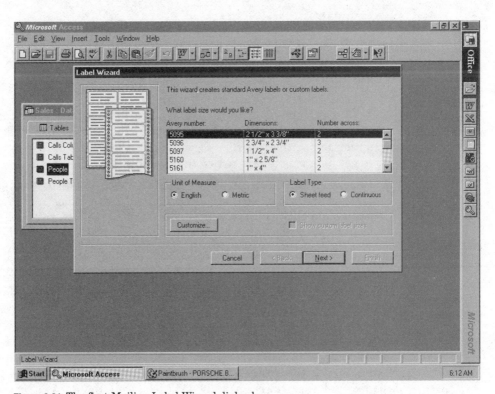

Figure 9.21 The first Mailing Label Wizard dialog box.

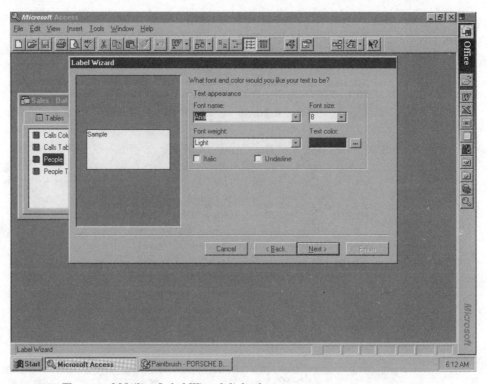

Figure 9.22 The second Mailing Label Wizard dialog box.

7. The last dialog box to appear informs you that the label design is complete, and it provides two buttons: See the labels as they will look printed and Modify the label's design. You can click the first option to see the labels in preview mode, or you can click the second option to see the report in Design view. (You must choose one of the two to get past this dialog box so that you can save the report.)

8. Choose File/Save to save the mailing label. If you are saving the report for the first time, you will be prompted for a name; enter the desired name, and click OK. You can then print the labels at any time just as you would print any other report, by clicking the report in the Database Window to select it and choosing File/Print.

Before you start to design your own mailing labels, you should know the size of the mailing label that you want to use, because mailing labels come in such a wide variety of sizes. The Report Wizards in Access make this easier by including the common Avery mailing label numbers in the choices. If you are not using Avery mailing labels and are unsure of the label dimensions, check the side of the box of labels to see if there is an equivalent Avery number. You should also be sure to use the correct type of labels designed for your printer. Labels designed for laser printers usually don't feed well into dot-matrix printers, and labels designed for dot-matrix printers might damage laser printers.

Mailing Label Tips and Traps

Microsoft designed the Mailing Label Wizard to work as well as possible with standard mailing labels and with a wide range of printers. To do its job, the Mailing Label Wizard makes certain assumptions about your printer, which might or might not be true in your case. Every printer has its own "printable area," or the rectangle on the sheet of paper that the printer can print into. The printer's printable area might not be the same size as the area defined by Access, and when this is the case, problems can occur.

One example of such problems arises with early-generation Hewlett-Packard LaserJet printers, which were designed to print to within ½ in. of the paper's edges. The Mailing Label Wizard, on the other hand, assumes that it can print to within ¼ in. of the paper's edges. If the mailing labels created by the wizard cause text to be cut off when you print the labels, you'll need to go into Design view for the labels and make needed modifications to get the text to print. You can try making the items smaller, you can use smaller fonts, or you can move the fields closer together. You can also try changing the top margin under `Print Setup` so that Access skips printing the first label on each page (of course, this does waste a row of labels). If you can't get the last line of the bottom row of labels to print without getting cut off, you can use the same trick at the bottom margin.

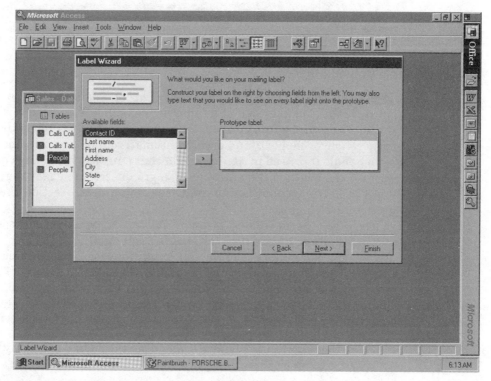

Figure 9.23 The third Mailing Label Wizard dialog box.

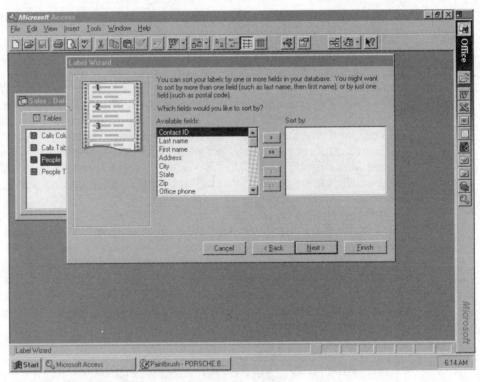

Figure 9.24 The fourth Mailing Label Wizard dialog box.

Creating Multiple-Column Reports

Another challenging type of report that's occasionally needed is a multiple-column report that makes use of a "snaking column." With such a report, your data prints down the first column, then starts again at the top of the page and continues down the next (and each additional) column on the same page. The way to handle this need in Access is to lay out a report with a page header that measures the width of the entire page, a group section header that measures the width of one column, and a multiple-column detail section that contains the snaking columns.

In the Print Setup dialog box for the report, you'll need to define the columns as either Vertical (or snaking columns) or Horizontal. As an example, you can make use of the following steps for 2-in. columns to provide space for three snaking columns on a sheet of 8½-in. by 11-in. paper. If you are using a different paper size, you can adjust your measurements to fit your paper size. These are the steps you can use to create a three-column report using snaking columns:

1. Open the report in Design view, and drag the right edge of any report section out to the report's desired width.

2. From the menus, choose View/Sorting and Grouping.

3. In the Field/Expression box, enter a field (or expression) that will be used to group the data.

4. In the Group Properties section of the Sorting and Grouping dialog box, choose Yes for the Group Header.

5. Use the Label tool in the Toolbox to create a label that will identify the page contents, and put that label in the Page Header section of the report. Click in the box, and enter the desired text for the label. Size the text box so that it is the same width as the Page Header section of the report.

6. Use the Text Box tool in the Toolbox to create a text box that's bound to the field used as the basis for the group. Place this text box in the Group Header section of the report. Place the left edge of the text box along the left edge of the group section, and size the control 2 in. or less in width.

7. In the Detail section of the report, add your desired bound controls (fields) inside the first 2 in. (For reports that use just two columns instead of three, you can make these sections 3 in. wide.)

8. Choose File/Print Setup from the menus.

9. When the Print Setup dialog box appears, click More to show an expanded version of the dialog box.

10. In the Items Across box, enter the number of columns that you want to appear in the Detail section of your report. If necessary, make any needed changes to the row and column spacing settings.

11. In the Item Size section, turn off the Same As Detail check box.

12. In the Width box, enter the number of inches desired for each column.

13. In the Item Layout section of the dialog box, choose Vertical, then click OK.

14. Click anywhere in the Group Header section, then and choose View/ Properties to open the Property window for the header. For the "New Row or Col" property, choose Before Section. Doing this will cause the group header to print once at the top of the column for each new group.

15. Save the report by choosing File/Save, and print it as needed.

Summary

This chapter has provided you with the techniques that you'll need to create reports for your Access applications, whether they are created with the aid of the Report Wizards or through the manual report design process. The chapter also detailed how you can work effectively with relational (or "multitable") reports, how you can handle report sections, and how you can work with mailing labels. With your tables, queries, forms, and reports completed, all you need to bind your Access applications together are macros and the necessary program code stored in modules; macros are covered in more detail in Chapter 11, and you can find the specifics of coding modules in Chapter 4.

10

Using Expressions in Forms and Reports

This chapter details the use of expressions in Access, with a specific view toward effectively using them in forms and reports. You make use of expressions throughout Access, particularly in queries where they form the basis of the criteria that selects a given set of records. In addition to their use in queries, Access expressions can accomplish much when properly used in various aspects of form and report design. In particular, you can use expressions for the following form and report-related tasks:

- Including sum totals or averages for page summaries, group summaries, or for an entire report
- Adding system variables like the current page number or the system date and time to a report
- Placing a calculated field in a form
- Performing validity checks on data entered into the controls of a form

What's an Expression?

Simply put, an expression is nothing more than a combination of values, operators, functions, and identifiers (or names of Access objects) that evaluates (or calculates) to some value. In forms and reports, expressions typically are used to provide a value that's not directly stored in a table but that can be obtained indirectly. Take, for example, a Cost field in a Sales table. If you need a form to display a value that includes a sales tax of 8%, you could place the following expression within a control on the form:

```
=[Cost] + ([Cost] * .08)
```

The result would be the current value in the Cost field, plus 8% of that value.

Note that the Access objects in the previous expression (the field name in this case) have been surrounded with square brackets. This isn't a requirement, unless the object names contain spaces. I recommend their use in all cases just to get in the habit of surrounding object names with brackets, so you don't accidentally omit them when they really are needed.

Operators

The parts of an expression that really do the work in describing what needs to be done are the *operators*; they perform the operations on the values that result in the eventual calculation. Besides the usual math operators for addition (+), subtraction (-), multiplication (*), and division (/), Access also provides operators used for logical (true/false) operations, for comparisons (greater than, less than, and the like), for concatenation (combining text strings), and for pattern matching. Table 10.1 shows the commonly used Access operators.

When it comes to using operators in your expressions, you need to keep the order of precedence in mind. In any expression, exponentiation (powers of) gets performed first, followed by negation (assigning a minus sign to a positive value), then multiplication and division, then concatenation, and finally logical operations. When operations have an equal precedence (as is the case with addition and subtraction), Access handles the order of precedence by working from left to right. Ignoring this order of precedence can lead to real problems in your calculations; for example, if you want to add an item cost plus a shipment cost together and then multiply the total by 6%, you wouldn't want an expression like this:

```
=[Item Cost] + [Ship Cost] * .06
```

because Access would multiply the shipment cost by .06, then would add the results of that calculation to the Item Cost. To force a change in the order of precedence, you add parenthesis wherever you need them. When you include parenthesis in an expression, Access calculates from the innermost pair of parenthesis and works outward. Using the previous example, you could force a correct calculation of the previous expression by including parenthesis to force the addition operation to be performed first, as in this example:

```
=([Item Cost] + [Ship Cost]) * .06
```

Identifiers

Identifiers are the actual names that you use to refer to the Access objects within your expressions, such as the names of fields in a table or the names of controls in a form. If, for example, you wanted to refer to a control named Cust ID in a form called Customers, the identifier you could use in an expression would be:

```
Forms![Customers]![Cust ID]
```

In another example, assuming two fields named Quantity Sold and Unit Cost exist in the current table, the expression:

```
=[Unit Cost] * [Quantity Sold]
```

Table 10.1

Math Operators	
Symbol	Description
*	Multiplication
+	Addition
-	Subtraction
/	Division
\	Integer division (divides numbers and returns integer part of the result)
^	Exponentiation (raises one number to the power of another)
Mod	Modulus (divides two numbers and returns just the remainder)

Comparison Operators	
Symbol	Description
<	Less than
<=	Less than or equal to
>	Greater than
>=	Greater than or equal to
=	Equal to
<>	Not equal to

Logical Operators	
Symbol	Description
And	Both comparisons are true
Or	Either comparison is true
Not	Comparison is not true
Xor	One comparison or the other is true, but not both ("exclusive Or")

Concatenation, Pattern-Matching, and Miscellaneous	
Symbol	Description
&	String concatenation (combines two text strings)
Like	String comparison (text matches a given pattern)
Between	Value falls within a specified range

could be used to calculate the product of both values. In this example, both [Unit Cost] and [Quantity Sold] are identifiers. They can be used as such to identify their respective Access objects, which in this case are fields of the current table. Remember that, when Access objects contain a space as part of the object name, you must surround the name by square brackets. (The brackets are optional if the object name has no spaces.)

Literals

Literals, as the name implies, are actual values. Text, numbers, and dates are examples of literals, as in the case of "George Washington," 42.157, or 04/15/96. Remember that literal text strings must be enclosed in quotes; if the quotes are omitted, Access assumes that the text string is a variable name. Also, dates must be surrounded with number signs, as in #04/15/96#.

Constants

Constants are statements representing string, logical, or number values that do not change. Examples of constants include Yes, No, True, False, and Null. As an example of the use of a constant, consider the DefaultValue property for a Yes/No control in a form. The default value for the control could be set to No by using the expression =No or =False in the DefaultValue property.

Functions

You can think of *functions* as special-purpose programs, designed to perform a calculation without the need to write the corresponding VBA code that would be needed to handle the calculation. Most functions accept data, perform a calculation of some kind based on the data supplied, and return some sort of value. A few functions (like the Date() function) don't need a value supplied, but nevertheless return a value. You can use the Access functions to perform complex math operations, to test for certain conditions, to return values integral to the system (like the current date or time), to convert data from one type to another, to manipulate data, and more. Access offers dozens of different functions, for handling tasks such as converting a string of characters to all lowercase, returning a value indicating the day of the week, calculating the sum of a group of values, or returning the current time.

Using Expressions in Forms and Reports

The expression that you need to accomplish a given task can be typed directly into a text box control or entered into the ControlSource property of the control. While typing the expression directly into the control is easier than opening the Properties window to get to the ControlSource property, the advantage of the second method is that it provides easy access to the Expression Builder if you want it. The Expression Builder (detailed in the steps that follow) can reduce the possibility of errors in your expressions, because it always correctly spells function names, object names, and the like. You can use the steps that follow to enter expressions into controls, with or without the aid of the Expression Builder.

To enter an expression into a text box directly, use these steps:

1. Open the form or report in Design view.
2. Choose the desired text box on the form or report.
3. In the text box, enter an equal symbol (=), then enter the text of the desired expression.

To enter an expression into the ControlSource property of the Property window, perform these steps:

1. Open the form or report in Design view.

2. Choose the desired text box on the form or report.

3. Choose View/Properties from the menus, or click the Properties button in the toolbar to open the Property window for the text box control.

4. Click in the ControlSource property.

5. To enter the expression directly, type an equal symbol (=), then enter the text of the expression. If desired, press Shift–F2 to open the Zoom box (Figure 10.1) to see the entire expression. (You also can use the Expression Builder, by performing the steps that follow.)

6. To use the Expression Builder, click the Build button to the right of the ControlSource property. In a moment, the Expression Builder appears, as shown in Figure 10.2.

Using the Expression Builder, you can build the needed expression by clicking desired operator buttons to add the operators where needed and by clicking desired items within the list boxes followed by the Paste button (you also can double-click the desired item in the list boxes). As you choose

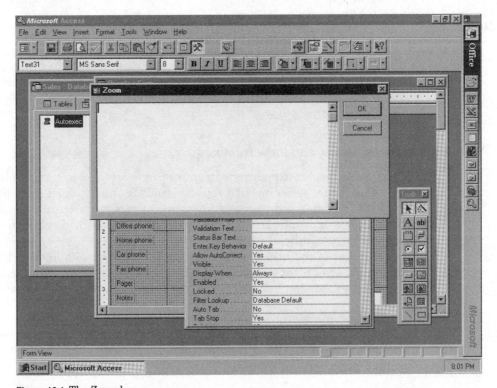

Figure 10.1 The Zoom box.

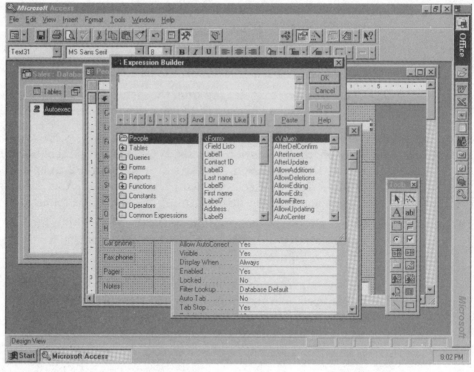

Figure 10.2 The Expression Builder.

the desired items, you will see them in the window at the top of the Expression Builder. When you are finished constructing the expression, click OK to put away the Expression Builder and insert the expression into the ControlSource property of the control.

Working with Dates, Times, and Page Numbers

One typical use for expressions in your forms and reports is to display the current date, time, or both. With reports, you also might need page numbers at the bottom of selected pages or all pages in reports. You can use the expressions shown in Table 10.2 within text box controls to display the date, the time, or page numbers.

In the case of the last two expressions, they can be combined to indicate the page number of a total number of pages in a report. For example, you might enter this expression in a text box control located in the Page Footer of a report:

```
="Page " & Page & " of " & Pages
```

If you were printing page 4 of a 12-page report, the text box would produce the text "Page 4 of 12" at the designated location in the Page Footer for the printed page.

Table 10.2

Expression	Displays
=Date()	Current date
=Time()	Current time
=Now()	Current date and time
=Page	Current page number in a report
=Pages	Total number of pages in a report

Using Concatenation

The concatenation operator (&) often is used in reports, especially with mailing labels, to combine text strings within a report. This technique usually arises when you need to combine fields such as a city, state, and postal code into a single text box. As an example, consider a table with fields named City, State, and Zip Code. With such a table used as the data source for a report, you might use an expression like this one in a text box control of the report:

```
=[City] & " " & [State] & ", " & [Zip Code]
```

which could produce a text string like "Hempstead, NY 11712."

As you work with text, remember that you can make use of the string functions within Access—such as Left(), Mid(), and Right()—to print a portion of text. As an example, if the table or query that you are using contains a field called Middle Name, and you want to show just the first character of the entry in that field, you would use an expression like =Left([Last name],1) to show the first character stored in the field.

Using the IIF Function

Access offers an Immediate IF function (IIF()) that can be helpful in expressions in forms and reports. You use the IIF() function when you need to display or print one set of data if one condition is true and another set of data if the condition is false. For example, a Yes/No field of a table named Insured would contain a logical value of 1 to indicate a yes entry, or 0 to indicate a no entry. In a report, if you wanted to show the value stored in the field using a text string rather than the logical values, you could use a text box containing an expression like the following:

```
=IIF(Insured = 1, "Patient is insured", "Patient has no insurance")
```

By placing the expression in the ControlSource property for the control (or by typing it directly into the text box), you would give the report the ability to display the proper text string depending on the contents of the logical field.

Adding Summary Controls

You can add summary calculations to your reports by including calculated controls at the desired locations in group footers, page footers, or report footers. Use the SUM() function to provide a sum total of a numeric value, the AVG() function to provide an average of a group of values, and the COUNT() function to provide a count of the values. For example, given a number field named Attorney Charges that's used to store a currency value for billing costs for every client in a table, you could include a text box with this expression in the page footer of a report:

```
=SUM([Attorney Charges])
```

When you use these functions in your reports, remember that the basis of the calculation is controlled by which footer you place the control into containing the expression. As an example, if you add the control to a group section of a report, the value would reflect all records in the group. If you add the control to the page section, the value would reflect all records printed on that page. If you add the control to the report header or to the report footer, the value would reflect all records printed in the report.

Summary

Expressions are an important aid in displaying information that users need within the forms and reports of an application. By putting the techniques detailed in this chapter to work, you'll ensure that your forms and reports provide your users with what they need. The chapter that follows details the use of Access macros, which are the last of the component pieces that you'll need to assemble your complete applications.

Implementing Macros in Access Applications

This chapter details the use of *macros*, which are a fundamental part of your work in creating applications in Access. Macros can be used for a wide variety of tasks in Access; they can help you automate routine operations and make better use of your tables, queries, forms, and reports. Macros are the key to providing much of any complete application in Access, as they can provide complete menu-driven systems that will shield novice users from the complexities of Access.

What's a Macro?

In Access, a macro is a list of actions that you specify in advance. When you run the macro, Access carries out the list of actions for you. As an example, if you routinely open two forms and three reports and work most with these throughout the day, a macro can be designed to automatically carry out these actions. Going further into the realm of applications development, a menu option that prints a report can do so by calling a macro that opens the desired report in Print view.

If you have used macros with other software products, you might be accustomed to the concept of *macro recorders*, where you activate a "recording" capability of the software, then carry out a group of actions (such as a series of menu selections). Later, when you play back the macro, it duplicates the actions that you recorded. If this is your idea of macros, be warned that Access is very different in its approach. There is no "recorder" feature. With Access macros, you must specifically tell the macro what actions you want performed by choosing actions in a macro window. While this initially might sound more complicated to some, the benefits of the Access approach go far beyond any apparent added complexities. It is this ability to specify a wide range of actions in an Access macro that gives macros the power to manipulate your database in so many different ways.

Creating a Macro

To create a macro, click the Macros tab in the Database Window, then click New. When you do this, a new Macro window opens, as shown in Figure 11.1.

The macro window can be divided into two areas: an upper portion, which contains *actions* and *comments*, and a lower portion which displays *action arguments*, as shown in the figure. Depending on how your display options have been set up, you also might see columns in the upper portion titled Conditions and Macro Names. (The use of these columns will be detailed later in the chapter.)

In the upper portion of the Macro window within the Action column, you select or list the *actions* that you want the macro to perform; how to do so is described shortly. In the Comment column, you can enter a comment describing what the macro does. Such comments are purely optional and provide a reference to help you remember how your macros operate.

When you open a macro in Design view, the toolbar takes on the appearance shown in Figure 11.1. Table 11.1 explains the purpose of the buttons in the Macro Window toolbar.

Specifying Actions

Much of your work in designing macros will consist of telling the macro what you want Access to do by means of *actions*. Actions are simply instructions that tell

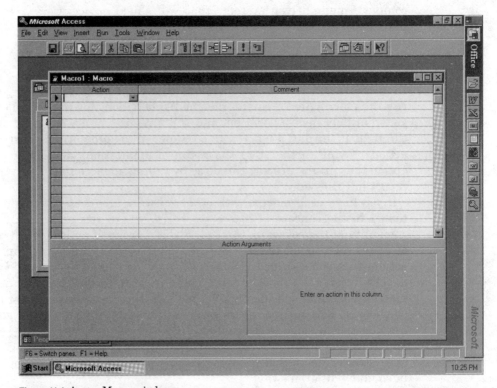

Figure 11.1 A new Macro window.

Table 11.1

Toolbar button	Meaning
Save	Saves current macro
Macro Names	Displays or hides Macro Names column
Conditions	Displays or hides Conditions column
Run	Runs the current macro
Step Into	Runs a single step of the macro at a time
Database Window	Displays the Database Window
Build	Displays the Expression Builder
Undo	Undoes most recent action
Cue Cards	Displays the Cue Cards main menu
Interface Help	Displays the Interface Help pointer used to obtain context-sensitive help

Access what type of task to perform. An action might be the opening of a particular form, the running of a query, or the selection of a series of menu commands. While actions are named using a specific syntax, you need not worry about the precise syntax, because you can choose the desired actions from a pull-down list. You specify the actions that you want the macro to perform in the Action column of the macro window. To specify an action, you perform the following steps:

1. In the Macro window, click the first empty cell in the Action column. Click the down arrow, or press Alt–down arrow to display the action list.

2. Choose the desired action from the list. (Note that you also can type the name of the action you want to add.) If desired, type an optional comment for the action in the Comment column.

3. In the bottom portion of the window, specify the arguments for the action (if any are desired).

As a simple example, perhaps you want a macro to open the People form in the Sales database and maximize the form so that it fills the Access window. In the first empty cell of the Action column, you would click the down arrow and choose Open Form from the list box. You then could enter an optional comment such as "Open the People form" in the Comment column. Then, in the Action Arguments area at the bottom of the macro window, you could click in the Form Name text box and type People or click the down arrow and select the form name, People, from the list box. This would complete the first action required by the macro.

Because the macro needs one more action (i.e., maximizing the form to full-size in the window), you would click in the next empty cell of the Action column, click the down arrow, and choose Maximize from the list. (Again, you could add a comment if desired, but remember that comments are optional.) At this point, your macro window might resemble the example shown in Figure 11.2.

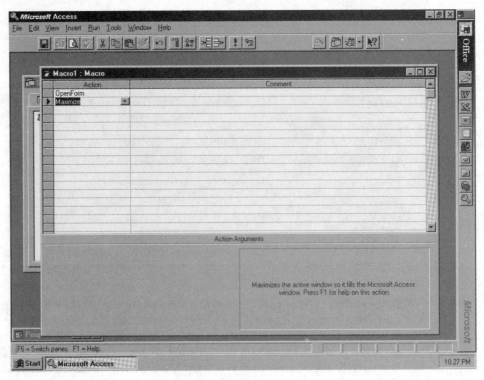

Figure 11.2 An example of a completed macro.

If you then save the macro (by choosing File/Save from the menus) and run the macro (by clicking the Run button in the toolbar), you'll see that the macro performs the specified actions. The People form is opened and maximized to fill the Access window. (For more on saving and running macros, see "Saving Macros" and "Running Macros" later in this chapter.)

Most macro actions have arguments that apply to the action. Arguments can be thought of as specific definitions for an action. Arguments provide additional information needed by Access to handle the task exactly as you prefer. As an example, the OpenQuery action, which opens a query, requires the name of the desired query as an argument. Arguments often also provide additional information. For example, in the case of a form, arguments can indicate whether the form should be opened in Form view, Design view, or Print Preview and whether the form should allow editing or be used in a display-only ("read-only") mode of operation. A few macro actions, such as Maximize and Minimize, have no arguments. Table 11.2 shows the available macro actions, along with their purposes and arguments.

Using Drag-and-Drop to Specify Actions

One way to specify actions is to choose them from the list box. Another way is to use a method called *drag-and-drop*, in which you click and drag an object

Table 11.2

Action	Purpose	Arguments
Add Menu	Adds a drop-down menu to a custom menu bar	Menu Name Menu Macro Name Status Bar Text
ApplyFilter	Applies a filter, query, or SQL statement to a table, form, or report to restrict available records	Filter Name Where condition
Beep	Causes a beep to sound through the PC speaker	(No arguments)
CancelEvent	Cancels the event that caused Access to run the macro	(No arguments)
Close	Closes an object by name, or if no specific object is specified, closes the active window	Object Type Object Name
CopyObject	Copies the specified object to another database Destination Database	New Name Source Object Type Source Object Name
DeleteObject	Deletes the specified object	Object Type Object Name
DoMenuItem (Run Command in Access 97)	Performs a menu command	Menu Bar Menu Name Command Subcommand
Echo	Determines whether the screen is updated as the macro runs	Echo On Status Bar Text
FindNext	Finds next record meeting criteria previously specified by the FindRecord criteria	(No arguments)
FindRecord	Finds the first record meeting criteria specified by the arguments	Find What Where Match Case Direction Search As Formatted
GoToControl	Move the focus to a specified control	Control Name
GoToPage	Move the focus to the first control on a specified page	Page Number Right Down
GoToRecord	Move the focus to a specified record	Object Type Object Name Record Offset
Hourglass	Change the mouse pointer to an hourglass	Hourglass On
Maximize	Maximize the current window	(No arguments)
Minimize	Minimize the current window	(No arguments)
MoveSize	Move or resize the current window	Right Down Width Height

Table 11.2 *(continued)*

Action	Purpose	Arguments
MsgBox	Displays a message box	Message Beep Type Title
OpenForm	Opens a form	Form Name View Filter Name Where Condition
OpenModule	Opens the specified Access Basic module	Module Name Procedure Name
OpenQuery	Opens a query	Query Name View Data Mode
OpenReport	Opens a report	Report Name View Filter Name Where Condition
OpenTable	Opens a table	Table Name View Data Mode
Print	Prints the current object	Print Range Page From Page To Print Quality Copies Collate Copies
Quit	Quits Access	Options
Rename	Renames the specified object	New Name Object Type Old Name
RepaintObject	Completes any screen updates for the specified object	Object Type Object Name
Requery	Requeries the source of the specified control	Control Name
Restore	Restores a maximized or minimized window to its prior size	(No arguments)
RunApp	Runs a Windows or DOS-based application from within Access	Command Line
RunCode	Runs an Access Basic procedure	Function Name
RunMacro	Runs another macro	Macro Name Repeat Count Repeat Expression
RunSQL	Runs a query using its corresponding SQL statement	SQL Statement

Table 11.2 *(continued)*

Action	Purpose	Arguments
SelectObject	Selects the specified object	Object Type Object Name In Database Window
SendObject	Sends the specified Access object in the form of a Microsoft Mail message	Object Type Object Name Output Format To Cc Bcc Subject Message Text Edit Message
SendKeys	Sends keystrokes to Access or to another Windows-based application	Keystrokes Wait
SetValue	Sets the value of a field, control, or property	Expression Item
SetWarnings	Turn system messages on or off	Warnings On
ShowAllRecords	Removes any filter currently in effect from the active table, dynaset, or form	(No arguments)
ShowToolbar	Displays or hides a toolbar	Toolbar Name Show
StopAllMacros	Stops all macros currently running	(No arguments)
StopMacro	Stops the current macro	(No arguments)
TransferDatabase	Imports or exports data between the current database and another database	Transfer Type Database Type Database Name
TransferSpreadsheet	Imports or exports data between the current database and a spreadsheet file	Transfer Type Spreadsheet Type Table Name File Name Has Field Names Range
TransferText	Imports or exports text between the current database and a text file	Transfer Type Specification Name Table Name File Name Has Field Names

from the Database Window into the Action column of the Macro window. While you cannot use this method for all types of actions, you can use it to perform actions that open any database object (such as a table, form, query, or report). To specify a macro action using drag-and-drop, perform the following steps:

1. Move and size the Macro Window and the Database Window so that you can see them both at the same time. (One quick way to make both windows visible is to choose Window/Tile Horizontally or Window/Tile Vertically from the menus.)

2. In the Database Window, click the tab for the kind of object that you want the macro to open. As an example, if you want your macro to open a report, you would click the Reports tab in the Database Window.

3. Locate the desired object by name, and click and drag the object to a cell in the Action column of the Macro window.

As an example, consider Figure 11.3. In the figure, the form named "Calls" has been dragged to the Action column of a new macro. As a result, Access has automatically entered "OpenForm" as an action. Within the Action Arguments portion of the Macro window, Access has entered "Calls" as the form name.

You can use drag-and-drop to have one macro run another macro. Whenever you drag an existing macro to the Action column of a macro window, Access adds an action that runs the existing macro as part of the new macro.

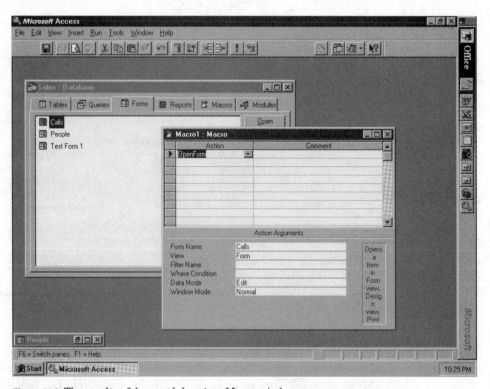

Figure 11.3 The results of drag-and-drop in a Macro window.

Changing Existing Arguments

You can change the existing arguments for any macro by performing the following steps:

1. Open the desired macro in Design view, and click in the row for the desired action to make sure that the row is the currently selected row in the macro.

2. Click in the desired Action Argument row at the bottom of the Macro Window. If a down arrow appears, you can click on the arrow, then choose an argument from the list. If no down arrow appears, you must type your desired argument into the box.

Tip: If you are unsure about what response is needed to an argument, you can click in the row for that argument, then press the Help (F1) key. The Help window that appears will contain specific details about the type of argument you are working with.

Moving and Deleting Actions

If you decide to change the actions that a macro uses, you can easily do so without starting all over again. Access lets you move or delete actions in a macro. To move an action, first click the row selector at the left edge of the Macro Window to select the row containing the desired action, then click again and drag the row to the new desired location. To delete an action, select the desired row by clicking the row selector at the left edge of the window, then press the Del key (or choose Edit/Delete).

Saving Macros

Macros must be saved before you can run them. You can save a macro by choosing File/Save or File/Save As from the menus. If you choose File/Save and you are saving the macro for the first time or if you choose File/Save As, Access will prompt you for a name for the macro by displaying the Save As dialog box (Figure 11.4).

You can enter any name of up to 64 characters, including spaces. Click OK, and the macro will be saved.

If you attempt to close a Macro window that contains a new macro that you haven't saved, Access will warn you that the macro has not been saved and will ask if you want to save it. If you click Yes, Access displays the Save As dialog box, and you can enter the desired name for the macro and click OK to save it.

Running Macros

There are a number of ways that you can run a macro. One way that's common with applications is to attach the macro to a command button so that the macro runs when the user clicks a button on a form. You also can design custom

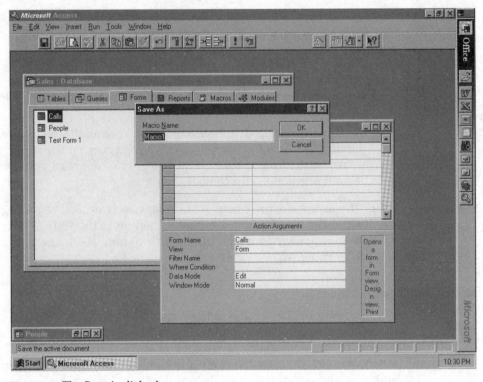

Figure 11.4 The Save As dialog box.

menus and attach your macros to commands on those menus. This topic also is detailed later in the chapter. To run a macro directly, use either of these methods you prefer:

- *To run a macro from the Database Window:* In the Database Window, click the Macros tab to display all your macros. Click the desired macro by name, then click Run. Note that you also can double-click the desired macro by name in the Database Window; double-clicking is the same as clicking a macro name to select it, then clicking the Run button.

- *To run a macro from the Macro Window:* If the Macro Window is the active window, click the Run button in the toolbar, or choose Macro/Run from the menus (in Access 95), or choose Tools/Macro/Macros and enter the macro name in the dialog box (in Access 97).

Copying and Deleting Macros

You can copy and delete existing macros. Copying macros saves time when you want to create a macro that is similar in design to an existing macro. Rather than creating the new macro from scratch, copy the macro to a new name, then make the desired changes to the new macro. To copy a macro, perform the following steps:

1. In the Database Window, click the Macros tab to display all your macros. Click the desired macro that you want to copy.

2. Choose Edit/Copy from the menus (or press Ctrl–C). Then, choose Edit/Paste from the menus (or press Ctrl–V).

3. In the Paste As dialog box that appears, type a name for the new macro, then click OK.

You can copy macros from one database to another. To do so, use the previous instructions; however, before performing Step 3, close the current database and open the database where you want to copy the macro to.

To delete an existing macro, in the Database Window, click the Macros tab to display all your macros. Click the desired macro that you want to delete, then press the Del key and click OK in the confirmation box that appears.

Adding Macros to Forms and Reports

A common use for macros in Access (and one that is emphasized heavily for applications development) is to attach them to forms or reports. Macros can be dragged from the Database Window onto the design surface of a form to add a command button. When the user clicks the button in the completed form, the macro runs. Macros also can be attached to forms or reports by naming the macros in various properties of the form or report.

As an example, you might want a macro to run when a certain event occurs, such as the opening of a report. The macro might provide a confirmation box that the user would have to accept before the printing of a report would begin. Another common use is in the validation of data; you might want a macro to validate data that is entered into a particular field of a form. Access recognizes events for forms, controls on a form, reports, and report sections. You can attach a macro to a form or a report with the following steps:

1. Open the desired form or report in Design view.

2. Choose View/Properties to open the Properties window, and type or choose the macro name in the appropriate property. The property determines when Access runs the macro.

One excellent way to get an idea of how macros can be attached to forms or reports is to examine examples of applications. Those provided on the CD-ROM further illustrate how you can attach macros to your forms and reports.

Note: If you are attaching a macro in a macro group to a property, be sure to include the name of the macro group, along with the name of the macro. In such cases, you would enter macrogroupname.macroname in the Property text box.

Synchronizing Forms Using Macros

One important ability of Access macros is to synchronize two forms. With this technique, you can show a record or records on one form and, at the same time, display related records on another form. (Another way to handle this kind of task is to create a form that contains a subform, as detailed in Chapter 5.) However, when, for one reason or another, you prefer to use separate forms, you must use this technique of synchronizing them with a macro.

As an example of this type of task, you might have one form that shows customer names and addresses. Each time that you display a different customer, you might want another form to show all orders (stored in an orders table) placed by that customer. You can synchronize two forms by performing these steps:

1. Create a macro that contains an OpenForm action. Use this action to open the second form that you want synchronized with the first form.

2. In the Where Condition action argument of the OpenForm action, specify the value of a control on the second form equal to the value of the same control on the first form. As an example, if the common field is named Customer ID and the first form is named Customers, you might enter an expression like this:

```
[Customer ID] = Forms![Customers]![Customer ID]
```

Attach the macro to the first form, using the OnPush property. When you click the command button, the second form will appear with the matching records displayed.

With this technique, the Where Condition argument that you specify in the macro is the key to synchronizing the forms. In the example described earlier, the Customer ID control on the second form is set to the value of the Customer ID control on the first form. When opened, the two forms show the record for the same customer.

Using Conditions in a Macro

Access lets you use conditional expressions in macros to determine whether the macro is carried out. By adding a condition, you force the macro to follow one of two paths, depending on whether a specified condition is true or false. As an example, you might have a macro attached to a form that contains fields for addresses. If you entered the expression [City] = "Dallas" in the Condition box of the macro, the macro would run only when Dallas was entered into the City field of the form. You can enter a conditional expression in a macro by performing the following steps:

1. From the menus, choose View/Conditions (or click the Conditions button on the toolbar). This causes the Condition column to appear in the Macro Window.

2. In the Condition column, enter an expression in the row where you want to place the condition.

3. In the Action column, choose the desired action that you want Access to perform when the specified condition is true.

Tip: If a macro action has a long argument or condition, remember that you can display it in the Zoom box by clicking the desired cell in the Macro Window and pressing Shift–F2. The expressions that you enter can contain operators, literals, functions, and/or identifiers. Operators identify the operations to be performed on the other parts of the expression. In a conditional expression, you can use the math operators (+ – * /), the comparison operators (= <> < > <= >=), the concatenation operator (&), the logical operators (AND, NOT, OR), and other operators (BETWEEN, IN, LIKE).

Identifiers can be used to refer to controls within forms and reports. Identifiers contain object names, separated by exclamation marks. You use the format, Forms![form-name]![control-name], to refer to a control within a form, and you use the format, Reports![report-name]![control-name], to refer to a control within a report. As an example, perhaps you want a macro to run if a value entered into the Salary field of a form named Employees is greater than $20.50. In such a case, you might use an expression like the following in the Conditions column of the macro:

```
Forms![Employees]![Salary] > 20.50
```

Literals are literal values and can be characters, dates, or numeric values. Character strings must be enclosed in quotes, and number signs (#) must be used around dates, as shown in the following expressions:

```
Forms![Orders]![Payment] = "VISA"
Forms![Employees]![Hire Date] >= #01/01/96#
```

How Conditional Macros Execute

When a macro runs, Access checks the Condition column for an expression. If none is present, the macro runs. If a condition is present, Access first evaluates the condition, and if the condition is true, the macro runs. Access continues to perform any additional actions within the macro, as long as an ellipsis is present in the Condition column for the additional actions. If Access encounters a blank entry in the Condition column, another expression, or the end of the macro, execution of the macro stops.

If the condition is false, Access skips ahead to the next blank row in the Condition column, to the next entry (other than an ellipsis), or to the next macro name. As an example, consider the macro shown in Figure 11.5.

If the condition shown in the Condition box, Forms![Employees]![Department] Is Null, is true, a message box that contains a warning message is displayed and the insertion pointer is moved to the Department field of the form. If the condition is false, only the last action of the macro (i.e., maximizing the form) is performed.

Using Macros for Data Validation

One useful task for macros is that of data validation in a form. As shown in Chapters 5 and 7, you can add validation rules to tables or to the fields that you place in a form. However, there might be times when you need a more complex

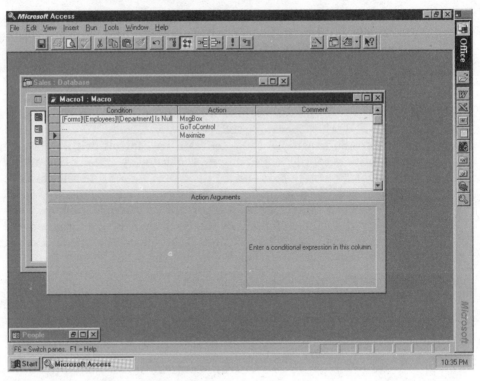

Figure 11.5 An example of a conditional macro.

type of validation than is possible with the validation rules present in tables and forms. As an example, perhaps a `Salary` field in a table of employees has different acceptable ranges, depending on which department an employee is assigned to. This type of validation cannot be handled with validation rules in a table or a form, but you can handle this task with macros.

In the Condition column of the macro, you enter the desired condition that will validate the data. To call the macro, you name the macro within the On Exit or the Before Update property of the control. If you always want the entry validated (even when there is no change to the data), use the On Exit property. If you want to validate the data only after it has been changed, use the Before Update property.

As an example, consider the form shown in Figure 11.6. In this example, there are multiple ranges of allowable salary amounts. Salaries for employees in the Admin department can range from 6.50 to 15.00; in the Manufacturing department, from 4.50 to 18.00; in the Sales department, from 7.00 to 22.00; and in the Service department, from 6.00 to 20.00. The different validations for each department are handled by the macro shown in Figure 11.7. The conditions test for the various departments and, if a value entered into the `Salary` field falls outside of the acceptable range for that department, an appropriate warning dialog appears.

The macro shown is named in the Before Update property of the Salary field in the form shown earlier in Figure 11.6. If a user enters an amount that is outside of the acceptable range, the CancelEvent action in the macro cancels the update made by the user.

Creating Macro Groups

As you grow proficient with designing macros, you will find that the collection of macros in the Macro window can grow quite large. This is particularly true when you are designing complete applications, because you might have a collection of macros used for common tasks, such as manipulating forms, moving to various records, and running different queries. To keep your collections of macros from getting out of hand, you can group related macros together.

Any number of macros can be stored in a *macro group*. A macro group is simply a macro window that contains more than one macro. You identify each macro by providing it with its own title in the Macro Name column of the Macro window. (By default, this column does not appear, but you can show and hide it at will by clicking the Macro Names button in the toolbar or by choosing View/Macro Names from the menus.) Note that it normally is not a good idea to group together macros that you want to run directly from the Database

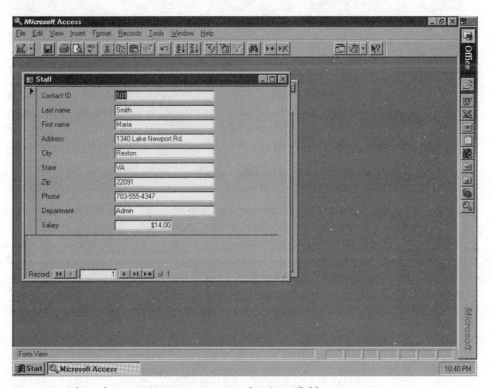

Figure 11.6 A form that contains Department and Salary fields.

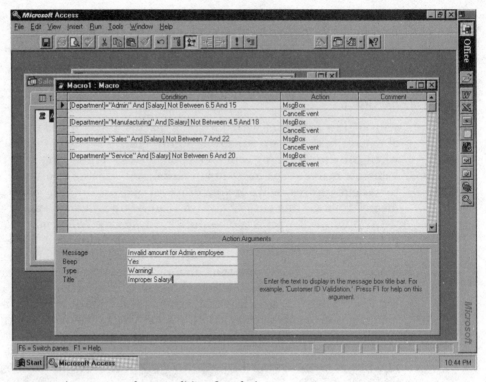

Figure 11.7 A macro to evaluate conditions for salaries.

Window, because running the desired macro gets a little more complex, as described shortly. You normally use this technique of placing multiple macros in a macro group when you want to run the macros from command buttons or menus options within an application. You can create a macro group by performing the following steps:

1. Click the Macro button in the Database Window, then click New to open a new Macro Window.

2. If the Macro Names column is not visible in the window, click the Macro Names button on the toolbar or choose View/Macro Names to display the Macro Names column.

3. In the Macro Names column, enter a macro name of your choosing for each set of actions that make up a macro. Whenever a macro contains more than one action, you should include the macro name only beside the first action. Leave the macro name column beside the other actions blank.

As an example, consider Figure 11.8. In the figure, the Macro window contains three separate macros. Each macro is identified by its name in the Macro Name column. The People Form macro opens the People form and maximizes it, the Calls Form macro does the same for the Calls form, and the People Report macro opens and prints the People report.

Running a macro that's stored in a macro group is somewhat different, because you need to identify which of the macros stored in the group should be run. You do this by referring to the macro by the macro group name, followed by a period, followed by the macro name. As an example, in Figure 11.8. the macro group is named "My Forms." If you wanted to run the macro named "Calls Form," you would need to use the title My Forms.Calls Form to refer to the macro name. *Don't* use the Run button in the Macro toolbar to run a macro that's in a macro group; the Run button will run the first macro stored in the macro window, regardless of which macro you actually might want to run.

Macros and Applications Design

As mentioned earlier in the chapter, macros make up much of the glue that binds the pieces of a complete application together. You can use macros to create various objects — such as custom menus, custom toolbars, and dialog boxes — that can be used throughout your applications. The objects that you can add to an application using macros include the following:

■ *Switchboards* — Forms that contain buttons for performing common tasks. Switchboards routinely are used as menus in an application. Figure 11.9 shows the switchboard that is provided with the Northwind Traders application, provided with your copy of Access.

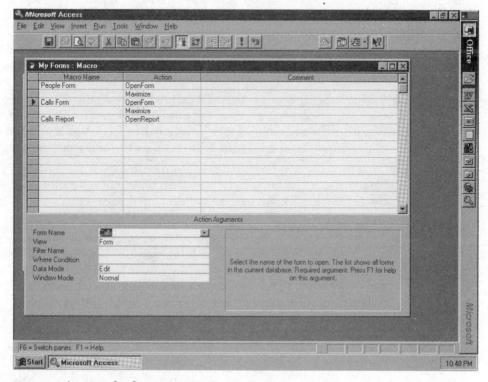

Figure 11.8 An example of a macro group.

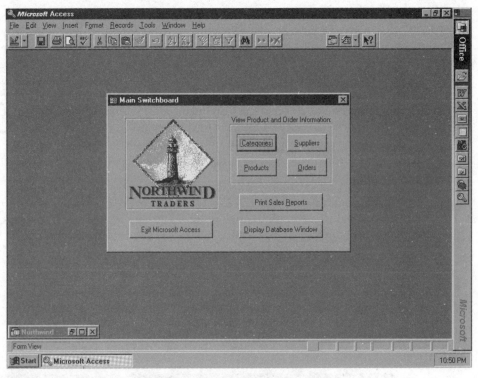

Figure 11.9 The switchboard used by the Northwind Traders application.

- *Custom menus*—Menu bars with pull-down menu options that you can use to replace the standard menu bar that Access provides.

- *Custom dialog boxes*—Forms designed to resemble dialog boxes. You can use dialog boxes to ask users for specialized input or for confirmation before performing an action (such as printing a report). You also could use custom dialog boxes for special functions, such as the entry of a password.

- *Custom toolbars*—Forms that contain buttons purposely designed to resemble a toolbar. The buttons can perform tasks not normally available through the Access menus. For example, you could design a toolbar with buttons that would display the Windows Calculator or Calendar when pressed.

- *Autoexec macros*—Macros that automatically run as soon as a database is opened. Whenever you open a database and a switchboard or a form with menus attached immediately appears, it is the result of an Autoexec macro stored as part of the database. As an example, you might use an Autoexec macro to open a switchboard containing command buttons and to hide the Database Window and the toolbar so that a novice user does not get into trouble with them.

The remainder of this chapter provides tips and techniques for designing all of these objects.

Creating Switchboards

Switchboards are simply blank forms that contain buttons that are used to perform the desired tasks (such as opening a form or printing a report). Because the buttons that you place on the switchboard call macros, you also will need to create the needed macros that respond to the buttons. Switchboard design generally is easier if you create the needed macros, because once they exist, you can easily create the buttons using the drag-and-drop method detailed shortly. (In a nutshell, you click on the macro name in the Database Window and drag the name to the switchboard to create the button.) You can create a switchboard by performing the following steps:

1. Create a macro for each button that you plan to include on the switchboard. For example, if you want to include a button for adding a new record through a form, you will need to create a macro that opens the desired form and moves to the blank record at the end of the table. (When you name your macros, try to give them the same names as you would like to appear on the buttons in the switchboard. Doing so will save you the effort of editing the names within the buttons later, assuming you use the drag-and-drop method of creating the buttons.)

2. In the Database Window, click the Forms tab, then click New to create a new form.

3. In the New Form dialog box that appears, leave the Select a Table/Query box empty, and click Design View, then OK, to open a blank form in Design view. Move and size the form window so that you can see both the form and the Database Window at the same time.

4. In the form's Design window, turn off the Control Wizards option in the Toolbox.

5. In the Database Window, click the Macros tab to display your macros.

6. Click a desired macro in the Database Window, and drag it over to the blank form. When you release the mouse button, a button appears in the form that will call the macro. Using the moving and sizing techniques detailed in Chapter 5, place the button in the desired location on the form and resize it if desired.

7. Repeat Step 6 for every button that you want to place on the switchboard.

8. Add any desired text, graphics, colors, or shading to the switchboard to improve its appearance. (Remember, the switchboard is no more than a blank form, so you can use the form techniques detailed in Chapter 5 to enhance the form's appearance.)

Using One Switchboard to Call Another

You can use one switchboard to call another; that is, you can design a macro to open a switchboard and drag that macro onto another switchboard to create a button. The button, when clicked by the user, will cause the second switchboard to appear. This technique is common in menu design for many applications, because most applications contain too many options to place on a single menu. As an example, a `Print` button on a switchboard could cause another switchboard to appear; the second switchboard could contain buttons for printing a variety of different reports.

To have one switchboard call another, design the second switchboard, using the design techniques outlined previously, and save the second switchboard under the desired name. Next, create a macro that opens the second switchboard. Finally, open (in Design view) the first switchboard, move and size the windows so that you can see both the form that contains the switchboard and the macro window, and click and drag the macro that opens the second switchboard onto the first switchboard. The command button that appears as a result can be used in the application to open the second switchboard.

If your application requires a number of switchboards, you probably will want to store your macros in macro groups, rather than storing each macro individually. Storing the macros in macro groups holds down the clutter in the Database Window and keeps your macros better organized.

Keep in mind that the use of multiple switchboards is not the only way to handle numerous menu options in an application. You also can create custom menus that replace the usual Access menus when your application runs. For more on this topic, see "Creating Custom Menus" later in this chapter.

Starting an Application with Autoexec Macros

Once your application has been completed and tested, you probably will want to automatically start the application's main menu switchboard whenever the database is opened. One way to do this is by means of an *autoexec* macro. (Another way is by setting the Startup options for the database, as detailed in the following chapter.)

An autoexec macro is nothing more than a macro saved under the name Autoexec. Whenever Access opens a database, it looks for a macro named Autoexec. If the macro exists, it is run automatically. To automatically start your application, first design the switchboard that will serve as the main menu for the application, as detailed earlier in this chapter, then create a new macro and place an OpenForm action inside that macro. You also might want to add a Minimize action before the OpenForm action to minimize the Database Window before opening the form; doing so gives the display a cleaner appearance. Under Form Name in the action arguments, choose the form that serves as your switchboard. Close the macro, and when prompted for a name, call the macro `Autoexec`. From that point on, whenever you open the database, the switchboard will appear.

Tip: You can disable an autoexec macro by holding the Shift key while you open the database.

Hiding the Database Window

If you want to clean up your screen area as an application runs, you probably will want to hide the Database Window. You can easily do so by writing a

macro that chooses `Window/Hide` from the menus while the Database
Window is the active window. It normally makes sense to do this immediately
after opening the database, because the Database Window is always the active
window right after the database has been opened. Create a new macro, and in
the Action column, choose `DoMenuItem`. Under Action Arguments, set the
arguments as shown in Table 11.3.

Save the macro under your desired name (such as "Hide Database
Window"). Then, open your form that serves as the main menu switchboard,
enter design mode, open the Properties window for the form, and set the On
Open property to the name of your macro that hides the Database
Window.

Tip: After hiding a Database Window, remember that you can redisplay it at
any time by pressing F11. If, for some reason, you want to redisplay the
Database Window under the control of your application, you can create a
macro that simulates pressing the F11 key. Create the macro, and in the
Action column, choose SendKeys as the action, choose Keystrokes under
Argument, and enter {F11} as a setting. (Remember to include the curly
braces around the key name.)

Assigning Macros to Hotkeys

You also can assign your macros to specific hotkey combinations. One popular
example is the assignment of the Ctrl–P key combination to print the contents
of the active window. In Access, you can assign any macro to a key combination with the following steps:

1. In the Database window, click `Macro`, then click `New` to start a
   new macro.
2. If the Macro Names column is not visible, choose `View/Macro Names` or
   click the `Macro Names` button on the Toolbar.
3. In the Macro Name column, type the key combination to which you want
   to assign the macro. (Table 11.4 shows the acceptable key combinations
   that you can use.) Each key or key combination can call one set of macro
   actions in the macro group.
4. In the Action column, choose the actions that you want to run when the
   key combination is pressed. You can select several actions in sequence, by
   leaving the Macro Name column blank for the rows that follow the key
   combination.

Table 11.3

Argument	Setting
Menu Bar	Database
Menu Name	Window
Command	Hide

5. Repeat Steps 3 and 4 as needed to make any additional assignments, assigning an action or combination of actions to each key combination.

6. Choose File/Save from the menus to save the macro group. When prompted for a name, call the macro AutoKeys. The key assignments will take effect when you save the macro, and they automatically will take effect when the database is opened. Table 11.4 shows the key combinations used to assign keys to macros.

Creating Custom Menus

When your application runs, you might prefer to replace the usual Access menus with a custom menu bar of your own design. (This is one way to provide a user with choices in an Access application; the technique of using switchboards, described earlier in this chapter, is another.) Figure 11.10 shows an example of a custom menu bar in an application.

You can add custom menus to your application with the aid of the Menu Builder. With the Menu Builder, you define the menus and commands that you want on the menu bar, and the Menu Builder creates a series of macros needed to display the menus. Also note that the Menu Builder can create menus that do more than run macros in response to the menu choices. You also can run VBA code or perform standard menu bar choices. Assuming that you have created a series of macros and you want to tie these macros to choices on a menu, you can start the Menu Builder by performing these steps:

1. Open a new, blank form. (The menu will be attached to this form.)

2. From the menus, choose Edit/Select Form to select the form.

Table 11.4

Syntax	Meaning
Carat (^) followed by a letter or number (Example: ^P or ^6)	Ctrl key plus that letter or number; hence, ^P would mean Ctrl–P
{FX}	Any function key named inside the braces
^{FX}	Ctrl plus any function key named inside the braces
+{FX}	Shift plus any function key named inside the braces
{INSERT}	Ins key
^{INSERT}	Ctrl plus Ins key
+{INSERT}	Shift plus Ins key
{DELETE} or {DEL}	Del key
^{DELETE} or ^{DEL}	Ctrl plus Del key
+{DELETE} or +{DEL}	Shift plus Del key

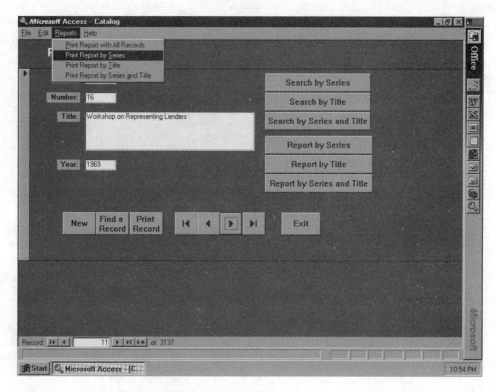

Figure 11.10 An example of a custom menu bar.

3. Choose View/Properties from the menus to open the Property window for the form.

4. Right-click the Menu Bar property, and choose Build from the submenu that appears. In a moment, you see the first Menu Builder dialog box, as shown in Figure 11.11.

5. With Empty Menu Bar selected in the list box, click OK. (The remaining choices let you use existing Access menus as templates for a new menu.)

When you click OK, the Menu Builder dialog box that now appears (Figure 11.12) is used in the construction of the menu. You use the options in this dialog box to define the captions for the menus and what actions should be taken by each of the menu choices that you add.

In the Caption portion of the Menu Builder dialog box, you enter the menu name or the command name as you want it to appear on the menu bar. Under Action and Arguments, you enter the actions that you want the command to carry out, plus any appropriate arguments. In the Status Bar Text box, you can enter optional text that appears in the Status Bar when the menu option is highlighted.

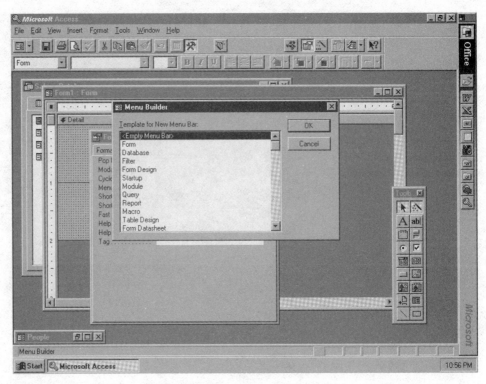

Figure 11.11 The first Menu Builder dialog box.

The lower half of the dialog box shows all of the menus and command that will appear on the menu bar. You can use the left and right arrows to indent and unindent items as you add them, and you use the up and down arrows to move among the available menu items in the lower half of the dialog box. Items that are flush left in the dialog box will appear as menu items at the top of the menu bar. Items that are indented to one level will appear as choices underneath a menu; and items that are indented to two or more levels become submenus of the prior menu.

To define the menu, you perform the following steps.

1. Fill in the caption for a menu or a menu item in the Caption box, then click Next. Repeat this step for all of the menu items.

2. Indent the items that are to represent commands on the menus. For each indented command, choose an action and fill in any needed arguments. The available menu actions are DoMenuItem (which runs a standard Access menu command), RunMacro (to run a macro), or RunCode (to run a VBA procedure).

3. When done with the menu's definition, click OK. Access displays a Save As dialog box; type a name for the menu. Click OK.

You then can save the form to which the menu is attached. When you open the form, the menu takes the place of the standard Access menus.

Creating Custom Dialog Boxes

You also can use blank forms along with macros to create custom dialog boxes. These can be used to query your users for specific information that's needed at a given time. For example, often in printing reports, you might need to ask for criteria that will limit the records printed. As discussed in Chapter 8, one way that you can do this is by means of *parameter queries*, which cause a query, when run, to stop and ask the user for information. However, you might want dialog boxes with a more attractive appearance or more detailed explanations than can be provided by parameter queries. You can create forms that serve as dialog boxes, and the responses typed into those forms can be used within the action arguments of a macro.

The dialog boxes that you create should be *modal,* and *pop-up.* When you design the form, open the Properties window, and set the Pop-Up property to Yes, the Modal property to Yes, the Record Selectors property to No, the Navigation Buttons property to No, and the Scroll Bars property to Neither.

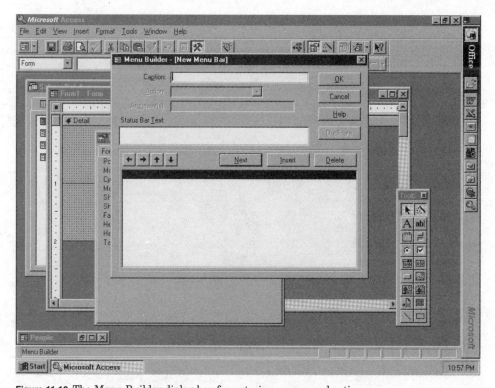

Figure 11.12 The Menu Builder dialog box for entering menus and actions.

Giving the form a modal property means that all other objects on the screen will be unavailable until you close the form, which is what normally is desired for a dialog box of any sort. Normally, you'll want to include one or more command buttons in the form with captions like Print, OK, or Cancel. You can use the following steps to create custom dialog boxes:

1. Create the form that will serve as the dialog box. Using the techniques outlined in Chapter 5, add the controls that will be needed in the dialog box.

2. Create a new macro, and add the desired macro actions that will respond to the buttons in the dialog box. Save the macro.

3. Open the form in design view, open the properties for the form, and in the OnClick property, type the name of the macro that should run.

As an example of a dialog box, consider the form shown in Figure 11.13. This form serves as a dialog box that asks the user to enter a starting date and an ending date in preparation for running a report. Once the user enters the information and clicks on the OK button, the report is printed with records based on the range of dates provided.

The unbound text boxes that will contain the starting and ending dates typed by the user are named (in this example) Start Date and Ending Date,

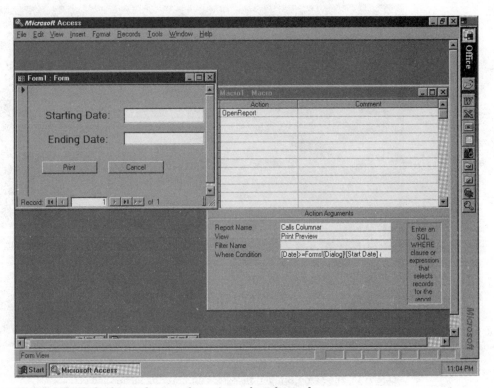

Figure 11.13 A dialog box and macro that prints selected records.

respectively. The desired macro name, "Print from Dialog," is entered in the OnClick property for the `Print` button; therefore, when this button is clicked, the macro named "Print Sales" executes. This macro also is visible in the figure. The macro actions contained in this macro are OpenReport, Print, and Close. Under the OpenReport macro action, a Where condition is specified that uses the values entered into the form. In this case, the Where condition stored in the macro is as follows:

```
[Date]>=Forms![Dialog]![Start Date] and [Date]<=Forms![Dialog]![Ending Date]
```

This condition is the key to obtaining the information from the dialog box. Once the user types the data into the dialog box and clicks OK, Access uses the information to set the condition in the report, and print the specific records.

You can activate the dialog box when needed with an OpenForm action in an appropriate macro. For example, a `Print` button on a switchboard might have an OpenForm action attached to it; the OpenForm action would open the dialog box you designed, and an OK button within the dialog box could call the actual report that then would be printed.

Copying Macros to Other Databases

When it is your job to construct applications on a company-wide basis or for other clients, you soon find yourself using similar macros from application to application. Rather than creating the same or similar macros over and over, you can save time by copying and modifying your macros as needed. You can copy macros from one database to another by using the following steps:

1. In the Database Window, click the `Macros` tab to display all the macros, then click the desired macro to select it.

2. From the menus, choose `Edit/Copy`.

3. Open the database that you want to copy the macro into.

4. In the Database Window, click the `Macros` tab to display all the macros.

5. From the menus, choose `Edit/Paste`. Access will prompt you for a name for the macro. Enter the desired name for the macro, then click OK. The copy of your original macro appears in the Database Window under the name that you've assigned.

You can create a library of your most commonly used macros. For example, in such a library, you might have macros designed to search a table for a given record or to print the current record from a form. Then, each time you design a new application, you can copy macros from your library as needed to handle these common tasks in the new application.

Summary

In Access, macros are an important part of your developer's toolkit. Many applications can be composed entirely of macros if desired, although as Chapter 4 emphasized, there often are reasons for the inclusion of VBA code as well. With macros, along with all the other Access objects detailed throughout this book so far, you can construct complete applications and then get them optimized for client/server use, as the following chapters will explain.

12

Putting the Application Together

Throughout this book so far, I've introduced all the bits and pieces that make up an Access application, and I've detailed how you can work with those various objects—tables, forms, reports, queries, macros, and module code—to design the parts that your application will need. This chapter will continue where Chapter 3 left off, with coverage of the various techniques you'll use to assemble those parts into a complete, working application.

Designing Your Startup Form

A popular approach to applications design is to initially present a startup form to the user. Microsoft uses this approach with all of the applications created by the Database Wizards; as an example, Figure 12.1 shows the startup form for an application created with the aid of the Database Wizards.

When you use this popular approach with your applications, it's important to remember that the startup form is the first thing that the user sees. Hence, you should visually lay out the form so that each possible path is clearly visible. It's also recommended that the users' main task be placed as close to the startup form as possible. For example, in a database that handles business contacts, users spend the most time viewing contacts for an individual in the database. Hence, it would make sense for a form used to view an individual's contacts to be placed no more than a command button or menu option away from the startup screen. In some cases (like this example just described), it might make sense to have a form that contains data serve as the startup screen and to provide buttons or menu options so that users can navigate to other areas. In other cases, where it is impossible to predict what task a user will want to take on first, it makes more sense to go with a startup form designed purely as a switchboard, like that shown earlier in Figure 12.1.

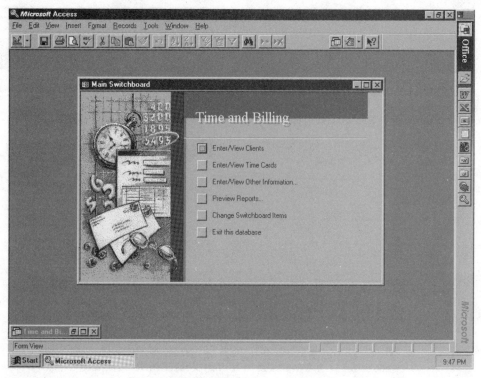

Figure 12.1 A startup form for an application.

Connecting the Dots

Once you have a collection of objects needed to form a complete application, you've still got to bind them together as needed—"connecting the dots," in a sense. To do this, you create the macros and the code needed for event procedures that will be used to open or run the various objects in your application.

As an example, a switchboard button, when clicked, might run an event procedure that runs a report. The report might use a parameter query as its record source, and the expression in the Criteria cell of the parameter query prompts the user for a criteria that limits the records to be printed. The report is tied to the query that is tied to the event procedure that's attached to the command button on the switchboard. It's this process of connecting various objects that will make for a complete Access application. Figure 12.2, for example, shows a startup form that contains data from a table, along with a command button for finding a record.

In Figure 12.3, you see the Properties window for the command button, which shows that the OnClick property is tied to a macro named FindIt. Hence, when the button is clicked, the named macro runs.

In Figure 12.4, you see the structure of the Visual Basic for Applications code used to start the find operation; the code simulates the Edit/Find command under Access to display the Find dialog box.

Because applications design in Access requires such a holistic, "big picture" approach, it makes sense to carefully lay out user options on paper during the applications design process. A written roadmap of sorts can be invaluable when you are designing macros or snippets of VBA program code to accomplish all the tasks that your application must handle.

Providing Navigation Throughout Your Application

One of the important design tasks you must plan and implement is precisely how users will navigate throughout the various tasks of your application. This is where you get to draw on the results of the planning process outlined in Chapter 2. If you put together any flowcharts while in those focus groups with end users, now's the time to drag them out. Much of the navigation that users need to perform inside of an application consists of navigation within a single form and navigation between forms.

Navigation Within the Form

For navigation while inside a form, you can control the natural flow of things by changing the AutoTab and Tab Index properties for a given field in the form.

Figure 12.2 A startup form with a Find button.

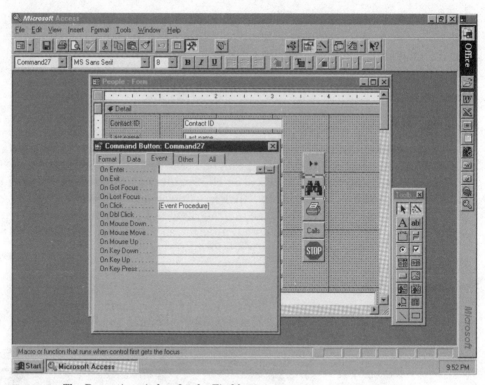

Figure 12.3 The Properties window for the Find button.

Both these properties can be found under the `Other` tab in the Properties window, as shown in Figure 12.5.

The AutoTab property determines whether a tab is generated when the last allowable character is entered into a field. When set to `Yes`, filling a field generates a tab, forcing the focus to move to the next field.

The Tab Index property specifies the control's place in the Tab Index for the entire form. Hence, a control with a Tab Index setting of 4 would be the fourth control reached on the form by pressing the Tab key. If you wanted to have a user move through five controls in succession while filling in data, those controls would have a tab order of 1 through 5, successively.

From a design standpoint, keep in mind that navigation from field to field should follow the natural flow of the task. Don't make users bounce around the form in a strange order to edit data, and group your controls in a logical sequence.

Navigation Between Forms

User navigation between the different forms of an application typically is done with menu options or with command buttons that call the desired forms when needed. Of the two options (menus versus command buttons), command buttons tend to be more readily noticed by the user. With menus, you're dependent on the user to open the appropriate menu to reach the desired choice that will bring up the needed form. However, if you have to provide the user with access to a large number of forms, menus probably will present a less cluttered interface than command buttons.

Tip: If your application needs to present a large number of forms to the user, consider opening all of the forms as the application loads, then hiding them all by using VBA code to set the Visible property of each of the forms to False. You then can use code to set a form's Visible property to True as the form is needed, then set it to False when it's time to hide the form again. Hence, the code for a button that displays a form named "Calls" might look like this:

```
Sub Button12_Click()
    Forms!Calls.Visible = True
End Sub
```

while a `Close` button placed on the Calls form to put away the form might have code like this attached to the button:

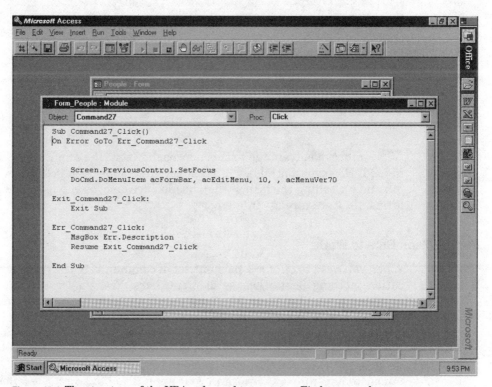

Figure 12.4 The structure of the VBA code used to execute a Find command.

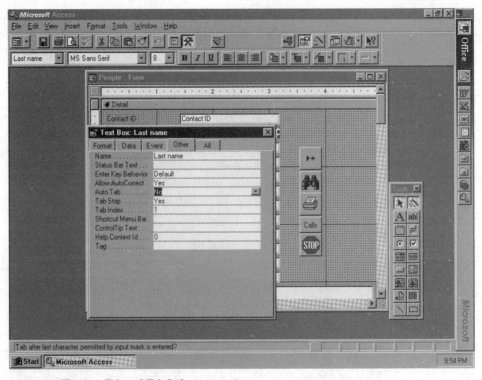

Figure 12.5 The AutoTab and Tab Index properties.

```
Sub Button17_Click()
    Forms!Calls.Visible = False
End Sub
```

The minor disadvantage to this approach is that the application takes longer to load. However, once loaded, response time appears much faster than loading and unloading the forms when needed because, as the user moves between forms, they are already in memory.

Putting Menu Bars to Work

When you need to offer a consistent set of commands to the users of your application, nothing beats the use of menu bars. Yes, they are more work than throwing a pile of command buttons onto a switchboard, but they do provide a familiar and Windows-compliant way for users to reach any point in your application. As Chapter 11 details, you can create menus with the aid of the Menu Builder, which lets you define each drop-down menu and name the macros (or VBA code) that gets called in response to each menu option. You can put custom menu bars to work in your application in any of the following ways:

- *Use the menu as the global menu bar throughout your application*—When you use the Tools/Startup menu command to specify a global menu for an application, Access displays that custom menu in all windows of your application, unless you've opened a form or report that has its own custom menu attached. (Any menus attached to forms or reports override any global menus when the form or report is open.)

- Attach the menu to a form or a report—You can attach a custom menu to any form or report. When you do so, the custom menu appears when the form is opened or when the report opens in preview mode.

- *Attach the menu as a shortcut menu to a form or to a form's control*—When you attach a custom menu to a form or to a control of a form as a shortcut menu, the menu appears when a user right-clicks on the form or control that the menu is attached to.

Using a Custom Menu as a Global Menu Bar

When you want a custom menu to appear as a global menu bar anywhere in your application, here are the steps you can use to do so:

1. From the menus, choose Tools/Startup.
2. Click within the Menu Bar box, then click the Build button to start the Menu Builder.
3. Use the Menu Builder to design the menu, using the steps outlined in Chapter 11.
4. When you are done creating the menu, click OK. Access sets the Menu Bar option to the same name as you assigned the menu bar. Whenever you start the application, the custom menu will appear.

Attaching a Menu Bar to a Form or Report

To create a menu bar that's attached to a form or to a report, you can open the form or report in Design view, then launch the Menu Builder. Access then will attach the custom menu to the MenuBar property of the form or report. Here are the steps you can use to do this:

1. Open the desired form or report in Design view.
2. Click the Properties button in the toolbar.
3. Select the MenuBar property in the Properties window.
4. Click the Build button.

The Menu Builder appears, and you can create the menu using the techniques outlined in Chapter 11. When you exit the Menu Builder, Access attaches the menu to the form or report.

Tip: You can attach an existing menu to any form or report by entering the name of the menu in the MenuBar property for the form or report.

Attaching a Shortcut Menu

You can modify the ShortcutMenuBar property for a form or for a form's control to attach a shortcut menu that appears whenever the user right-clicks on the control or on the form. Here's how you do this:

1. Open the form in Design View.

2. If you want to add the shortcut menu to the form, choose Edit/Select Form from the menus. If you want to add the shortcut menu to a control, click the desired control to select it.

3. Choose View/Properties from the menus to open the Properties window.

4. Select the ShortcutMenuBar property, then click the Build button to launch the Menu Builder.

5. Use the Menu Builder to design the desired menu. When you exit the Menu Builder, Access attaches the shortcut menu to the form or control.

Tip: You can attach an existing shortcut menu to any form or form control by entering the name of the shortcut menu in the ShortcutMenuBar property for the form or control.

Changing the Startup Options

Once you've designed and implemented your startup form and tied your menu options or command buttons to the other various Access objects, your application is nearly ready to run, at least in standalone mode. (It might not be ready for client/server, but successive chapters will get you there.)

You still need to tell Access how your application should appear when it starts. In previous versions of Access, this was commonly done with an Autoexec macro that launched an initial form and perhaps set various other options. You still can use that technique if you are comfortable with it, but Access for Windows 95 offers yet another way, with more flexibility than an Autoexec macro; you can make use of the options in the Startup dialog box. These options control various aspects of a database, when the database is initially opened. From the menus, choose Tools/Startup. When you do this, the Startup dialog box appears, as shown in Figure 12.6.

As you can see from the dialog box, you can specify a form to open automatically (under Display Form) and a global menu bar (under Menu Bar). You also

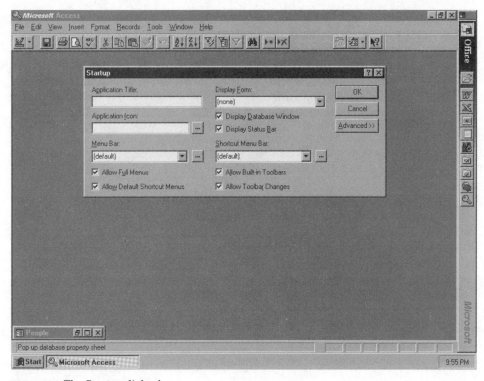

Figure 12.6 The Startup dialog box.

can provide a title for the application in the Application Title text box. You also have various options that let you enable or disable the built-in toolbars, display or hide the Database Window, and determine whether or not to allow the use of full menus and default shortcut menus. Make the desired selections in the dialog box, then click OK.

Creating a Shortcut to Start Your Application

One last touch that you might want to add is to provide your users with a way to easily launch the application. One way that you can do this is to create a shortcut under Windows 95. Open the Windows 95 Explorer or My Computer, and find the database file (.MDB file) that contains your application. Right-click the database name, and choose Create Shortcut from the menu that appears. When the shortcut appears under a new name in Explorer or My Computer, drag the shortcut onto the Windows 95 Desktop. From that point on you can load Access and open the database simultaneously by double-clicking the shortcut on the desktop.

Summary

By using the techniques presented in this chapter, you can complete the initial design of your application, and proceed on to the debugging and testing stage, which is detailed further in the following chapter. After the application appears relatively bug-free (or as close as we can come to such a state in today's complex world), you can move the application to the client/server environment and optimize it for client server. You'll find tips and techniques on how to accomplish all of this in the chapters that follow.

Debugging Your Applications

This chapter examines the techniques that you can put to use in debugging your Access applications, including ways in which you can implement error-trapping in your Visual Basic for Applications code. Like any modern-day high-level language, Visual Basic for Applications offers a number of aids that will assist you in the hunt for program bugs.

Get the Big Picture

Before getting into any discussion of the debugging tools in Access, it is worth noting that the very term "debugging" must be taken in a different context with Access than with earlier database development tools that ran a more linear style of program code.

Because Access takes a holistic approach to applications development, you'll need to look at the big picture when debugging an application. Your VBA code is just one small part of an application's design, and the code might or might not be where the bugs are. A complete and thorough use of the debugging tools for VBA will not find a poorly designed query, nor will it help you debug a report that supplies the wrong data because the Sorting and Grouping properties for the report haven't been correctly set. As long as you're able to keep all parts of your application in mind, the VBA debugging and error-handling tools will fall into their proper place.

VBA Errors, Defined

When it comes to errors in your code, Access does a lot to minimize these from the start by means of its built-in syntax checking. As you enter statements into a module window, Access checks the syntax of each statement, and if it finds an error, it will let you know about it very quickly by displaying a dialog box. In addition to syntax errors, there are three kinds of errors you can have in your program code, which can't be detected by the built-in syntax checking. They are *compiler errors*, *runtime errors*, and *logic errors*.

Compiler errors are errors in program code that are detected when Access tries to compile the code, which it must do before the code can be run. Compiler errors typically are the result of a misspelling or a syntax error that can't be detected by the built-in syntax checking.

Runtime errors are errors that are detected when Access runs the compiled code, and as a result of the code, it tries to perform an operation that simply isn't valid. As an example, a line of your VBA code might make a reference to a memory variable that doesn't exist at the time that the code runs; this type of error can't be detected until Access actually tries to carry out the operation. Another example is the common case of an attempted division by zero; if a VBA statement in your application attempts a divide by zero operation, the code will compile just fine but it will halt during execution, and Access will report an error.

Logic errors are errors in the logic, or "thought process," of your application, and they can be the hardest of all errors to track down. With logic errors, there is nothing wrong with the syntax of your VBA code or with the way the code carries out the requested operations. Instead, the fault lies somewhere in the overall design of what you're trying to accomplish. An example of a logic error might be if you have VBA code that attempts to execute a make-table query, and the user doesn't have read/write rights to the network directory where Access tries to create the table. The code that executes the make-table query is valid, but the operation fails at runtime for reasons that have nothing to do with the integrity of your code. Logic errors require you to step back and view that "big picture" of what the code is trying to accomplish before you can make the needed corrections to the code's design.

Tracking Compiler Errors by Compiling First

Compared to the other two types of errors, compiler errors are relatively easy to detect and fix. Access, like most high-level languages, makes use of a compiler. The compiler compiles the VBA code that you write into object code, which is run by Access when the code is called. By default, Access compiles any object that contains VBA code whenever the object runs. For example, if a report contains a line of VBA code in one of its properties, that code will be compiled when the report is opened for the first time. If a module contains VBA code, the code is compiled when another Access object calls the code contained within the module.

However, you don't have to wait for Access to run code that you write in a module window. You can check for compilation errors while you still have the Module Window open by choosing Run/Compile Loaded Modules (or, in Access 97, Debug/Compile Loaded Modules) from the menus. When you do this, Access will compile all the code that's stored within the module. If a compiler error does occur, the offending code appears in the Module Window, and Access displays a dialog box like the one shown in Figure 13.1.

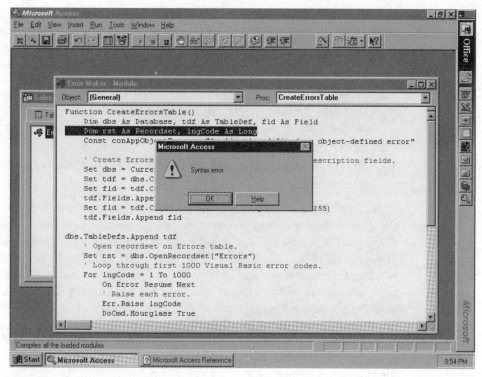

Figure 13.1 A compiler error dialog box.

You can click OK in the dialog box, then correct the cause of the error by correcting the code displayed in the Module Window.

Using the Run/Compile Loaded Modules or the Debug/Compile Loaded Modules option to check your code as you go along is a wise idea that can save you debugging time later, because if you use the option as you write the code, any errors found are displayed while you still have the code in view (and fresh in your mind). If you wait until after you've written several modules and are testing the entire application, it might be difficult to remember precisely what is happening with one particular module of VBA code.

Tracking Runtime and Logic Errors by Single-Stepping

Because runtime and logic errors occur after compilation and when the code actually runs, you need different techniques to help track down these errors. One technique that's useful with both these error types is to use *single-stepping* to step through the execution of the VBA code, one executable line at a time. You do this by first setting *breakpoints*, which are places in the code where the code stops running. Once Access halts at the location of a breakpoint you've set, you can continue program execution with the Run/Single Step command (or, in Access 97, the Debug/Step Into command) from the menus (or with the equivalent Run button in the toolbar). You can use these steps to set breakpoints, then use them to step through your program code:

1. In the Module Window, place the insertion pointer at the line where the breakpoint should appear.

2. From the menus, choose Run/Toggle Breakpoint (or Debug/ Toggle Breakpoint, in Access 97) or click the Breakpoint button on the toolbar. The line of program code changes color, indicating the presence of a breakpoint.

3. Repeat these steps for any additional breakpoints that you want to set in the module.

Once you have set the desired breakpoints, you can run the code by calling the Access object to which the code is attached. When the compiler reaches the breakpoint and execution of the code is halted, you can look at the status of variables (using the Debug Window, which will be discussed shortly), and you can examine the state of the various objects in the database to help pinpoint the cause of the errors. You now can single-step through the program code by choosing Run/Single Step (or Debug/Step Into, in Access 97) from the menus or by clicking the equivalent Single Step button on the toolbar. Each time you do this, Access executes the next statement in the program code. Remember that, at any time, you can go into the code in the Module Window and make any desired changes to it. If you change the code, when you try to close the Module Window, Access will ask if it can reset the halted code so that changes to the code can be saved. Click Yes in the dialog box, and you then can perform the necessary actions to run the code again.

Once you are done stepping through the program, you can choose Run/Continue from the menus (or you can click the Continue button on the toolbar) to continue program flow normally. When you are done with a breakpoint, you can clear it by placing the insertion pointer on the line containing the breakpoint and again choosing Run/Toggle Breakpoint (or clicking the Breakpoint toolbar button).

Keep in mind that, in addition to setting breakpoints, you also can use the Stop statement (just the word Stop on a single line by itself) anywhere in a program to force the program to halt at that point. In effect, setting a breakpoint and using a Stop statement produce the same result, the halting of the code at a desired place in the program. The difference is in the more permanent nature of the Stop statement. Breakpoints are in effect only as long as you don't close the database or exit from Access; when you close the database or exit from Access, the breakpoint is lost. Stop statements, on the other hand, are in the program code until you take them out. So if you plan to do some long-term debugging of complex code, you might want to use Stop statements in the code instead of setting breakpoints.

Note: Some languages provide *variable breakpoints*, which are breakpoints that are conditional, based on the value of some variable; for example, if the value of X is greater than 5, a breakpoint occurs. Access does not offer anything of this sort in its stable of programming tools. However, you can duplicate the effects of a variable breakpoint by inserting a `Stop` statement in the code, followed by a `MsgBox` statement that reports on the value of the desired variable. For example, code like the following might be used in such a case:

```
If X > 5
   Stop
   MsgBox "Value of X", X
Endif
```

Working With the Debug Window

Another tool provided for debugging VBA code is the *Debug Window*. With the Debug Window, you can test the value of variables after you've halted program execution, you can change the values of variables, you can check the contents of fields or controls in forms and reports, and you can execute VBA commands. (Those who have written programs under variations of xBASE can compare the Debug Window to the dBASE dot prompt or the FoxPro Command Window.) Here's how to make use of the Debug Window for your debugging:

1. Open a Module Window.

2. From the menus, choose `View/Debug Window`, or click the `Debug Window` button in the toolbar.

When you perform these steps, the Debug Window appears, similar to the example shown in Figure 13.2.

In the Debug Window, you can check the value of a property or a variable by entering the `?` command, followed by the needed expression. As an example, you could check the value of the record source property of a report named Calls by entering this expression in the Debug Window:

```
? Reports![Calls].RecordSource
```

To check the value of a field or a control on a form or in a report, enter the question mark, followed by the field name or the control's identifier. For example, if you open a form called Customers that contains a field called `Company ID` and you bring up a specific record, you then can open a module and choose `View/Debug Window`, then enter this expression in the window to view the control's contents:

```
? Forms![Customers]![Company ID]
```

You also can use the `Debug.Print` object and method to test Function or Sub procedures in the Debug Window. To test Function procedures, type `Debug.Print` followed by the function name and parenthesis. To test Sub procedures, type `Debug.Print` followed by the Sub name and parentheses.

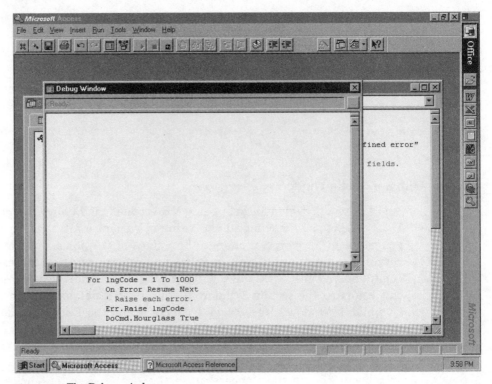

Figure 13.2 The Debug window.

Using Error-Handling with VBA

One area of applications development that's too often overlooked is that of *error-handling*. Because the Windows environment does a nice job of presenting users with a friendly face when errors occur, many Access developers leave error-handling up to what is built into Windows, or they give minimal attention to error-handling. However, Access does provide the needed tools—in the form of the On Error statement and the Err(), Erl(), and Error$() functions—to write effective error-handling routines. When you include error-handling in your VBA code, you provide your code with (hopefully) the ability to recover cleanly from errors.

In writing VBA code, the foundation for error-handling is the On Error statement, which comes in the following three flavors:

```
On Error GoTo labelname
On Error Resume Next
On Error GoTo 0
```

The On Error statement initializes an *event handler*, or a system-wide loop that continually checks for errors as the program executes. Once an error occurs, what Access does next depends on how you structured the On Error statement. With On Error GoTo *labelname*, control passes to the first executable line following the label named by *labelname*. With `On Error Resume`, control passes to the statement immediately after the line where the error occurred. The use of `On  Error GoTo 0` disables any previous use of the `On Error` statement.

As an example of a very rudimentary error-handling capability, a portion of a module's code might look like the following:

```
On Error GoTo Bombed
Function AddThem(TableName)
Dim db as Database, tb as Table
    Set db = CurrentDB()
    Set tb = db.OpenTable(TableName)
    ...additional code here...
Bombed:
    MsgBox Err.Description
    Resume Next
```

Note the emphasis on "very rudimentary" here; this error-handling routine accomplishes virtually nothing more than Access would manage all by itself, but it does demonstrate error-handling by trapping the error through the use of the `On Error` statement.

A better strategy than simply trapping the error and displaying it to the user is to provide a complete routine that attempts to pinpoint the cause of the error and perhaps respond accordingly (or at least give the user a concrete idea of what went wrong so that useful feedback can be given to you, the developer). With this technique, an error-handling routine might resemble the following:

```
On Error GoTo Bombed
Function AddThem(TableName)
Dim db as Database, tb as Table
    Set db = CurrentDB()
    Set tb = db.OpenTable(TableName)
    ...additional code here...
Bombed:
Static TheCode as Integer
TheCode = Err.Number
Call FixIt
```

Then, in a separate routine called FixIt stored in the same module, you could use code like this:

```
Select Case TheCode
  Case 53
  BugNote = MsgBox("Error","Program can't find a file that's needed!")
  Case 61
  BugNote = MsgBox("Error","Disk is full! Erase unneeded files.")
 Case 71
 BugNote = MsgBox("Error","Device failure. Notify network personnel.")
    ...additional code here...
End Select
```

With code like this, once an error occurs while the code runs, Access transfers program control to the label named `Bombed:`. The first executable statement after that label declares a variable to store the value of the error, and the next line assigns the error code to that variable. The third line, `Call FixIt`, transfers control to the error-handling routine. The error-handling routine makes use of a series of `Case` choices inside a `Select Case` statement to give the user an appropriate message, depending on the cause of the error.

About the Err Properties

Within your error-handling routines, you'll need to use the appropriate error properties of the Err object where they are needed. The error properties are `Err.Number` and `Err.Description`, and each property returns information regarding the specifics of the error that occurred. The `Err.Number` property returns a numeric value that represents the type of error; available values for errors are shown in Table 13.1. The `Err.Description` property returns a text string that contains the error message. (Access Basic, the predecessor to Visual Basic for Applications, made use of the `Err()` and `Error$()` functions for this purpose; you still can use those functions in VBA code, but the newer use of the object-and-property approach is more in line with the added features of Visual Basic for Applications.) You can use these properties in your error-handling program code, as shown in the code examples throughout this chapter, to trap for errors and to display informative messages to the user.

As an example of the use of error properties, consider the following simple error-handler routine. The code is simple, but it does the job of rudimentary error-handling:

```
On Error GoTo HandleIt
...more code here...


HandleIt:
If MsgBox("The following error occurred-  " & Trim(Str(Err.Number)) &
        ":" & Chr(13) & Chr(10) & Err.Description, 17) = 1
Then
    Resume
    Next
Else
    Stop
End If
```

Note that the two lines following the `HandleIt:` label actually would comprise a single line of code. They appear on two lines here because it's not possible to print the line as a single line in this book.

A Few Final Hints

When it comes to the overall topic of debugging applications, the following final hints might be in order to help you with this mundane but necessary task:

Table 13.1

Code	Message
3	Return without GoSub
5	Invalid procedure call
6	Overflow
7	Out of memory
9	Subscript out of range
10	This array is fixed or temporarily locked
11	Division by zero
13	Type mismatch
14	Out of string space
16	Expression too complex
17	Can't perform requested operation
18	User interrupt occurred
20	Resume without error
28	Out of stack space
35	Sub or Function not defined
47	Too many DLL application clients
48	Error in loading DLL
49	Bad DLL calling convention
51	Internal error
52	Bad file name or number
53	File not found
54	Bad file mode
55	File already open
57	Device I/O error
58	File already exists
59	Bad record length
61	Disk full
62	Input past end of file
63	Bad record number
67	Too many files
68	Device unavailable
70	Permission denied
71	Disk not ready

Table 13.1 *(continued)*

Code	Message
74	Can't rename with different drive
75	Path/file access error
76	Path not found
91	Object variable, or with block variable not set
92	For loop not initialized
93	Invalid pattern string
94	Invalid use of Null
322	Can't create necessary temporary file
325	Invalid format in resource file
380	Invalid property value
423	Property or method not found
424	Object required
429	OLE Automation server can't create object
430	Class doesn't support OLE Automation
432	File name or class name not found during OLE Automation operation
438	Object doesn't support this property or method
440	OLE Automation error
442	Connection to type library or object library for remote process has been lost
443	OLE Automation object does not have a default value
445	Object doesn't support this action
446	Object doesn't support named arguments
447	Object doesn't support current local setting
448	Named argument not found
449	Argument not optional
450	Wrong number of arguments or invalid property assignment
451	Object not a collection
452	Invalid ordinal
453	Specified DLL function not found
454	Code resource not found
455	Code resource lock error
457	This key is already associated with an element of this collection
458	Variable uses an OLE type not supported in Visual Basic
481	Invalid picture

- Misspelling variable names is a common cause of program errors. Watch your spelling, and make use of the `Option Explicit` statement in each module that you create. Adding an `Option Explicit` statement will cause Access to flag variables that it thinks are undeclared (which will include any that you've misspelled).

- Use the Debug Window and `Debug.Print` statements to show in the window results of expressions that you might suspect are causing problems.

- Break up your program code into Function and Sub procedures that have a clear, definite purpose. Doing so will better help you localize your errors.

- Use plenty of comments! Comments don't just serve as an aid to other programmers who must follow your work, but they can help you immeasurably months after you've written code and you can no longer remember precisely why you wrote it that way in the first place.

Summary

In this chapter, I've explored a variety of techniques that you can use to debug your application, making it as ready as possible for the first steps of launching it as a network-ready, client/server application. The chapters that follow will help you take your application to that final state.

14

Network Techniques

This chapter details network topics, with a view to how the setup of your application's network options affect the users (and the use of your application) on a network. Because Access comes ready for single-user or multiuser use out of the box, there's often a tendency to throw applications "out there on the server" and leave network planning and implementation to a minimum. However, you'll get better performance from your multiuser applications if you take advantage of the various options present in Access to tailor the environment to the needs of your users and the design of your network.

Given that the focus of this book is on developing applications for eventual use in a multiuser, client/server environment, I'll assume that you're using Access on a server-based network with a dedicated server operating system (such as Novell NetWare, Microsoft Windows NT Server, or Banyan VINES). While each server operating system uses techniques that are unique to that operating system, the techniques discussed in this chapter (which you implement under Access) will apply regardless of which server-based network you are using.

Exclusive? Shared?

Before you work with Access in a multiuser environment, it's important to understand how Access does things when it comes to sharing data. This is true even if you come from the world of xBASE development and you feel that you have a solid handle on working with shared records, because Access does some things differently than does dBASE and FoxPro.

By default, the File/Open command opens a database for exclusive use, meaning no one else can get to it while you have it open. This behavior of Access is controlled by the Exclusive setting in the Open Database dialog box. When you first start Access and choose File/Open, you see the Open Database dialog box, shown in Figure 14.1.

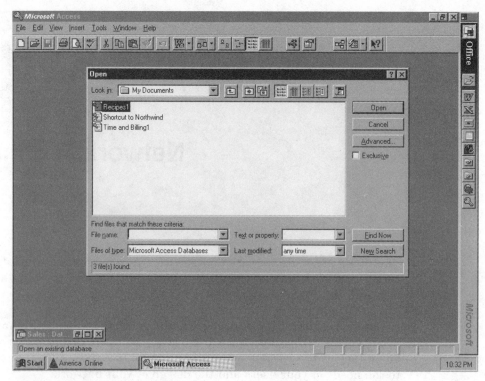

Figure 14.1 The Open Database dialog box.

Note that, at the right side of the dialog box, the Exclusive option is checked. Leaving this option turned on causes Access to open any database in exclusive mode. While the database is open, other users cannot open it. To change this option so that it is turned off by default, choose Tools/Options from the menus. In the Options dialog box that appears, choose the Multiuser category, and change the Default Open Mode for Databases option to Shared. Then, click OK.

Remember that, while you are in "development mode," you'll need exclusive access to the database. Access won't let you change the design of any objects unless you have the database opened for exclusive use. (This shouldn't be a problem because end users should never have access to a database that you still are developing!) Once the database leaves the debugging stage and begins to undergo user testing, you'll need to provide shared access by setting up the users' copies of Access to open tables in shared mode by default.

Setting the Multiuser Options

Because every network differs with regard to the number of users present and how often they contend for use of the same data, it makes sense to set up the multiuser options of Access so that the software will perform best for your particular scenario. Microsoft designed Access so that the multiuser options would default to what would be best on an overall basis, but this might or might not be what's best for you. To get to the multiuser options, choose Tools/Options from the menus. When the Options dialog box appears, click Advanced to view the multiuser options, as shown in Figure 14.2. Table 14.1 explains the purpose of each of the multiuser options.

It's important to remember that any changes that you make to the multiuser options apply to the copy of Access that you are currently running. If multiple users have their own copies of Access on separate workstations, any desired changes to the multiuser options must be made at each users' workstation.

Deciding on a Record-Locking Strategy

Whenever you edit a record in Access, by default the program automatically locks that record (and possibly, some others located near it) until you are done with the changes, then the record gets unlocked. How Access performs a lock to protect shared data from corruption is determined by one of the settings listed in Table 14.1, the Default Record Locking option. This option offers three choices: No Locks, All Records, and Edited Record.

With No Locks selected, any user can edit any record at the same time that another user is editing that record. When two users edit the same record simultaneously, the first user to close the record is allowed to save it. When

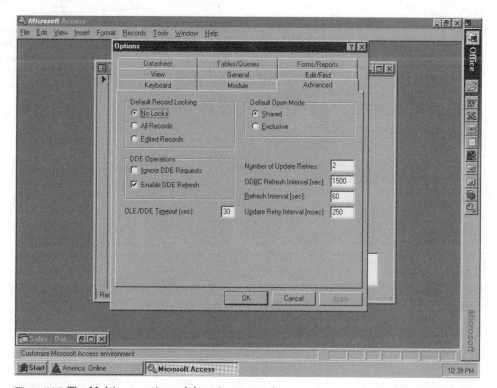

Figure 14.2 The Multiuser options of the Advanced tab.

Table 14.1

Option	Settings	Result
Default Record Locking	`No Locks`, `All Records`, or `Edited Record`	Doesn't lock records, locks all records underlying open objects, or locks the current edited record in tables, queries, or new forms. When this option is set to `All Records`, you can't view records in attached SQL Server tables. You can specify how records in a form or report's underlying tables or queries are locked by setting the Record-Locks property.
Default Open Mode for Databases	`Exclusive` or `Shared`	Opens an existing database for exclusive or shared access automatically. To open a database with a different access mode, choose `Open Database` from the File menu and select or clear the Exclusive dialog box option.
Refresh Interval	1 to 32,766	Sets the interval (in seconds) after which Microsoft Access automatically refreshes records in the current form or datasheet. To refresh records immediately, choose `Refresh` from the Records menu.
Update Retry Interval	0 to 1000	Sets the time interval (in milliseconds) after which Microsoft Access automatically tries to save a changed record that is locked by another user.
Number of Update Retries	0 to 10	Sets the number of times Access automatically tries to save a changed record that is locked by another user.
ODBC Refresh Interval	1 to 3600	Sets the interval (in seconds) after which Access automatically refreshes records that you are accessing using ODBC drivers.

the second user tries to save the record, a dialog box appears warning the user that the record has changed since it was opened. The user then can choose whether to save the changes (and overwrite the changes made by the other user) or discard the changes. For network applications that routinely have large numbers of users vying for the same record, this might be the best choice.

With All Records selected as the locking option, Access will lock all of the records in the underlying data source for the form or dynaset whenever it is opened. Obviously, this setting won't win you any friends on the network, and it should be avoided at all costs.

With Edited Record selected as the locking option, Access locks the record as you begin editing and unlocks it when you're done. On networks that rarely have two users attempting to work with the same record, this often is a wise choice.

Implementing Network Security

In addition to customizing your multiuser options for optimal network performance, you also might choose to implement security by means of the security features that are designed into Access. In Access, security is based on a system of *users* and *groups*, with each user belonging to a specific group. Each user gets his/her own user name, a PIN (personal identification number), and a password. When you initially install Access, no security is in effect, and all users automatically log in under the name "Admin" to a group called "Admins." You can add groups and password protection to all user accounts, and you can specify what rights users will have when working with the various Access objects. First, you'll want to set the passwords for your users, then you can set up the permissions that determine what they can and can't do within a database. Securing a database involves the following general steps:

1. Create or choose a workgroup in which the database is to be used. (The workgroup is defined by the system database, usually the SYSTEM.MDA file, which Access uses at startup.)

2. Create one or more user accounts, or choose one or more existing accounts, to administer the workgroup and to own the database and its objects. (It is important to have Administrator and Owner accounts, because these have permissions that can't be deleted. These accounts replace the unrestricted Admin account, which is the default account installed with Access.)

3. Activate the logon procedure.

4. Change the database and object ownership to the owner account.

5. Create user accounts for each user of the database, and create groups to store your user accounts in.

6. Remove the default permissions, and assign new permissions for the database and its objects.

You can use the more detailed steps that follow to carry out these tasks.

Establishing Passwords

First, you'll want to establish password security for the database. You can do this by performing these steps to add a new user and password, then delete the old Admin user:

1. Open the database.

2. Choose Tools/Security/Set Database Password from the menus. When you do this, the Set Database Password dialog box appears, as shown in Figure 14.3.

3. In the Password field, enter a desired password.

4. Re-enter the new password in the Verify field, then click OK.

5. Choose Tools/Security/Users and Group Accounts from the menus. When the Users and Group Accounts dialog box appears, click New.

6. In the New User/Group dialog box that now appears (Figure 14.4), enter a login name and a PIN, then click OK.

7. Under Available Groups in the Users dialog box, select Admins.

8. Click Remove, then click OK.

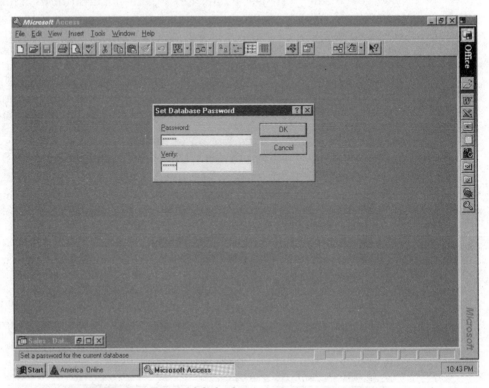

Figure 14.3 The Set Database Password dialog box.

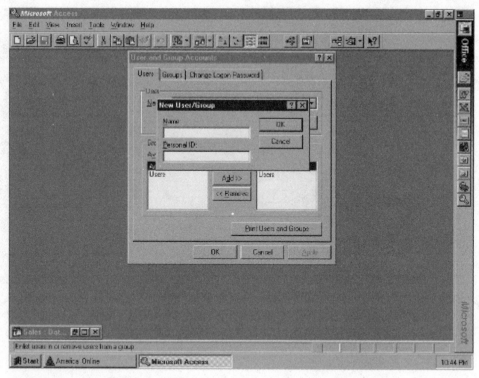

Figure 14.4 The New User/Group dialog box.

Once you've completed the prior steps, you will be the only authorized user of Access. Next, you can use the following steps to set up which groups and users can make use of Access:

1. Choose Tools/Security/Users and Group Accounts from the menus.
2. In the dialog box that appears, click the Groups tab, then click New. When you do this, the New User/Group dialog box appears, as shown earlier, in Figure 14.4.
3. In the Name box, enter a name for the group.
4. In the Personal ID Number box, enter a PIN for the group.
5. Click OK to close the dialog box and return to the Groups dialog box.
6. Repeat Steps 2 through 5 for each group that you want to add. When done adding groups, click OK in the Groups dialog box to close it.

After adding all the necessary groups, you can proceed to add users to the system by performing the following steps:

1. Choose Tools/Security/User and Group Accounts from the menus. When you do so, the User and Group Accounts dialog box appears (Figure 14.5).

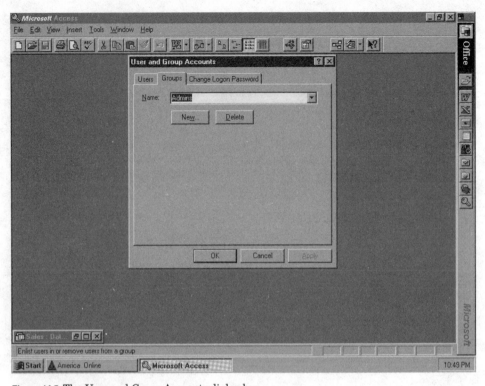

Figure 14.5 The User and Group Accounts dialog box.

2. Click New. When you do so, the New User dialog box appears, as shown earlier.

3. Enter the name and the PIN number for the user in the respective fields.

4. Click OK.

5. Repeat Steps 1 through 4 for each additional user you need to add to the system.

These steps will add new users to the Users group, which by default must contain all users of Access. In addition to belonging to the Users group, users can belong to any other group that you've added, and you can set read/write permissions for each group individually. To add a user to another group that you defined earlier, use these steps:

1. Choose Tools/Security/User and Group Accounts, and click the Users tab.

2. Click the down arrow beside Name, and select the desired user.

3. Under Available Groups, select the desired group.

4. Click Add.

5. Repeat Steps 3 and 4 if you want to add the selected user to any other groups.

6. Click Close.

Establishing Permissions

Once your users and groups have been established, you can proceed to define the permissions that will determine what rights users have to the objects in the database. When doing this, keep in mind that you must remove the permissions of the Admin user and Users group, which includes all users in a workgroup. Until you remove those permissions, users might have unintended permissions for objects. Once you have removed these permissions, users will have only the permissions that you assign. You can assign or remove permissions by performing the following steps:

1. Open the database that contains the objects that you want to assign or remove permissions for.

2. With the Database Window active, choose Tools/Security/User and Group Permissions from the menus.

3. In the Permissions dialog box that appears (Figure 14.6), choose the type and name of the object and the group or user whose permissions you want to assign.

4. Select the permissions that you want to assign to the group or user, then click OK. Table 14.2 shows the permissions, and what they mean.

To assign default permissions for new objects, perform these steps:

1. Open the database that contains the objects that you want to assign or remove permissions for.

2. With the Database Window active, choose Tools/Security/User and Group Permissions from the menus.

3. Choose the type of object in the Object Type box, and choose the <New object> selection in the Object Name list. (The <New object> selection will depend on the type of object you've selected, being either New Tables/Queries, New Forms, New Reports, New Macros, or New Modules.)

4. Choose the group or user whose permissions you want to assign.

5. Choose the default permissions that you want to assign for that object type, then click OK.

Encrypting a Database

As part of the security process, you might want to encrypt a database so that others who have their own copy of Access installed cannot get to your data in

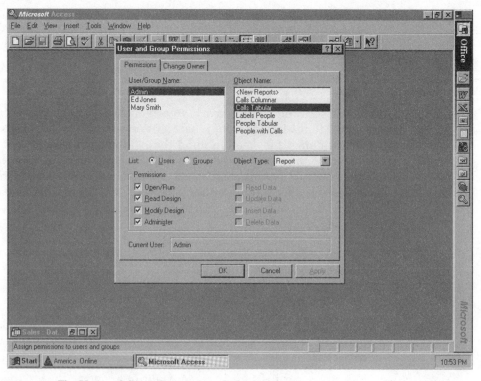

Figure 14.6 The User and Group Permissions dialog box.

Table 14.2

Permission	Permits a user to	Applies to
Open/Run	Open a database, form, or report, or run a macro.	Databases, forms, reports, and macros.
Read Design	View objects in Design view.	Tables, queries, forms, reports, macros, and modules.
Modify Design	View and change the design of objects, or delete them.	Tables, queries, forms, reports, macros, and modules.
Administer	Have full access to objects and data, including ability to assign permissions.	Tables, queries, forms, reports, macros, and modules.
Read Data	View data.	Tables and queries.
Update Data	View and modify but not insert or delete data.	Tables and queries.
Insert Data	View and insert but not modify or delete data.	Tables and queries.
Delete Data	View and delete data but not modify or insert data.	Tables and queries.

any way. Access lets you encrypt databases to add another layer of protection. You can encrypt a database by performing these steps:

1. Start Access without opening a database. (Access won't let you encrypt a database that is open. On a network, the encryption attempt will fail if another user has the database open.)

2. From the menus, choose `Tools/Security`, then choose `Encrypt/ Decrypt Database`.

3. Select the database that you want to encrypt or decrypt, then click `OK`.

4. Indicate a name, drive, and folder for the encrypted or decrypted database, then click `OK`.

Summary

In this chapter, you've learned about the steps that you can implement to optimize your Access databases for use on a network and how you can implement security across your database objects. The chapters that follow will detail how you can move your completed, secure application to the client/server environment.

Moving the Access Application to Client/Server

This chapter details the final part of the application development process (i.e., moving the application to the client/server environment). At this point, your application should be fully developed, debugged, and operational either in a standalone environment or on the network but with the data still residing in Access tables under the direct control of Access. The last step involves moving those tables to the server (or re-creating the tables on the server and attaching to them) and optimizing the application to run smoothly in the client/server environment.

Adding the ODBC Drivers

If you haven't done this already, you'll need to install the ODBC Drivers so that Access can communicate with your particular database server. The default installation for Access does *not* add these drivers to your hard disk, so you'll probably need to run Setup again and add the drivers. You can use these steps to add the ODBC Drivers to your installation of Access:

1. Insert Setup Disk 1 (in the case of a floppy disk package) or the Access Setup CD-ROM (in the case of a CD-ROM package) in the appropriate drive.

2. On the Windows 95 Taskbar, choose Run from the Start menu.

3. In the dialog box that appears, enter X:\SETUP where X is the letter of the drive containing your Setup disk or CD-ROM.

4. When the Setup dialog box appears, click Change Options. In a moment, you'll see the Maintenance dialog box, as shown in Figure 15.1.

5. Click Data Access in the list, then click Change Option. If you're using Access 97, select Database Drivers, then click Change Option. Next, you'll see the Data Access dialog box in Access 95, or the Database Drivers dialog box in Access 97. (Figure 15.2).

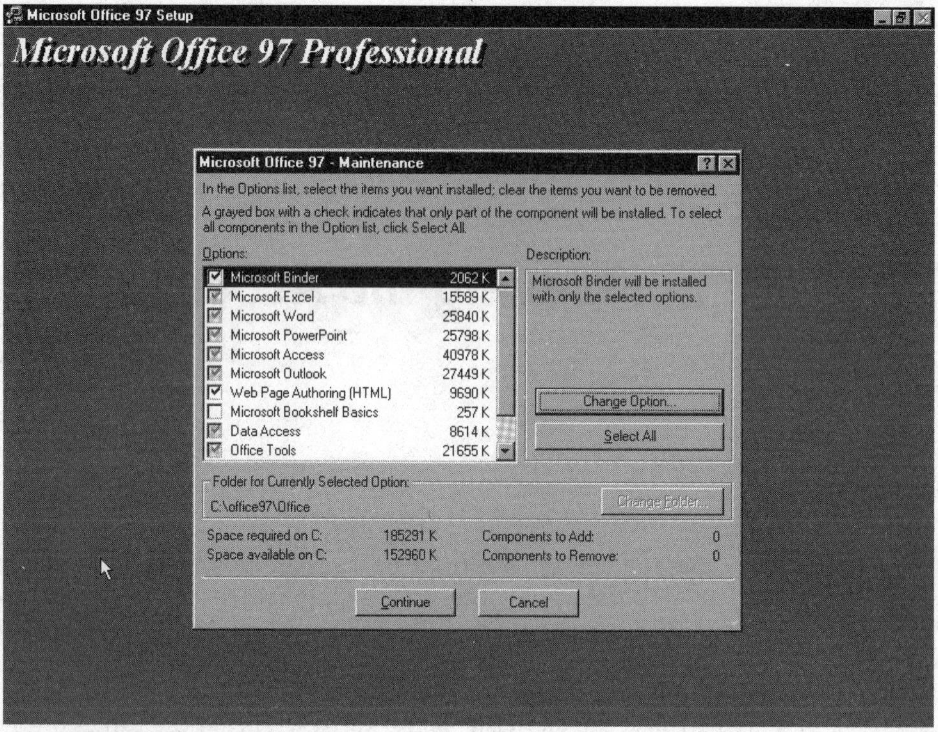

Figure 15.1 The Maintenance dialog box.

6. Turn on the SQL Server ODBC Driver option, then click OK.

7. When the Maintenance dialog box reappears, click Continue.

The Setup program will prompt you for additional disks as needed, and it will proceed to install the ODBC drivers.

Once you've installed the drivers, one more step is needed before you can attach to data that resides on the server. You'll need to identify the ODBC *data source* that's appropriate to your server. The ODBC data source identifies the SQL database, its location (which server it resides on), and the network used to reach the server. You use the ODBC Manager to set up the data source by performing these steps:

1. On the Windows 95 Taskbar, choose Settings/Control Panel from the Start menu.

2. In the Control Panel window, double-click the ODBC icon.

3. To specify a new data source, click Add.

4. In the Add Data Source dialog box that appears, select SQL Server, then click OK. When you do this, the ODBC SQL Server dialog box appears, asking for a Data Source Name, a Description, a Server Name, and an (optional) Network Address and Network Library.

5. Under Data Source Name, enter a name that you'll want to use to identify the data source (this name can be whatever you want).

6. Under Description, enter any desired description of the data source.

7. Under Server, enter the name that identifies SQL Server on your network.

8. Under Network Address, enter the location of the SQL Server DBMS. (For installations using Microsoft SQL Server, you can generally leave this option set to <default>.)

9. Under Network Library, enter the name of the SQL Server Net Library DLL that the SQL Server driver uses to link to the network software. (If you leave this option set to <default>, the SQL Server driver uses the default library that's specified in the SQL Server Client Configuration Utility.)

10. After filling in all desired options in the dialog box, click OK.

Separating the Tables

When you move an Access application to client/server, one part of the process involves separating the application's tables from the other objects in the database. You initially need to move to a two-database approach, in effect, creating

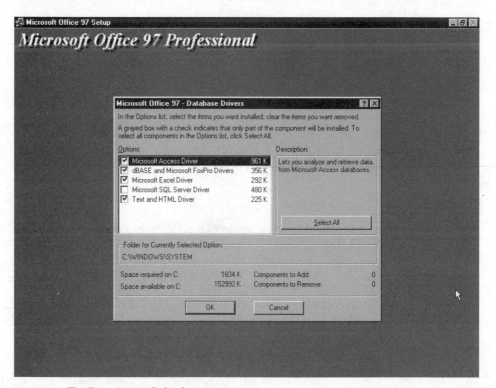

Figure 15.2 The Data Access dialog box.

one database that holds all of the data (the tables used by your application) and another database (let's call it the *application database*) used to store the queries, forms, reports, macros, and modules. Once both databases exist, in the application database, you *attach* to the tables in the data database.

With this done, as you complete the testing and debugging stage, you can open and work with the application database. Because the objects (such as the queries and reports) in the application database are based on tables that are attached, any changes that you make to the data change the tables in the data database. This approach prepares the way for the final move to client/server, when you'll attach to data tables that reside on the server by means of the ODBC drivers. Even if the application isn't destined for client/server, this approach to applications development has significant advantages, in terms of maintaining the finished application.

With the application split into a data side and an application side, you can make wholesale nontable-related changes to the application at any time, even after it's been given to end users, without disturbing the application's data. Trust me, the first time a networked application with 30 users needs a minor change to a report's design, you'll be glad you took this approach. You can use these steps to split an application after you've created it (and hopefully debugged most of it):

1. Create a new database, and open it. (This database will become the data database.)

2. Import all of the tables from the original database into the new database.

3. Create any necessary relationships between the tables in the new database.

4. Delete the tables from the original database.

5. In the original database, attach to the tables in the new database.

Once the application has been split in this manner, you can complete any necessary testing and debugging and afterward attach to the final data tables on your particular SQL server.

Attaching to the External Tables

Once you've installed the needed ODBC Drivers and set up the SQL data source (as detailed earlier in this chapter), you can attach to tables stored on your SQL Server just as you would attach to any foreign tables from within Access. Here are the steps that you can use to attach to tables in a SQL database:

1. In Access, open the data database (i.e., the database that you will use to store the attached SQL tables).

2. From the menus, choose File/Get External Data/Link Tables. When you do this, the Link dialog box appears, asking for the name of the data source, as shown in Figure 15.3.

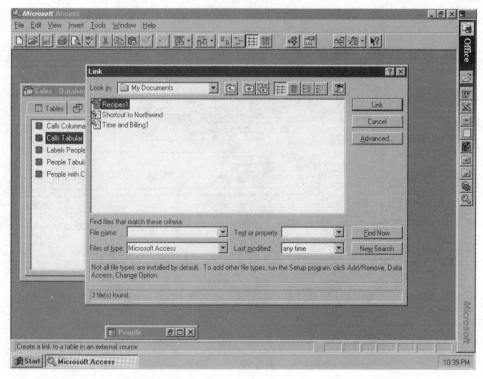

Figure 15.3 The Link dialog box.

3. In the dialog box under Files of Type, select <SQL Database>, then click OK. In a moment, the SQL Data Sources dialog box appears, as shown in Figure 15.4.

4. In the SQL Data Sources dialog box, choose the SQL data source that contains the desired tables, then click OK. When you do this, Access will connect to the SQL Server, and you will see an Objects list box that contains the available SQL tables. (Depending on which variant of SQL Server you are using, you also might be prompted for a login name and password.)

5. In the Objects list box, click the desired table to select it. Then, click Attach to attach to the table. Access will display a dialog box indicating that the SQL tables have been attached successfully, and you can click OK to close the dialog box.

6. Repeat Steps 4 and 5 for each additional table on the SQL Server that you want to attach to.

But What If It Doesn't Work?

Often when you are trying to attach to SQL tables, Access will report an error of some type, and you're left with the task of tracking down the cause of the

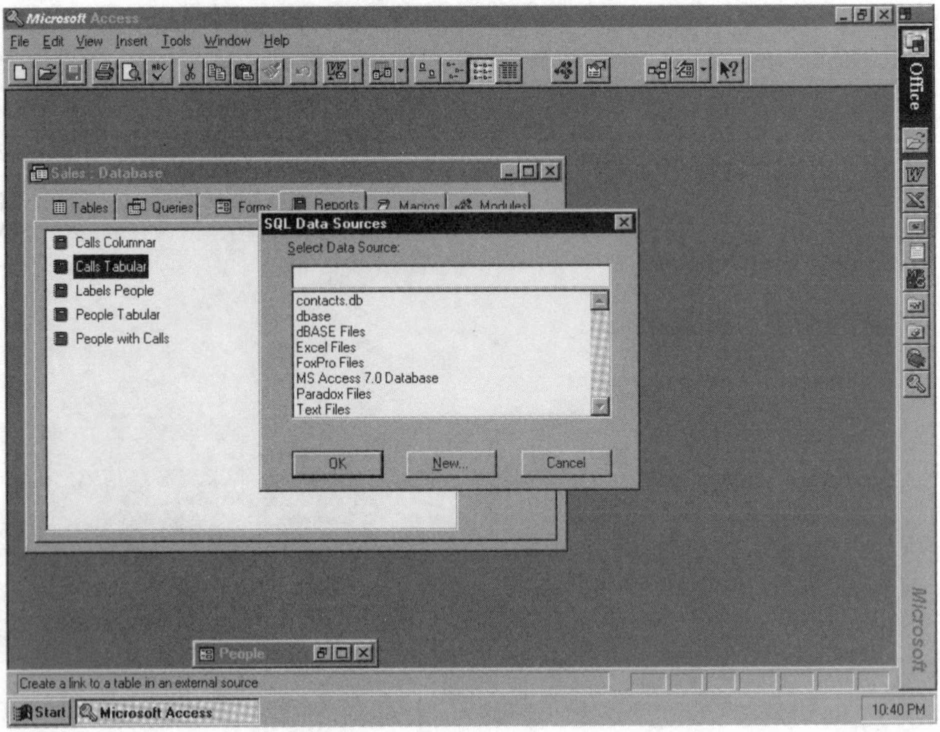

Figure 15.4 The SQL Data Sources dialog box.

problem. Given the variation in possible SQL Servers out there, it's not possible to say here exactly where your problem might lie, but one common area to look closely at is with the access rights you've been given on the SQL Server. Under no circumstances will Access bypass the rights set by the server, and any attempt to get at data that you don't have rights to will generate an error message. You might need to check with the network administrator and verify that you have the access rights that you need. Another point to check in avoiding problems is to make sure that you've got plenty of available disk space on your local hard drive. This is important because the temporary indexes that Access creates while running queries off attached SQL Server tables get stored on your local hard disk. If you try to execute queries and run out of disk space in the process, you'll get errors (at the least) and at worst, you'll see bizarre behavior, such as Access locking up completely.

Dealing with Server Data

Given that the whole purpose of a client/server application is to improve performance by keeping the data on the server, at some point you'll need to place your tables on the server. However, the flexibility that's built into Access means that, as the developer, you get to choose when during the development process this takes place. You can start out by creating all of your tables on the server, using the back-end database definition tools for your particular server package. You also can create the tables in Access on a local hard drive and leave them there during the application process. The second option is more commonly used when the application is not making use of existing data as it is a simple matter to work with your tables in Access, especially while the application is in a state of flux. However, note that there are some points to be aware of if you choose to create the tables locally and move them later:

- *Table names and field names*—Most servers won't let you get away with the kind of flexibility that Access offers in naming tables and fields. In particular, spaces usually aren't allowed in names, and very long names often aren't permitted. You can avoid potential problems by sticking to the server's naming conventions for your server as you create the tables in Access.

- *Security*—The security options that you set up in Access have absolutely no effect on the security that's enforced at the server level, and server-level security will always be enforced in addition to any security that you implement in Access. Hence, if you are going to implement security locally, it makes sense to use the same permissions and passwords as are used at the server level. This makes things easier on your users, as they'll only need to log in once.

- *Indexes*—If a table that you create locally has secondary indexes and you export that table to a server, the indexes won't exist on the server side. Access can't automatically create remote indexes on the server. You'll want to use the database definition tools appropriate to your server to create any needed remote indexes.

- *Relationships*—Many servers let you define relational integrity at the table level, with rules regarding cascading updates and deletions. Note that Access has no way of knowing what these rules are, although of course it won't let you violate the rules at the server level.

Preconnecting to the Server

When you open any form or report that uses attached server tables as a data source, Access will attach to the server, if it hasn't done so already. However, often in applications, you'll want to get the process of attaching out of the way as the application is launched. You can do this by *preconnecting* to the server, and all this takes is a small amount of VBA code. As an example, the procedure shown here could be called from a RunCode action stored within an Autoexec macro that launches an application. The routine prompts for a server user name and password, then connects to a server named "ServerName" and opens a database called "DbName":

```
Function PreConnect (TheUserName as String, ThePassword as String)
   Dim wrkRemote as Workspace, dbsRemote as Database
   Dim TheConnect as String
```

```
        TheUserName = InfoBox("Enter user name:")
        ThePassword = InfoBox("Enter password:")
        TheConnect = "ODBC";DSN=ServerName;DATABASE=DbName; &_
                    "UID=" TheUserName & "PWD=" & ThePassword & ";"
        Set wrkRemote = DBEngine.Workspaces(0)
        Set dbsRemote = wrkRemote.OpenDatabase("",False,False,TheConnect)
        dbsRemote.Close
End Function
```

When you aren't sure which ODBC data source the user must connect to, you can use the term ODBC; as the connection string argument. Then, when the code runs, Access will display a dialog box listing all the registered ODBC data sources, and the user can select the desired data source from the list.

Using Pass-Through Queries

Depending on your application, you might prefer to use regular Access queries, or you might prefer to use queries based on SQL statements written in the SQL variant of your particular server. When you use regular Access queries on attached server tables, Access compiles and runs the query just as it would if the data were stored locally in the form of Access tables, but you get the added power and security of the client/server environment. On the other hand, with pass-through queries, you enter SQL statements, and Access passes those statements directly to the server without compiling the query beforehand. (Hence, with pass-through queries, it is important to use a syntax that is acceptable to your particular server.)

Pass-through queries improve performance in many cases, because more processing takes place on the server, and network traffic is reduced. You also can take advantage of features offered by the implementation of SQL on your server that might not be available in Visual Basic for Applications. (Keep in mind, however, that pass-through queries return snapshots of data and therefore are *not* updatable.) You can use these steps to create a pass-through query:

1. In the Database Window, click the Query tab, then click New.

2. In the New Query dialog box that appears, select Design View, then click OK.

3. When the Show Table dialog box appears above the blank Query Window, click Close in the dialog box.

4. Choose Query/SQL Specific from the menus, then choose Pass-Through from the submenu. When you do this, a SQL Pass-Through Query Window appears, as shown in Figure 15.5.

5. Choose View/Properties from the menus to open the Properties window for the query.

6. Set the ODBCConnectStr property to the connection string appropriate for your SQL Server. (You can click the Build button at the right of the property, and Access will prompt you for the needed information.)

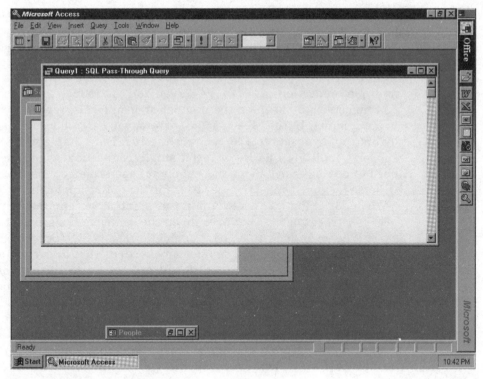

Figure 15.5 The SQL Pass-Through query window.

7. Set the ReturnsRecords property to Yes if the query returns records, or set it to No if the query does not return records.

8. Close the Property window, and enter the desired SQL statement in the Query Window.

9. Save and run the query using the same techniques that you would use for saving or running any query. Note that saved pass-through queries will appear with a globe icon beside the query name in the Database Window.

Optimizing Client / Server Applications

With your application up and running using the attached tables that are stored on your server, you've finally reached your goal of having a Microsoft Access application running in the client/server environment. However, before you move on to developing your next application (and moving through this process all over again), there are some points that you can consider to ensure that your application is running at optimal efficiency. In a nutshell, you'll want to minimize the number of connections necessary and design your queries to be as efficient as possible.

Each connection that's established between a client (in this case, Access) and a server requires usage of both memory and network resources, and Access doesn't necessarily use just one connection per user to work with your server data. Depending on the type of SQL Server that you are using and what tasks Access is performing in your application, a single user can have multiple connections open to the server. You can reduce the number of needed connections by keeping the number of open forms, reports, and dynasets to a minimum. In the case of some servers, you can reduce connection usage by limiting dynasets to 100 or fewer records. Note that, if your SQL Server supports multiple queries using a single connection, you generally won't need to be concerned about the number of open connections, because Access will use just one connection per user for the entire application.

When designing queries to run in the client/server environment, your goal is to construct queries that execute on the server to the greatest degree possible. Whenever you run a query against attached SQL Server tables, Access will evaluate the query's design for any portions that aren't compatible with your brand of SQL Server, and it will process those portions of the query locally. This can slow things down considerably, not to mention requiring large amounts of disk space in the \TEMP directory of the user's PC. You can minimize such delays by restructuring your queries to avoid clauses in the resulting SQL statements that are incompatible with your brand of SQL Server. Most servers don't support operations that you can't express within a single SQL statement or any operations, functions, or SQL extensions that are specific to Microsoft Access.

Tip: Some servers support outer joins, and some don't. You might want to check the documentation for your brand of server before making extensive use of outer joins in an Access application. For specifics about the types of joins in Access queries, see Chapter 8.

When designing relational forms for use in the client/server environment, try to use single forms based on relational queries, as opposed to multitable forms that contain both a main form and a subform. The reason is that, with a single form that's based on a relational query, the server only has to deal with the single query (which draws data from more than one table). However, with a form that contains a subform, Access must pass two queries to the server: one for the main form and a separate query for the subform. If your users don't need to see subforms, use single forms based on relational queries.

Finally, when designing forms that use attached tables as a record source, try to put any memo and/or OLE fields on a second form page, and add command buttons to display that page only upon a user's request. The retrieval of memo field and OLE field data from a server is time-consuming; therefore, if users are given the option to skip those fields in the display of a form, your application's performance can improve considerably.

Summary

This chapter has examined the topic of attaching to your data tables on the server and the various ways in which you can optimize your completed Access applications to work more efficiently in the client/server environment. You can use the techniques presented here and throughout this book in developing client/server applications in Access for use within your organization. Look on each application's development as a new learning experience. With each development task, you'll grow more comfortable with techniques that you'll use repeatedly in the world of client/server application development.

Chapter

16

Sharing Data with OLE

This chapter is optional for many developers, as it deals with using OLE within Access applications. The use of OLE (Object Linking and Embedding) is by no means required in an Access application, but on those occasions when it is needed, there's generally no way around it. Much earlier in the book, in Chapter 7, the concept of OLE Object fields was introduced, and Chapter 5 showed how you could place containers for displaying and editing OLE Object fields in your forms. By means of the use of OLE, you can store other Windows data—such as spreadsheets, word processing documents, or sound clips—in your Access tables. However, with OLE Automation, you can go beyond the simple storage of Windows data in fields of a table. You can pass data back and forth between Access and other Windows applications, and you can control other Windows applications from within Access.

OLE, Defined

If you've done any significant amount of work with different Windows applications, you've probably had some interactions with OLE. If you've pasted pictures from a Windows drawing package like Corel Draw or Harvard Graphics for Windows into OLE Object fields of an Access table, you've used the capabilities of OLE. In a nutshell, object linking and embedding is a Windows protocol (a clearly defined set of rules of communication) that enables data in the form of objects stored in one Windows application to be used (by means of linking or embedding) within documents in another Windows application. You can create OLE objects in any Windows application that supports OLE, and most Windows applications do provide OLE support.

Windows applications that do support OLE can be OLE *clients*, OLE *servers*, or both. OLE clients can accept OLE data from other Windows packages, and OLE servers can provide OLE data to other Windows packages. Windows Paint, for example, is an OLE server, as it can provide OLE data to another Windows package, but you cannot store OLE data in a Windows Paint image.

Microsoft Access can act as both an OLE client and an OLE server. As you work with OLE, you'll also hear the terms *source document* and *destination document*. The source document is the document that is providing OLE data, and the destination document is the document which is receiving the OLE data.

OLE objects can consist of portions of documents (such as a paragraph of a Word for Windows document or a range of cells in an Excel spreadsheet), or they can consist of entire files (such as a complete document in Word). Because you have a choice of linking or embedding when you store the Windows data in Access, it makes sense to have a clear understanding of the difference between the two, because each method of storage has its advantages and disadvantages.

With *linking*, the OLE object remains stored in a separate file, and a link (or pointer to the file) is established between the OLE object in Access and the original file. For example, if part of an Excel spreadsheet is stored in an OLE Object field of an Access table by means of linking, the Access field contains a reference to the original Excel spreadsheet file. Linking is the preferred method to use when you want the OLE objects in Access to reflect any changes made to the original data under the control of the source application.

With embedding, on the other hand, the data from the other Windows application is *embedded*, or literally inserted into an Access object; hence, it becomes part of the Access database. (The data still might exist in the original file where it was created by the source application, but the embedded object within Access becomes a copy of the data in the source application.) Once other Windows data has been embedded in an Access database, there is no direct connection between the original (source) data and the embedded copy. You can make changes to the embedded data, and the original data will remain unchanged. An advantage of embedding is that it is easier to maintain portability, as when you move data around, you don't have to worry about breaking links between drive locations of linked objects. However, be warned that embedding consumes large amounts of disk space when compared to linking, especially if you are storing objects such as sound clips or video.

Using Object Linking and Embedding

As far as where you can utilize your OLE data within Access, you have two general choices: in the fields of a table or in controls placed in forms and in reports. When you display OLE data by means of OLE containers in forms and reports, the data can be *bound* (or tied to OLE Object fields of a table where that data is stored) or *unbound* (not stored in any table, but simply linked or embedded directly from another Windows application). With tables that contain OLE Object fields, you can use forms that contain controls for those fields to serve as a method for data entry and editing. You also can use the steps that follow to link or embed data in the OLE Object fields of an Access table.

Note: If you're going to use OLE Object fields in an Access application within the client/server environment, you'll probably need to decide how to split your data where necessary so that you can store the tables that contain the OLE data in native Access format. Most SQL Servers do not support the OLE Object field type, so you'll need to create and maintain a table or tables in Access just for the purpose of storing your OLE data.

Linking an Object to a Field

When you want to store OLE data in an OLE Object field, you can use these steps to do so:

1. Open the file within the source application (the one providing the OLE data), and use the appropriate Windows selection techniques to select the desired data.
2. From the menus, choose Edit/Copy.
3. Switch back to Access (you can use the Windows 95 Taskbar to do so).
4. Open the form that contains the OLE Object field in form view (or open the datasheet for the table or query that contains the OLE Object field).
5. Find the desired record where the link to the OLE data should be placed.
6. Click within the bound object frame (or in the OLE Object field of the datasheet) where you want to place the link.
7. From the menus, choose Edit/Paste Special. When you do so, the Paste Special dialog box appears, as shown in Figure 16.1.
8. Turn on the Paste Link option in the dialog box.
9. Click OK. When you do so, Access creates the link and stores the OLE data in the underlying field of the table. If you are using a bound object frame in a form or report to display the data and the data is a graphic, you see the graphic in the frame; if the data is a Word or Excel document, you see the text of the document or the spreadsheet cells. In the case of PowerPoint presentations, you see the actual presentation.

Embedding an Existing OLE Object in a Field

You can embed existing OLE data in a field of an Access table by performing the following steps:

1. Open the file within the source application (the one providing the OLE data), and use the appropriate Windows selection techniques to select the desired data.
2. From the menus, choose Edit/Copy.
3. Switch back to Access (you can use the Windows 95 Taskbar to do so).
4. Open the form that contains the OLE Object field in form view (or open the datasheet for the table or query that contains the OLE Object field).

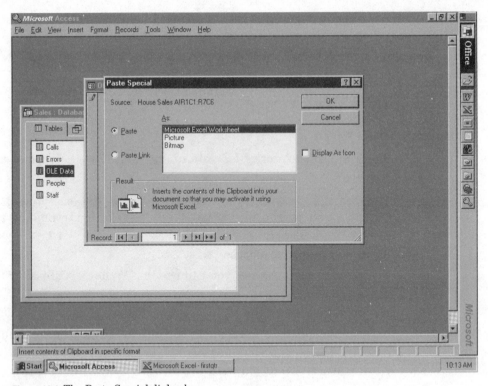

Figure 16.1 The Paste Special dialog box.

5. Find the desired record where the link to the OLE data should be placed.

6. Click within the bound object frame (or in the OLE Object field of the datasheet) where you want to place the link.

7. From the menus, choose `Edit/Paste`.

Once you do this, Access shows the data within the bound object frame (if you are viewing the data in a form or a report's preview mode). If you are viewing the data through a table or query's datasheet, the name of the data type (such as "Paintbrush Picture") appears in the field of the record.

Embedding a New OLE Object in a Field

You can create and embed OLE data in a field of an Access table by performing the following steps:

1. Open the form that contains the OLE Object field in form view (or open the datasheet for the table that contains the OLE Object field).

2. Move to the desired record of the table where you want to add the OLE data.

3. Click within the field where the data should be added.

4. From the menus, choose `Insert/Object`. When you do this, you will see the Insert Object dialog box, as shown in Figure 16.2.

5. Leave the `Create New` option selected in the dialog box.

6. In the Object Type list box, select the type of object that you want to embed, then click `OK`. Access will launch the source application for the chosen type of object.

7. Create the object in the source application, using the techniques applicable to that application.

8. If the application supports OLE2, you can click anywhere outside the OLE Object field to leave the source application. If the source application does not support OLE2, then while still in the source application, open the File menu, and choose `Exit and Return`. (If there is no such command under the File menu, choose `File/Update`.) When you leave the source application, the object will be stored in Access.

Embedding OLE Files in Unbound Frames

In some cases, you'll have OLE data that exists in the form of a complete file and want to place it into a form or report, but the data is not bound to any

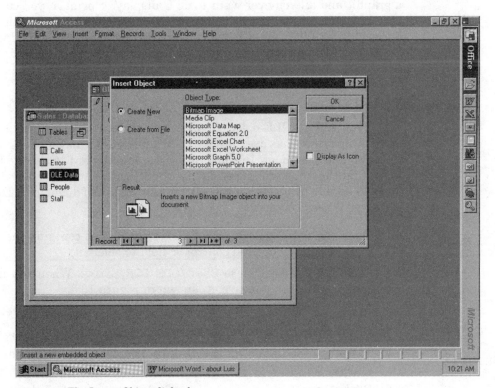

Figure 16.2 The Insert Object dialog box.

field of a table. (This is commonly the case with graphic images that appear as design elements of forms or reports.) You can embed OLE data in the form of files and place them as objects in forms or reports using the following steps:

1. In Access, open the desired form or report in design view.
2. In the Toolbox, click the Unbound Object Frame tool to select it. (If the Toolbox isn't visible, choose View/Toolbox from the menus to display it.)
3. In the Design window for the form or the report, click and drag at the desired location to the desired size for the frame. When you release the mouse, you will see the Insert Object dialog box, as shown earlier in Figure 16.2.
4. Click the Create From File button, then click Browse.
5. Use the Drives and Directories list boxes to navigate to the directory where the desired file is stored.
6. Select the desired file in the File Name list box, then click OK.

Note that, if you are inserting graphic OLE objects as design elements, it's probably a good idea to leave them in OLE format only if you need the benefits of OLE (for example, in being able to double-click on the object and play a sound or video or edit the original object while in Design view). If the object is a graphic and all you ever want to do is display or print it, you can speed the response time of your form or report by pasting it in as a static bitmap as opposed to an OLE object or by converting it to a bitmap after inserting the graphic OLE object (open the Edit menu, and choose Edit/Picture Object/Convert to Picture from the menus).

Changing a Link's Update Settings

When you add an OLE object to an Access table, form, or report by means of an OLE link, the links are automatically updated whenever changes are made in the source document. In some cases, you might want to change this behavior so that the links are updated only when you tell Access to update the data. You can do this by changing the settings in the Links dialog box. Here are the steps you'll need to do this:

1. Open the form, report, or table datasheet that contains the OLE data, and click in the desired control or field to select it.
2. From the menus, choose Edit/OLE DDE Links. When you do this, the Links dialog box appears, as shown in Figure 16.3.
3. In the list box, select the link that you want to change the settings for.
4. At the bottom of the dialog box, change the Update setting to Manual.
5. To update the link, click the Update Now button at the right side of the dialog box.
6. Click Close when done changing link settings to close the dialog box.

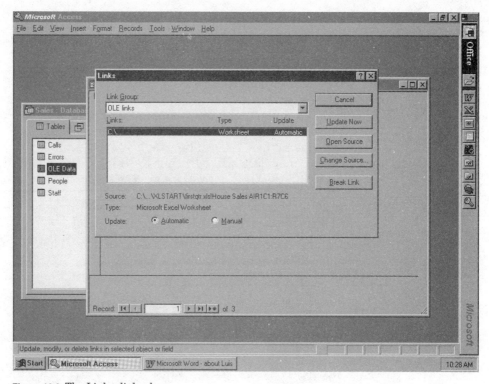

Figure 16.3 The Links dialog box.

Remember that, once you've changed the link status for any link from Automatic to Manual, you will need to open the Links dialog box (choose Edit/OLE DDE Links), select the desired link, and click the Update Now button whenever you want to update the OLE object in Access with the most current data.

Breaking and Restoring Links

There also might be times when you purposely want to break an existing link between OLE data stored in Access and the source document. As an example, you might have an Excel worksheet stored in an OLE Object field of a table, and you are sure that you won't need updates of the data. So, you want to make the data "static" to improve the response time of viewing the data in Access. You can break a link by performing these steps:

1. Open the form, report, or table datasheet that contains the OLE data, and click in the desired control or field to select it.

2. From the menus, choose Edit/OLE DDE Links. When you do this, the Links dialog box appears as shown earlier, in Figure 16.3.

3. In the list box, select the link that you want to break.

4. Click the Break Link button at the right side of the dialog box.

5. In the confirmation box that appears next, click Yes to break the link.

Note that, when you intentionally break a link, it has the same effect as converting the object to a picture. You won't be able to re-establish a link that you break intentionally.

Some breaks of links might be intentional, and others might happen accidentally if the file that contains the OLE data is moved from one directory on the hard drive to another. You can re-establish a broken link that is the result of inadvertently moving a file by using the Links dialog box to tell Access where it can locate the OLE data. Here are the steps that you use to do this:

1. Open the form, report, or table datasheet that contains the OLE data, and click in the desired control or field to select it.

2. From the menus, choose Edit/OLE DDE Links. When you do this, the Links dialog box appears as shown earlier.

3. In the list box, select the broken link.

4. Click the Change Source button at the right side of the dialog box. When you do this, the Change Source dialog box appears, as shown in Figure 16.4.

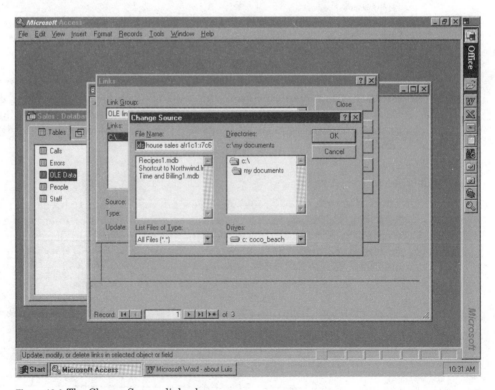

Figure 16.4 The Change Source dialog box.

5. Use the Drives and Directories list boxes as necessary to navigate to the desired drive and folder that contains the file with the OLE data.

6. Select the desired file in the File Name list box, then click OK to re-establish the link.

Editing Embedded Objects

When you embed objects in Access, you can edit them as you would edit any OLE object stored in any Windows application. Go to the location of the data (in this case, the control in the Access table, form, or report), and double-click on the OLE object. One of two things then will happen, depending on whether the source application supports the latest version of OLE (OLE2 at the time of this writing) or not. If the source application supports OLE2, the object will become active in a window, and the menus of Access will change to the menus of the source application. If the source application does not support OLE2 but supports OLE, the source application will be launched, and a copy of the object will appear in a window. In either case, you can make the desired edits to the embedded object. When you are done with the edits, if the source application supports OLE2, click anywhere outside of the OLE Object field to return to Access. If the source application supports OLE only, open the File menu and choose Update (this menu choice might be called Save Changes and Return or Exit and Return in some Windows applications).

Inserting Sound and Video

Because sound and video are stored as OLE data, you can insert these into Access, assuming your hardware supports the use of sound or video. (If your PC doesn't not have sound or video drivers installed, you won't be able to play sound or video.) You can add sound or video to an Access OLE Object field with the following steps:

1. Open the form that contains the OLE Object field in form view (or open the datasheet for the table that contains the OLE Object field).

2. Move to the desired record of the table where you want to add the OLE data.

3. Click within the field where the data should be added.

4. From the menus, choose Insert/Object. When you do this, you see the Insert Object dialog box, as shown earlier in Figure 16.2.

5. In the Insert Object dialog box, choose Media Clip, Video Clip, or Wave Sound to add the clip using the menu options of the Windows Media Player, or click Create From File if you want to add the sound or video based on an existing file. If you choose Create From File, a dialog box will appear where you can navigate to the desired drive and/or folder that contains the sound or video file. Windows sound files have a .WAV extension, and video files have a .AVI extension.

To play the sound or video, select the OLE object in Access, open the Edit menu and choose the last option on the menu, then choose Play from the submenu that appears.

Using OLE Automation in Access Applications

When you want to go beyond the use of Access as a storage medium for OLE data and actually automate the manipulation of other Windows applications, you can do so by means of *OLE Automation*. Ever since the release of OLE2, Microsoft has offered OLE Automation as an integral part of object linking and embedding. You can write VBA code that uses OLE Automation to control other OLE2-compatible Windows applications from within Access. For example, you could open a Word document under remote control, pass Access data to that document, print the document, save it to a file, and exit from Word, all while under the control of the Access application.

As a direct example of the use of OLE Automation, consider the form shown in Figure 16.5.

In this case, the controls in the form are bound to a table of customer data. The button labeled Build Memo in the form, when clicked, launches Word for

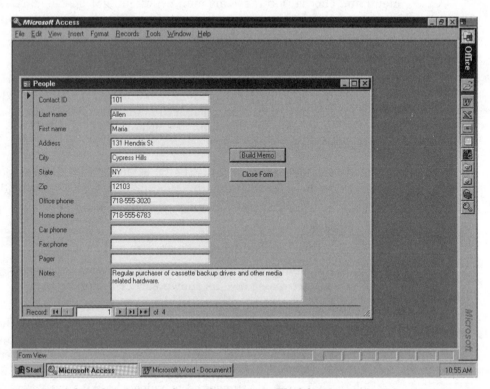

Figure 16.5 A form that contains a button for creating a Word document

Windows, opens a new document, and inserts the customer's name and address for the current record into the document. Here's the code that is attached to the Click event procedure for the button:

```
Private Sub MemoMaker_Click()
Dim objWord As Object
On Error Resume Next
AppActivate "Microsoft Word"
If Err Then
    Shell "C:\MSOffice\Winword\Winword"
End If
On Error GoTo 0
Set objWord = CreateObject("Word.Basic")
With objWord
    .AppMaximize "", 1
End With
objWord.Insert "Name: " & [Last name] & ", " & [First name]
objWord.Insert Chr(13) & Chr(10)
objWord.Insert "Address: " & [Address]
objWord.Insert Chr(13) & Chr(10)
objWord.Insert "City: " & [City]
objWord.Insert Chr(13) & Chr(10)
objWord.Insert "State: " & [State]
objWord.Insert Chr(13) & Chr(10)
objWord.Insert "ZIP Code: " & [Zip]
End Sub
```

In this code, the DIM statement declares a variable, objWord, as an object-type variable, suitable for storing OLE objects. The On Error Resume Next statement that follows tells Access to jump to the line after one causing an error, if an error occurs. This is done in case the next line, which attempts to activate an already running copy of Word, finds that Word is not running. If Word is not already running (in which case an error does occur), the If Err Then...End If statements that follow make use of the *Shell* statement to launch Word for Windows. The Set objWord=CreateObject("Word.Basic") statement uses OLE Automation to assign the Word document to the object variable called obj.Word. The lines that follow, serve to maximize the Word application window:

```
With objWord
    .AppMaximize "",1
End With
```

The objWord.Insert statements that follow that block insert the contents of the fields of the current record into the Word document.

This is just one example of what you can do by means of OLE Automation. While this example involves transferring just a small amount of data, you can use techniques like this to automate the exchange of massive amounts of information between Access and other Windows applications that support OLE. This book wasn't written to delve into the programming statements behind OLE Automation in detail, but you can find additional specifics by viewing the help screens in Access; search under the help topic "OLE Automation."

Using OLE Custom Controls

Since the release of version 2.0 of Access (the predecessor to Access for Windows 95), Access has supported the use of *OLE custom controls*. This section of the chapter details how you can put OLE custom controls to use in your Access applications. OLE custom controls resemble the standard controls that are available through the Toolbox when you are designing a form, in that you add them to forms and move and size them as desired like you do with standard controls. The difference with OLE custom controls is that they are stored in separate files that have an .OCX extension. All OLE custom controls make use of object embedding, hence they are sometimes referred to as *embedded controls*. OLE custom controls are available from a variety of vendors, and a number of shareware custom controls have been included on the CD-ROM that accompanies this book.

There are a wide variety of OLE custom controls, and each control has its own properties, methods, and events. As the developer, you'll need to refer to the documentation packaged with the OLE custom control that you are using to see what properties, events, and methods apply to that particular control. The remainder of this chapter often refers to the Calendar control that Microsoft supplies with Access, as it serves as a good example of a typical OLE custom control. Note that, to use the Calendar control in an application, you'll need to install the OLE custom controls provided with Access. These are *not* added as part of the default installation of Access. You'll need to rerun Setup, choose `Custom Installation`, and enable the Developer's Tools option. Figure 16.6 shows an example of the Calendar control in a form.

Adding OLE Custom Controls to Forms

While in Design view for any form, you can add an OLE custom control to that form by means of the `Insert/Object` menu option. You can use these steps to add the desired control:

1. Open the form in Design view.
2. From the menus, choose `Insert/Custom Control`. The Insert OLE Custom Control dialog box appears, as shown in Figure 16.7.
3. Choose the desired OLE custom control in the dialog box, then click OK.

Once you complete these steps, the OLE custom control appears in the form in Design view. Figure 16.8 shows the Calendar control's appearance in Design view.

Working with the Custom Control

Once you've added the control to the form, you can move it and size it using the same techniques that you would use with any control. You also can change the properties for the control itself either by means of VBA code or by right-clicking the control, choosing *<name>* `Control Object` from the

Figure 16.6 An example of the use of the Calendar control.

shortcut menu that appears (where *name* is the name of the custom control), and choosing `Properties` from the submenu. Note that, if you select the control and choose `View/Properties` or click the `Properties` button in the toolbar, you won't get the properties for the custom control; instead, you'll get the properties for the object frame that contains the control. To get to the properties for the control, you'll need to right-click it and use the shortcut menu as described above.

The VBA code that you'll use with each custom control will vary, depending on the design of the control itself. The examples described here apply to the Calendar control that Microsoft supplies with Access. In all cases, you can use the Object property to set the properties for a custom control. For example, the `Last Year` button shown in Figure 16.6 has the following code attached to it:

```
Sub LastYear_Click ()
    TheCalendar.Object.PreviousYear
End Sub
```

In this case, the name `TheCalendar` refers to the name assigned to the custom control, and `Object.PreviousYear` applies the PreviousYear method to the property of the control. The other buttons make use of similar code, using

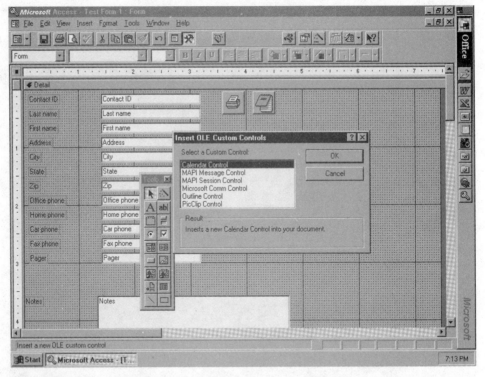

Figure 16.7 The Insert OLE Custom Control dialog box.

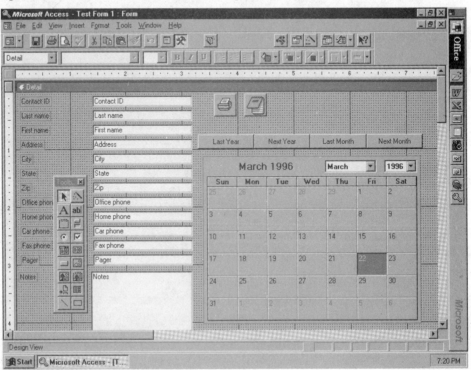

Figure 16.8 The Calendar control added to a form in Design view.

methods that apply to the Calendar control. (A full listing for the methods appears under the help screens for the Calendar control.) Keep in mind that every unbound object frame supports an Object property, and you can make use of that property to manipulate the control, using the methods that are applicable to that particular custom control.

Summary

This chapter has detailed the various ways in which the powers of OLE — Object Linking and Embedding — can be utilized within an Access application. While the inclusion of OLE is by no means a requirement with any application, its use can enhance your applications, giving users the power to do tasks that are beyond the scope of Access alone.

Index

Illustrations are indicated in **boldface**.

ABOUT THE AUTHOR

Ed Jones is an applications development analyst for Schulte, Roth & Zabel, a major New York law firm. One of the leading authors of database guides, Jones has written books that have sold over one million copies. Among his more than 30 books are the bestselling *Paradox 4 for DOS Made Easy, Paradox for Windows Made Easy, Ready-Made Powerbuilder Applications,* and *dBASE IV Inside and Out.*

SOFTWARE AND INFORMATION LICENSE

The software and information on this diskette (collectively referred to as the "Product") are the property of The McGraw-Hill Companies, Inc. ("McGraw-Hill") and are protected by both United States copyright law and international copyright treaty provision. You must treat this Product just like a book, except that you may copy it into a computer to be used and you may make archival copies of the Products for the sole purpose of backing up our software and protecting your investment from loss.

By saying "just like a book," McGraw-Hill means, for example, that the Product may be used by any number of people and may be freely moved from one computer location to another, so long as there is no possibility of the Product (or any part of the Product) being used at one location or on one computer while it is being used at another. Just as a book cannot be read by two different people in two different places at the same time, neither can the Product be used by two different people in two different places at the same time (unless, of course, McGraw-Hill's rights are being violated).

McGraw-Hill reserves the right to alter or modify the contents of the Product at any time.

This agreement is effective until terminated. The Agreement will terminate automatically without notice if you fail to comply with any provisions of this Agreement. In the event of termination by reason of your breach, you will destroy or erase all copies of the Product installed on any computer system or made for backup purposes and shall expunge the Product from your data storage facilities.

LIMITED WARRANTY

McGraw-Hill warrants the physical diskette(s) enclosed herein to be free of defects in materials and workmanship for a period of sixty days from the purchase date. If McGraw-Hill receives written notification within the warranty period of defects in materials or workmanship, and such notification is determined by McGraw-Hill to be correct, McGraw-Hill will replace the defective diskette(s). Send request to:

Customer Service
McGraw-Hill
Gahanna Industrial Park
860 Taylor Station Road
Blacklick, OH 43004-9615

The entire and exclusive liability and remedy for breach of this Limited Warranty shall be limited to replacement of defective diskette(s) and shall not include or extend to any claim for or right to cover any other damages, including but not limited to, loss of profit, data, or use of the software, or special, incidental, or consequential damages or other similar claims, even if McGraw-Hill has been specifically advised as to the possibility of such damages. In no event will McGraw-Hill's liability for any damages to you or any other person ever exceed the lower of suggested list price or actual price paid for the license to use the Product, regardless of any form of the claim.

THE McGRAW-HILL COMPANIES, INC. SPECIFICALLY DISCLAIMS ALL OTHER WARRANTIES, EXPRESS OR IMPLIED, INCLUDING BUT NOT LIMITED TO, ANY IMPLIED WARRANTY OF MERCHANTABILITY OR FITNESS FOR A PARTICULAR PURPOSE. Specifically, McGraw-Hill makes no representation or warranty that the Product is fit for any particular purpose and any implied warranty of merchantability is limited to the sixty day duration of the Limited Warranty covering the physical diskette(s) only (and not the software or in-formation) and is otherwise expressly and specifically disclaimed.

This Limited Warranty gives you specific legal rights; you may have others which may vary from state to state. Some states do not allow the exclusion of incidental or consequential damages, or the limitation on how long an implied warranty lasts, so some of the above may not apply to you.

This Agreement constitutes the entire agreement between the parties relating to use of the Product. The terms of any purchase order shall have no effect on the terms of this Agreement. Failure of McGraw-Hill to insist at any time on strict compliance with this Agreement shall not constitute a waiver of any rights under this Agreement. This Agreement shall be construed and governed in accordance with the laws of New York. If any provision of this Agreement is held to be contrary to law, that provision will be enforced to the maximum extent permissible and the remaining provisions will remain in force and effect.